Integrating College Study Skills

Reasoning in Reading, Listening, and Writing

Books of Related Interest

Essential Skills for Reading College Texts
  Diane W. Creel, Tompkins Cortland Community College

Critical Thinking: Reading and Writing across the Curriculum
  Anne Bradstreet Grinols, Parkland College

Opportunity for Skillful Reading, Fifth Edition
  Irwin L. Joffe, formerly Phoenix College

Reading Skills for Successful Living, Third Edition
  Irwin L. Joffe, formerly Phoenix College

College Reading I, Second Edition
  Minnette Lenier, Los Angeles Pierce College
  Janet Maker, formerly Los Angeles Pierce College

College Reading II, Third Edition
  Janet Maker, formerly Los Angeles Pierce College
  Minnette Lenier, Los Angeles Pierce College

College Reading III
  Janet Maker, formerly Los Angeles Pierce College
  Minnette Lenier, Los Angeles Pierce College

Integrating
College Study Skills
Reasoning
in Reading, Listening, and Writing
Second Edition

Peter Elias Sotiriou
Los Angeles City College

Wadsworth Publishing Company
A Division of Wadsworth, Inc.

Belmont, California

Production: Del Mar Associates
Print Buyer: Randy Hurst
Designer: Joe di Chiarro
Copy Editor: Andrea Olshevsky
Cover: Steve Harrison

Printed in the United States of America

1 2 3 4 5 6 7 8 9 10—93 92 91 90 89

ISBN 0-534-09564-X

Library of Congress Cataloging-in-Publication Data

Sotiriou, Peter Elias.
  Integrating college study skills.

  Includes index.
  1. Study, Methods of.   I. Title
LB2395.S597 1989   378'.17'02812   88-17413
ISBN 0-534-09564-X (pbk.)

Contents

Part Two: Basic Reading, Listening, and Writing Skills   27

Chapter 3   Locating the Main Idea   29

Chapter 4   Locating Major and Minor Details   54

Chapter 7   Reading Graphs and Tables   120

Chapter 8   Summarizing and Paraphrasing   139

Part Three: Taking Lecture and Study Notes   159

Chapter 9   Characteristics of Lectures   161

Chapter 10   Traditional Note-taking Techniques   169

Preface

In the second edition of *Integrating College Study Skills,* I have attempted to refine what has proven to be a successful study skills text. First and foremost, many users have asked for more exercises using textbook material, so I have included a textbook exercise at the end of the exercises in Chapters 3–8. I have also extensively revised the exercises on making inferences in Chapter 6, on paraphrasing in Chapter 8, as well as the exercises on condensing and using abbreviations in Chapter 10, in order to give students a better context in which to answer these questions. And in those exercises that I have kept from the first edition, I have updated and changed about 30 percent of the material. Finally, you will find two new study reading selections at the end of the book.

I have also revised all of the introductions—including updated research in study skills, language instruction, and cognitive psychology. In addition, I have condensed wherever I could; you will find that the introductions are shorter and more concise. I hope this change will make the introductions easier for students to read and easier for instructors to teach from.

What I have kept from the first edition is the text's careful sequencing and its challenging, college-level material. I still find the sequence of chapters from "Locating the Main Idea" to "Applying SQ3R to Textbooks" to be a sound pedagogy. Also, I have retained the sequenced progression of exercises in each chapter, so that each exercise is more challenging than the previous one. Finally, I continue to use in my exercises and examples topics that incoming college students will find in their courses—issues from the humanities, social sciences, and sciences.

I hope that this second edition will even more effectively accomplish what I set out to do in the first edition: to make students better readers, listeners, and writers of college material and to make them aware of how reading, listening, and writing use similar thinking skills.

To the Student

You have no doubt come to a study skills course for several reasons. For one, you probably need to upgrade your textbook reading skills. Two, you may want to improve your note-taking skills to capture the key points your instructors make. And three, you likely want to improve your test-taking skills. If you complete the exercises in this book, you will become a more successful college student—more efficient in reading, note taking, and taking exams.

How This Book Is Organized

Before you begin to do the exercises in this book, you need to know how it is put together. Part One is called "Skills for Beginning Your College Career." Here you will learn about the basic survival skills that college students need to know: how to use your college's counseling services, when and what to study, how much time to devote to your studies, and other equally important skills. This first part will point your college career in the right direction.

Part Two is the longest, dealing with the essential reading, listening, and writing skills you will need to master. In this part, "Basic Reading, Listening, and Writing Skills," you will learn several key reasoning skills. You will be shown how to locate the main idea, how to identify and use details, and how to read or listen for inferences. You will also learn how to read graphs and tables and how to summarize and paraphrase text and lecture material. Throughout this part, you will see how these skills apply to reading, listening, and writing. This is a unique feature of *Integrating College Study Skills*. As the title suggests, you will learn to integrate each study skill into the three activities of reading, listening, and writing.

In Part Three, "Taking Lecture and Study Notes," you will be using the skills learned in the previous part to improve your note-taking skills. You will learn how to condense information and use abbreviations. You will also be introduced to mapping—a visual way of taking notes that is especially helpful when you are studying for a major exam.

In Part Four, "Study Skills Systems and Strategies," you will be given guidelines for taking various kinds of tests—objective, essay, and math or science. Most important, you will learn about the SQ3R study system, a successful method for learning and remembering what you read from textbooks. Finally, in Part Five, "Applying SQ3R to Text Excerpts," you will use this method and all the previous skills you have learned to read and understand textbook excerpts.

How to Use This Book

Integrating College Study Skills follows a similar format throughout. Each chapter is divided into two parts—an "Explanation of Skills" and exercises that allow you to apply these skills. Follow these steps as you work through each chapter:

1. Read the "Explanation of Skills" carefully. The information presented in these sections will give you the skills to complete the exercises.

2. Before you begin an exercise, read the directions carefully. Know what you have to do before you begin.

3. Record your answers in the answer box that accompanies most exercises.

4. After you complete the exercise, check your answers. You will find the answers to most odd-numbered exercises at the end of the book. Your instructor will provide the answers to the even-numbered exercises. You will also need to consult your instructor for the correct answers to all exercises involving paragraph writing and for answers to many short-answer questions. Finally, your instructor will provide all of the answers for the examinations that follow the study readings in Part Five.

5. Follow the directions for scoring each exercise. Compare your score with that printed directly underneath it. This percentage is the acceptable score—one that shows mastery of the material. If you score below the acceptable one, check your errors to see what went wrong. You may want to ask your instructor for help.

When You Finish This Book

When you have finished *Integrating College Study Skills,* you will likely be ready for the demands of college work. You will be able to read textbooks better, take accurate lecture and study notes, use test-taking strategies, and write an organized paragraph explaining what you have learned. Most important, when you have completed this book you will be able to use the identical reasoning skills in your reading, listening, and writing. Rather than completing each assignment in isolation, you will be able to see your work in college more as an integrated activity.

Acknowledgments

My thanks go to Steve Rutter, who carefully followed the production of this second edition; to Nancy Sjoberg, the production editor, who made sure I met all deadlines; and to my wife Vasi and my sons who lovingly gave me the hundreds of hours I needed to complete this second edition.

I am thankful for the comments made by my reviewers of the first edition: Nancy C. Cook, University of Arkansas; Pat John, Lane Community College; Denise McGinty, University of Texas at Austin; Penney Miller, Clayton Junior College; Linda Pounds, Georgia State University; and Margaret Rauch, St. Cloud State University. I would like to thank the reviewers of the second edition: Nancy Hoover, Bellarmine College; Allan Jacobson, Los Angeles Harbor College; Lorita Manning, Baylor University; and Melaine Evans Summey, Abraham Baldwin Agricultural College.

Skills for Beginning Your College Career

In this part of the book, you will become acquainted with the services that your college provides, you will complete schedules for your short- and long-term projects, and you will learn how to manage your study area. This information and these skills provide a necessary foundation for your college career.

1

Getting to Know Your School

Explanation of Skills

The first week at a new college is frequently the most hectic. You have to pay tuition and fees, buy books, enroll in your classes, and organize a study and work schedule. Many students find colleges, particularly large ones, impersonal. Yet most colleges provide students with materials and services that can make their first semester a bit less trying.

College Catalog and Schedule of Classes

Weeks before you enroll in your classes, you can become familiar with your school by obtaining a college catalog and a schedule of classes. The catalog is usually published every year. It outlines college policies, gives a short history of the school, lists the services provided to students, names the departments and the courses offered, and names the faculty of each department. Reading the catalog is a smart way to begin your college career. Look for services that the college provides: scholarships, financial aid, tutoring, and so on. Read through the course offerings in those departments in which you plan to take classes. You will find out how many courses are offered, what kinds of courses are offered, and when during the calendar year courses are taught.

After most course titles, the catalog lists the prerequisites and the unit value of each course. Prerequisites list the course that you must have taken or the exams that you must have passed in order to enroll. Knowing whether you fulfill the prerequisites is important. An introductory chemistry course, for example, may give as one of its prerequisites: "appropriate score on placement test." If you do not take and pass this test before the first meeting, you may not be allowed to enroll. Some students enroll in courses without being aware of the prerequisites and are turned away the first day of class.

The catalog also lists next to the course title its unit value. A unit is usually equal to one hour per week of lecture or discussion. Many courses are three units, so you attend class three hours a week. Some foreign language and science courses are five units and usually require daily attendance or the equivalent of five hours a week. In most cases, if you are enrolled in fifteen units, you will be attending class fifteen hours a week.

The schedule of classes lists each course that will be offered for that semester, the time it is offered, its unit value, and the instructor of the course. This schedule is an important tool for you because it provides all the necessary information that you will need to set up your study list for the semester.

Counseling Services

Most colleges and universities offer some sort of counseling service to all their students. If you are new to the college, you need to make an appointment to see a counselor. At this meeting, discuss your educational and career goals with your counselor. If you have transcripts of course work completed in high school or at other colleges, bring them to this appointment. Ask your counselor what exactly is required to complete a degree or certificate in your chosen major and what your job opportunities are once you graduate.

Your counselor may advise you to take a battery of tests. The results of these tests will often show you which courses you are qualified to take in English, math, and science. Many colleges also have career centers where you can go any time during the semester to get information about your intended career or any career you may be interested in.

Financial Aid

Well before you begin the semester, start planning your finances. Many students must drop out of college because they cannot pay all of their school bills. Almost all colleges and universities have a financial aids office. Go to this office before the semester begins to learn of benefits available to you. If you have already been awarded a scholarship or grant, find out when you will be given the allowance and what grade point average and unit load you need to maintain to keep your funding. Also find out from the financial aids people what the cost of your education will be each semester or quarter. Then determine whether you can afford your education without having to work.

Job Placement Office

Most colleges and universities provide job placement services. Many students cannot afford to attend college without having to work. If you don't have a job and need extra money, see what jobs are available at the job placement office.

For most students who are serious about their college studies, being a student is a full-time job. Working full time and going to school full time is simply too much for them. School, work, or your health will suffer if you try to do too much. Part-time work of less than twenty hours per week is a reasonable work load for a college student. If you need to work full time, you may want to delay your full-time education until you have adequate savings. Many full-time workers go to school part time, often taking one or two courses at night. Taking twelve units is considered a full load, and you are advised not to work full time if you are also carrying a full load.

Orientation Activities

Many colleges and universities set aside a day or several days before the semester begins for orientation. At this time, new students are given a tour of the campus and are introduced to the various social and cultural activities the college provides. Take part in orientation activities, particularly if the college you have chosen is large. At the very least, on your first day of class you will know your way around the campus. You may also find out about a club or group that may interest you.

The First Class Meeting

The first class meeting for any course is an important one. The instructor officially enrolls you and usually gives you the course requirements: topics you will study, reading materials, exam dates, due dates for essays or projects, and the grading policy. Your instructor will also post office hours—hours when he or she will be able to meet with you outside of class. All of this information is usually presented in a syllabus, a calendar of course topics and a statement of class requirements. Save your syllabus, because you will be referring to it all semester.

Class Materials

You should take both pens and pencils to class. Take most of your notes in ink, but use pencil in math and science courses, where you will often be recalculating and erasing. You should have a separate notebook for each class, or at least a separate divider in a three-ring binder. Three-ring notebooks are particularly useful because you can add material for each course at any time during the semester, and you can keep your lectures in chronological order.

Buy your books during the first week of the semester or even before the semester begins. Be sure you know which books are required and which are recommended. Your syllabus will carry this information, and the bookstore will probably post "required" or "recommended" after each book title. After the first week of class, the bookstore may run out of some titles, and you may have to wait several weeks for the new order to arrive.

If you can afford it, buy new books. But if you buy used books, try to find those that have few or no markings. If you buy a heavily underlined book, you will be reading someone else's comments, which may not agree with yours.

Take only those books to class that you will use during lecture or lab or that you will want to study from during the day. Instructors often read from the textbook or refer to specific pages while lecturing. You will want to read along with the instructor or mark those important pages during the lecture. To carry those books that you will need for the day, you will need a briefcase, an attaché case, a large purse or satchel, or a backpack.

Making Class Contacts

During the first week of class, you should get to know at least one reliable classmate in each class. You should get this student's phone number and give yours to him or her. Whenever you cannot attend lectures, you can call this student to find out what you missed. You may also want to read over this student's notes whenever your notes are incomplete.

Most students enjoy studying with a classmate and find that they learn more than when studying alone. Often four or five students form a study group to prepare for a major exam. These groups are especially helpful if your instructor assigns several review questions before an exam. Students in the study group can divide up these questions, then meet to share their answers.

Try working in a study group to see whether you learn more easily this way. If you don't find study groups helpful, you may be one of those students who learn best alone.

Summary

Preparing for the first day of class takes work. By talking with a counselor, taking placement tests, and attending orientation meetings, you will get a clearer picture of your abilities and of the college you have chosen. The first day of class is also important because you will find out what your instructors expect you to do during the semester or quarter. Finally, getting to know a few fellow classmates early in the semester will help you, so if you cannot attend class, you can call them to find out what you missed.

Summary Box   *Getting Started in School*

What do you need to do?	Why are these activities important?
Read the catalog and schedule of classes.	To learn something about your school.
Meet with a counselor.	To plan your career goals.
Attend orientation meetings.	To familiarize yourself with the campus.
Get the phone number of at least one student in each class.	To find out what happened in class when you are absent.

Skills Practice

Exercise 1.1
Checklist of
Activities to
Complete

The following is a list of activities that you need to complete before the semester begins or soon after. When you complete each activity, enter the date. Check the "Does Not Apply" space for those activities that do not concern you.

Does Not Apply	*Date Completed*	*Activity*
1. _____	_____	Buy and read through the college catalog.
2. _____	_____	Buy and read through the schedule of classes.
3. _____	_____	Make an appointment to see a counselor.
4. _____	_____	Take placement tests.
5. _____	_____	Go to the financial aids office.
6. _____	_____	Go to the job placement office.
7. _____	_____	Go to orientation activities.
8. _____	_____	Buy paper, pens, and pencils for classes.
9. _____	_____	Buy textbooks.
10. _____	_____	Get the phone numbers of classmates.
11. _____	_____	Additional activities: _____

Exercise 1.2
Setting Goals for the
Semester

Answer the following questions that pertain to your plans for the current semester. Your answers should help you set reasonable goals for this and later semesters. Write "Does Not Apply" if the question does not pertain to you.

1. What, according to your placement tests, are your strengths and weaknesses?

2. What, according to your career tests, are your vocational interests?

3. What courses have you decided to take this semester as a result of talking to a counselor?

4. What is your intended major?

5. How many units are required for you to complete your major? How many semesters do you need to complete your major?

6. Do you plan to complete all of your course work at your present college, or do you intend to transfer? If you plan to transfer, what school do you intend to transfer to?

7. Did you find, after meeting with people in the financial aids office, that you are eligible for aid, or do you need to work? If you need to work, how many hours a week do you plan to work?

2

Managing Your Time and Your Study Area

Explanation of Skills

Being a student carries many responsibilities. In carrying out the job of being a student, you would be wise to prepare a schedule that indicates what you will be doing each day. A successful executive would be lost without a calendar of business and social appointments. So will you. As a student, you need to keep track of every hour that you spend in and out of school. Students who schedule their time find that there are many wasted hours during the day. Students also need to analyze their study areas to see whether these places are most conducive to concentration.

Incoming freshmen will find they will have many more free hours during the day than they had in high school, where they were often in classes five or six hours each day. Some days a college student may have only two hours of class, and the rest of the day will be free. For this reason, it is especially important for freshmen coming directly from high school to set up schedules that they plan to follow.

Setting Up a Schedule of Nonschool Activities

Your first job in establishing a study schedule is to determine which hours during the day you cannot study. Be detailed. Include the time it takes for you to get ready for class in the morning and get ready for bed at night, to eat your meals, and to take care of family matters. List all of these activities and the time allotted to each on a 3 × 5 card, as shown in Figure 2-1.

If you do not already follow a routine of getting up at a certain time, eating at set hours, and exercising regularly, start now. You will not be productive if you do not eat, sleep, and exercise well. Students who don't eat breakfast often become exhausted by midday. Similarly,

6–7 A.M.: Shower, get ready for school, eat breakfast.
7–7:30 A.M.: Drive to campus.
noon–12:45 P.M.: Eat lunch on campus.
10–11 P.M.: Exercise and get ready for bed.

Figure 2-1 *Activity card.*

students who do not exercise feel lethargic as the day wears on. Recent studies have shown that exercise gives your body more energy and fights depression. A half-hour to an hour of jogging, swimming, or brisk walking each day is time well spent. Finally, sleeping at least seven hours a night is important. Staying up late catches up with you. Even though it is tempting to stay up late, particularly if you live on campus, try not to. If you have slept little during the week, you will find yourself dozing off in class or sleeping through your morning classes.

Setting Up a Schedule of School Activities

Now that you have established regular times to eat, sleep, and exercise, you are ready to identify those hours you can devote to school. First, enter your hours of nonschool activities on a sheet of paper, listing the days of the week and the hours in each day. Also on this list include those hours that you must work, if part-time work is part of your daily schedule. Your schedule should look something like the one in Figure 2-2. In this schedule, the nonschool activities have been listed in the appropriate hours; for the moment, Saturday and Sunday have been left open.

If on this sample schedule you count the number of blank spaces in each day, you will find twelve hours that you can devote to school. Twelve hours well spent can make you an excellent student. You now need to include in this schedule the hours that you spend in class. In Figure 2-3, see how this same student has included fifteen hours of class time.

Notice that the student has spaced the classes. If you do not have to work, spacing your classes is wise. The more hours you are on campus during the day, the more time you will have to study. You will also have time to review your lecture notes right after class. If you check the schedule for Monday, you find that this student has the following hours to study: 9–10 A.M., 11–12 A.M., 2–6 P.M., 7–9:30 P.M., and 10:30–11 P.M.—a total of nine hours.

Many instructors will tell you that for every hour of lecture you should spend two hours outside of class studying for that course. This may be true, but a more realistic estimate will have to be made by you. For each course, assess your background knowledge; if your background is limited in a particular course, you may have to devote more time to studying for that course than for your other courses. If you

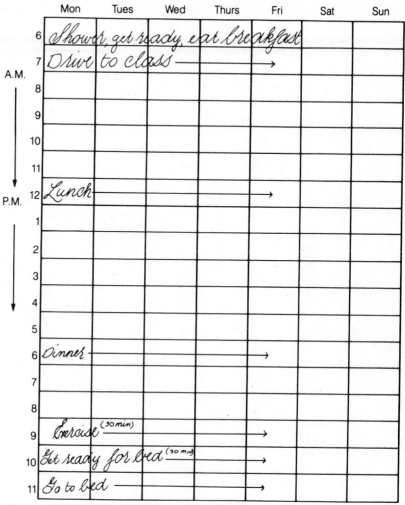

Figure 2-2 *Weekly schedule with nonschool activities.*

are carrying fifteen units, you may need to study fifteen, thirty, or even more hours during the week to be prepared.

It is best to write out a study schedule for each day. See how this same student has completed a schedule for Monday, including three hours of study on campus (Figure 2-4). In Exercise 2.2 you will determine your own study hours.

Writing Out Study Goals the Night Before Class

Each day you will have different school tasks to do. The night before, jot down the work you need to complete for the next day. Figure 2-5 is a sample list of goals; note that the activities are specific and that each one can likely be completed in one hour.

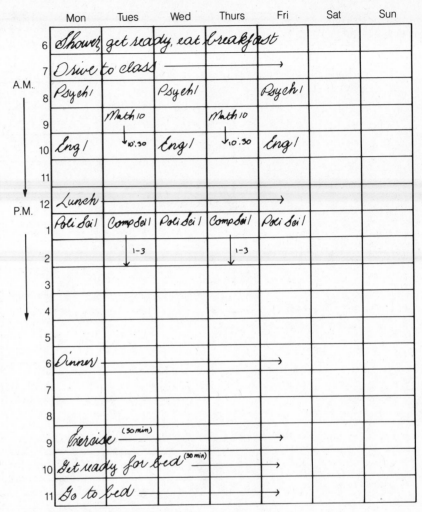

Figure 2-3   *Weekly schedule with school activities.*

When you look at a class syllabus at the beginning of the semester, you may feel overwhelmed, thinking that you can never get through all of the assignments. But breaking up large assignments into smaller tasks of no more than one hour each is an effective way of getting things done. Psychologists call the breaking up of larger activities into smaller tasks *successive approximations*.

**Schedules for
Long-Term Projects**

During the semester, you will likely be assigned large projects—term papers, critical papers, lab reports, and so on. You will also have to prepare for midterms and finals—exams that require more than just a night or two of study. It is best to place the due dates of these larger

Mon	
8	Psych 1
9	Study ////
10	Eng 1
11	Study ////
12	Lunch
1	Poli Sci 1
2	Study ////

Figure 2-4   *Schedule showing study hours.*

9/27
1. Read carefully pp. 12–22 in Psych.
2. Complete 10 homework problems in Math.
3. Make an outline for Poli Sci paper.

Figure 2-5   *Assignment schedule.*

tasks on a monthly calendar. You may want to buy a large calendar that you can place on the wall or desk where you normally study. On this calendar, enter the dates of the major projects and tests for that month. Look at how the month of May is marked in Figure 2-6. With this calendar, you can calculate the number of days you have to finish each assignment. On May 1, for example, on the sample calendar, note that this student has no more than eight days to finish a research paper and all month to study for a computer final.

What to Do on Weekends

If you keep up during the week, your weekends should not end up as study marathons. On weekends, you should relax as well as study; you should complete any late work, get a jump on assignments for the following week, and work on larger projects. It is best to set aside three or four hours on a Saturday or Sunday to work on an essay assignment. Writing requires more concentrated, uninterrupted time.

If you have to work, weekends are best. Without having to attend classes on the weekend, you will be able to work and not feel rushed.

Be Good to Yourself

The average student has ample time to study each day. You can therefore set aside some part of each day for fun. Psychologists have shown that students who vary their activities during the day actually retain more than those who study nonstop. So do not feel that you are wasting your time when you are not doing schoolwork. Give yourself

	Sun	Mon	Tues	Wed	Thurs	Fri	Sat
May							1
	2	3	4	5	6	7	8
	9	10 *Eng. paper due*	11	12	13	14	15
	16	17	18 *critical paper in Poli Sci due*	19	20	21	22
	23 / 30	24 *Math final* / 31	25	26	27	28 *Computer final*	29

Figure 2-6   *Deadlines marked on the calendar.*

some time each day to relax. On weekends, take advantage of the movies, plays, and concerts available to you on or off campus. If you come back to your studies refreshed, you will have a more positive attitude toward the new material.

What has been said so far about scheduling your time and making lists and calendar deadlines may seem tedious to you, and some of it is. But being organized is one of the most important characteristics of a successful student. If you stick to your schedules and continue to meet your deadlines, you will begin to enjoy the pleasures of being a successful student. Once being organized becomes a habit for you, you may want to dispense with written lists and goals entirely.

You are now ready to consider specific suggestions about managing your time and setting up your study area. With these suggestions, you will be able to make even better use of each study hour.

Setting Up a Course Priority List

At the beginning of each semester, you should look at all your courses and select the one or two that you think are most important. These courses may be the ones in your major or prerequisites to your major. You should list your courses in order of importance and then anticipate the grade you will earn in each. Then you can better predict the time you should devote to each course.

Study the following course priority list, designed by a student majoring in computer science:

	Course	*Predicted Grade*
1.	Computer Science 1	A
2.	Mathematics 10	A
3.	English 1	B
4.	Political Science 1	B
5.	Psychology 1	C

It is clear that this student will be exerting more effort in the computer science and math courses. Because she realizes the need to do very well in the computer science and math courses, the anticipated grade of "C" in psychology is realistic. She is not pressuring herself to do exceptionally well in all courses.

If you set up such a priority list, you should be able to set some realistic goals early on in the semester. If, during the semester, you are not doing as well as you had predicted, you need to determine what is going wrong. Do you need to study more? Do other activities conflict with your studies? Or have you chosen a major that is ill suited for you?

In Exercise 2.5 you will be able to determine your own priority list.

When Do You Study Best?

When should you study for each course? You should study for your priority courses when your mind is freshest. Each student's most productive hours vary. Some find the mornings best, others the evenings or late nights. Find out when you work best, and study for your most important courses then.

How to Study

In this book you will be introduced to several study hints and learn a successful study reading system called SQ3R. But first, consider the following general study hints:

1. Never study with distractions. Music, although soothing, is often distracting. When you are doing concentrated studying, avoid listening to music.

2. Do not begin studying if you are more concerned about something else. Your study hours need to be concentrated ones. A brisk walk, run, or swim before you study can often clear your mind of daily problems.

3. Try to divide up your studying into one-hour blocks. During this hour, you can take a ten-minute break either at the end or in the middle of the hour. Gauge your breaks according to the difficulty level of the material. The key to a successful study hour, though, is to put in fifty concentrated minutes of study.

4. After your hour is up, do something different. Either study for a course unrelated to what you have just studied or do something

not related to school. Studying during spaced intervals is more productive than cramming your studying into a few days.

5. Devote some time during your school hours to reviewing what you have learned for that day. You need to review your lecture notes or the study notes you have taken from your textbooks. You tend to forget more of what you have learned during the first twenty-four hours, so it is important to review soon after you have learned something new. More will be said about how you remember in Chapter 13, "Mnemonic Strategies."

6. Be sure to complete your reading assignments soon after they are assigned. Listening to a lecture on completely new material can confuse and frustrate you. So make your reading assignments a study priority item.

How to Study for Difficult Assignments

Sometimes your study material is difficult, and studying for a concentrated hour may be exhausting. If this happens, break your studying into shorter activities. Write these goals out before you begin studying. For example, if you have five difficult math problems to do, you can write out a list of shorter tasks, something like the following:

1. Complete problem #1.
2. Read and think about problem #2.
3. Take a four-minute break.
4. Come back to problem #2.

You will find that you will achieve your goals if you make them short and realistic. Instead of focusing on five difficult problems, reward yourself for completing one problem at a time.

Studying for Tests

Much will be said in this book on how to study for tests, including objective tests (Chapter 14) as well as essay and math or science tests (Chapter 15). For now, read the following time-management hints, which apply to preparing for any test.

1. Before you begin studying for a test, you should have completed all of your reading assignments. In addition, you should have reviewed your notes each day.

2. For a weekly quiz, take two days to study, one day to do your reviewing, and a second to let the material settle. If the course is difficult, you may need more days to learn the material.

3. For a midterm test, study for three or four days. On the last night, do not cram; review only the general concepts.

4. For a final examination, reserve about a week to study. As with the midterm, review only the general points the night before.

Making a Schedule for Your Longer Projects

Do not wait until the last few days of the semester to complete a project such as a term paper. You need to divide up these larger assignments into smaller tasks and assign yourself deadlines to complete them.

If, for example, you are assigned a 500-page novel to read in ten days, you need to divide up the number of pages by the days you have to complete the reading. With this novel, you need to read fifty pages a day. For a research paper, you can divide up your work into the following smaller tasks: (1) finding library material, (2) taking notes on this material, (3) writing an outline for the paper, (4) writing a rough draft, and (5) writing a final draft. Look at this sample schedule for completing a research paper on the Hopi Indians:

Hopi Indians (30-Day Project)

1. Go to library, make up a bibliography.	5 days
2. Take notes from the book.	8 days
3. Write an outline	2 days
4. Write a rough draft.	7 days
5. Type a final draft.	4 days
	Total = 26 days

You may have noticed in this schedule that, although it is for a thirty-day project, the student has estimated twenty-six days for completing the project. The extra four days give him some breathing room in case one task takes longer to complete. Often these projects take longer to finish than you had originally planned. Generally it takes three to four weeks to complete a research paper. Once you have completed your first research paper, you will be able to estimate more accurately the time required to complete the next one.

Analyzing Your Test Results

You can also learn much about your progress as a student by studying your test results, particularly your first test scores of the semester. Study your errors; try to determine why you made them. You may find that you need to study more or study in a quieter area.

By studying your results, you can also determine the kinds of tests your instructor gives and what study materials he or she emphasizes: lecture notes, textbook material, class discussion, and so on. Does the test emphasize details or concepts? Are any of the questions tricky? If the test is essay, what does the instructor seem to be looking for? An organized essay? Accurate details? New ideas? The instructor's ideas? By answering these questions, you will likely do better on the next exam.

If you receive a low or failing score, try to figure out what went wrong. Did you fail to study enough? Is this course too difficult for you? Do you need tutoring, or should you drop the class? Make an appointment to see your instructor. See what he or she has to say. Take these suggestions seriously.

Remember, a test score is more than a grade. By analyzing it, you become a more serious student.

Your Study Area

Finally, a successful student needs an organized study area. Ideally, you should have your own desk in a quiet area. On your desk, you need a dictionary, and all the texts and notes that you need to use for that hour should be at arm's reach. Your desk should also have scratch paper, lined paper, and typing paper, as well as several pens and pencils. If possible, you should have a typewriter or word processor on your desk. Finally, your chair should not be too comfortable, because you want to stay alert while you study. A chair with an upright back support is effective. With these materials, you will be able to stay in one place during your study hour.

If these ideal conditions are not possible for you, you should still be able to create an organized study area. You may be living at home with younger brothers and sisters disturbing you. Or you may be living in a small apartment with several roommates. So it may be impossible for you to have your own desk in a quiet area. But you still can find a large box for all your books and notes for the semester. Keeping all of your material in one area is a must. Students waste precious time looking for books or notes.

If you cannot study without interruption where you live, you need to find a quiet study area either at a local library or your college library. If you go to the library with friends, sit away from them when you study so you will not be distracted.

Summary

Setting up schedules is a key to success in and out of school. To organize your time, you must first list those activities not related to school. Once you have listed nonschool activities, you then include those hours when you attend school. Try to space your classes throughout the day. On this same schedule, you can then mark those hours that you reserve for study. You must plan your hours of study the night before and stick to your plan. Finally, you need to place long-term projects on a monthly calendar so that you know how much time you have to complete them.

To become a successful student, you also need to devise successful study strategies. Set up class priorities to determine which courses you need to concentrate on; then project the grade that you intend to receive in each of these courses. During your study hours, you should concentrate only on your school assignments. When you are working on large projects, you should break them up into smaller tasks, then set up a deadline for completing each one. Finally, you need to create a quiet study area for yourself, one that has all the materials you will need for that study hour.

In the rest of this book, you will be working on improving specific reading, listening, and writing skills. You may already be familiar with some of these skills; others may be new to you. All of these skills are necessary for you to do well in college.

Summary Box   *Managing Your Time and Your Study Area*

What is time and study-area management?	*Why should you manage your time and your study area?*
A way of analyzing how you spend your day so that you can set aside certain quiet hours to study. Some ways to manage your time and study area are: 1. Making nonschool schedules 2. Making on-campus schedules 3. Making daily activity schedules 4. Making time schedules for longer projects 5. Making course priority lists 6. Analyzing test results 7. Designing a study area.	To develop order in your life as a student. To provide time to complete reading assignments, study for tests, and complete term projects. To assess your progress in school. To get the most out of college.

Skills Practice

Exercise 2.1
Setting Up a
Schedule of
Nonschool Activities

Answer the following questions. Then transfer the answers to these questions to the weekly activity schedule shown in Figure 2-7.

1. When do you get up each morning for school?

2. When do you eat breakfast, lunch, and dinner during the week (excluding Saturday and Sunday)?

3. When do you exercise?

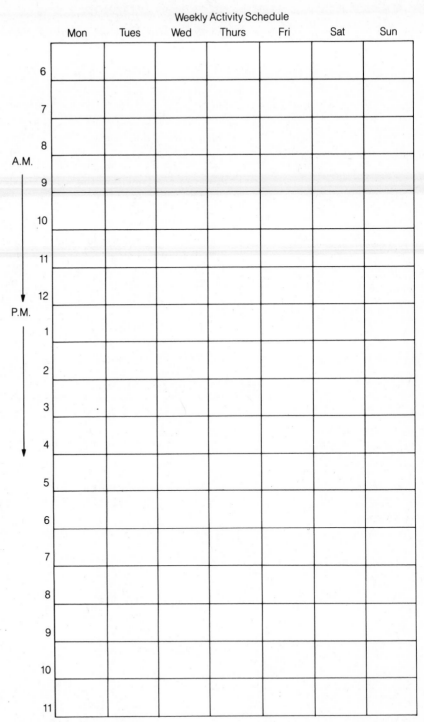

Figure 2-7   *Weekly activity schedule.*

4. When do you go to bed during the week (excluding Saturday and Sunday)?

5. If you work, what are your hours?

Exercise 2.2
Setting Up a
Schedule of School
Activities

Answer the following questions concerning your school activities. Then transfer the answers to these questions to Figure 2-7.

1. How many units are you carrying this semester?

2. List your classes and the time they meet.

	Class Name	*Time Class Meets*
a.		
b.		
c.		
d.		
e.		
f.		
g.		

3. When do you study? In Figure 2-7, shade in the boxes of those hours you regularly reserve for study.

4. How many hours have you reserved for study? Do these hours equal or exceed the number of units that you are carrying? Have you reserved enough hours each week for study?

Exercise 2.3
A Calendar for
Long-Term Projects

In Figure 2-8, you will find a calendar for a typical month. Fill in the current month and the appropriate dates. Then enter the due dates for longer projects and major exams for this month.

   Use this calendar to remind yourself of important due dates for this month. At the end of the month, ask yourself whether this calen-

Month:	Sun	Mon	Tues	Wed	Thurs	Fri	Sat

Figure 2-8   *Typical month's calendar.*

dar was a useful reminder for you. If you found it helpful, continue using it.

Exercise 2.4
Setting Up Daily
Schedules

Use the following activity reminders for the next three days. Remember to write out each task so that you can complete each one in an hour. At the day's end, see if you have completed each task. If you haven't, try to figure out why.

```
1. First Day    Date: _____
To Do:
1. _____
2. _____
3. _____
4. _____
```

Figure 2-9   *First activity reminder.*

Did you accomplish your goals? If not, why do you think you did not?

```
┌──────────────────────────────────────────────┐
│ 2. Second Day   Date: _____ │
│ To Do:                                         │
│ 1. _____ │
│ 2. _____ │
│ 3. _____ │
│ 4. _____ │
└──────────────────────────────────────────────┘
```

Figure 2-10   *Second activity reminder.*

Did you complete your goals? If not, why not? _____

_____

```
┌──────────────────────────────────────────────┐
│ 3. Third Day    Date: _____ │
│ To Do:                                         │
│ 1. _____ │
│ 2. _____ │
│ 3. _____ │
│ 4. _____ │
└──────────────────────────────────────────────┘
```

Figure 2-11   *Third activity reminder.*

Did you complete your goals? If not, why not? _____

_____

Exercise 2.5
Setting Up Course
Priorities

In this exercise, set up a priority list of your courses. List courses in their order of importance. Then predict the grade that you will receive in each.

	Course	*Predicted Grade*
1.		
2.		
3.		
4.		
5.		

Course   *Predicted Grade*

6.

7.

Save this exercise; then, at the end of the semester, compare your predicted grade with the one you actually received. If they were different, try to figure out why.

Exercise 2.6
Assessing Your Time
Management and
Your Study Area

The following ten questions concern your ability to manage time and your study area. Read each question carefully; then answer it by writing yes or no after the question. After you have answered all ten questions, you will be asked to use these results in determining where you need to improve your time management and study area.

1. Does your mind wander when you study? _____
2. Do you often take study breaks that are too long? _____
3. Do you often study for the same kinds of courses back to back? _____
4. Do you fail to review your reading and study notes frequently? _____
5. Do you often go to lectures without having completed the reading assignment? _____
6. Do you get frustrated when you read difficult material? _____
7. Do you wait until the last day to study for your exams? _____
8. Do you wait until the last days to complete longer projects? _____
9. Do you look only at your test score when you get an exam back? _____
10. Is your study area disorganized? _____

If you answered yes to any of these questions, you need to go back to the introduction and reread the section that applies to the skill in question. Now make a list of those skills that you intend to improve during this semester.

Skills Needing Improvement

1. _____

2. _____

3. _____

4. _____

5. _____

6. _____

7. _____

8. _____

This semester, make it your goal to sharpen the skills you listed.

Basic Reading, Listening, and Writing Skills

In Part Two, you will learn skills that will help you read, listen, and write better in college. These are very important skills for you to acquire in order to succeed. So read each Explanation of Skills carefully, and do as many of the exercises as you can. When you finish Part Two, you will have some very useful study skills at your disposal.

3

Locating the Main Idea

Explanation of Skills

Determining the main idea in textbooks and in lectures is perhaps the single most important study skill that you will learn. Without the main idea, you will be unable to follow the train of thought in a chapter or in a lecture. Once you lose the main idea, details become confusing and meaningless. On the other hand, if you have the main idea in mind, your textbook chapter or lecture becomes both organized and informative. Consider the main ideas as umbrellas under which all significant details are included.

Determining the Main Idea

There are several ways to locate main ideas. Some methods are direct, others indirect. Let's look at some strategies to use in finding main ideas.

Locating the Topic. The first step in locating the main idea is to determine the *topic* of your reading or lecture material. In a reading selection the **topic** is generally easy to find, because it is the title of the material. Most titles clearly tell you what the selection is about. An article with the title "Jean Piaget—His Contributions" will almost definitely tell you what Piaget did. "Albert Einstein—Scientist or Philosopher?" will no doubt try to analyze Einstein's contributions to determine whether he should be considered a philosopher, a scientist, or both. It is best to lock the title in your mind before you start reading, to begin determining what the material will cover.

In some articles, the title may be more indirect. The writer may use a quotation as a title. In this case, you may understand the meaning of the title only while reading or after reading the selection. You will find this to be a problem when you read poetry or fiction. Ernest Hemingway wrote a novel titled *A Farewell to Arms.* In this novel, you understand the title only after carefully reading the book, when you discover that the word *arms* refers both to the hero's lover's arms and to his guns. When you do not immediately understand the title, you should read through the first chapter of the novel or the first page or two of the short story and then write out in a phrase what the novel or story is about. Don't write out involved sentences—just a few words such as "a true adventure set in Africa" or "a teenage girl's thoughts on growing up in New York City." If you determine the topic early on in your reading or listening, you will be on your way to identifying main ideas.

Locating the topic of a lecture is usually quite easy, because most instructors list the subject for that class meeting in the syllabus, next to the class date. For example, a psychology instructor might write: "Monday, January 7—Recent Learning Theory." Write this title on the first line of your page of lecture notes for that day. You should then see how this topic fits into what your instructor said in the previous meetings. Did he discuss the history of learning theory on January 5? Or is this the first lecture on theories of learning? As you start seeing connections among lectures, you will derive more meaning from each lecture.

What if your instructor does not provide a syllabus or does not begin the lecture with a stated topic? Then the responsibility for determining the topic is on you. Give yourself no more than five minutes of listening to the lecture to determine the topic. Then write your own title on the first line of your lecture notes.

The Main Idea in Outline Form.   With your topic in mind, you are now ready to read or listen for main ideas. Perhaps you can best see the main ideas as Roman numerals in an outline, where:

I. = the main idea

and

$\left.\begin{array}{l} \text{A.} \\ \text{B.} \end{array}\right\}$ = the supporting details

If you have already learned this traditional outline form, you know that the main ideas, preceded by Roman numerals, are placed farthest to the left on your page of notes. You may also have learned that the farther to the right you go, the more detailed you get. The main idea, then, is more general than its details but more specific than the topic. See how the main idea is sandwiched between the topic and the details of support in the following outline on note taking.

Note-taking Strategies

I. What is the main idea?

    A. More specific than the topic
    B. More general than details
    C. Sometimes written in a word or phrase

Notice that "I. What is the main idea?" is one issue under the topic "Note-taking Strategies," and that A., B., and C. are the characteristics of main ideas. Whether you are reading or listening, visualize the main idea as the category between the topic and the details. Let this "I., A., B., C." organization be in mind when you are locating main ideas in writing or lectures. And remember that every paragraph and every group of statements in a lecture must contain one main idea and one or more details. When you are comfortable with this "I., A., B., C." structure, you will be able to locate main ideas automatically.

Seeing and Hearing Main Ideas at the Beginning.   In about half of the paragraphs you read, you will find the main idea in the first sentence. In the sentences that follow the first sentence, you will usually read details that support this main idea. Study the following paragraph to see how the first sentence expresses the main idea, while the sentences that follow present details:

> The color of a star tells you its temperature. The hottest stars are blue, sometimes reaching a surface temperature of over 60,000° Fahrenheit. Yellow stars, of which the sun is one, have a surface temperature of about 10,000° F. The coldest and oldest stars in the universe are red ones, whose surface temperature may be as low as 3,500° F.

Did you note that the first sentence is the most general—the umbrella under which the other three sentences fall? Did you also note that in each detail sentence specific colors and temperatures are given? In main-idea sentences, you do not usually read facts and figures. Main-idea sentences are more general. Thus in the main-idea sentence of the paragraph, a temperature is introduced, not a specific temperature.

Similarly, instructors will present main ideas at the beginning of the various parts of their lectures. So you need to listen carefully when they begin a presentation or when they introduce new ideas during the lecture. These introductory remarks will usually be the I., II., and III. of your notes.

Seeing and Hearing Main Ideas at the End.   In a small number of paragraphs, the main idea is presented at the end of the paragraph. In these cases, the detail sentences are presented first. The process of presenting specific information that leads to a general statement is called an *induction*. Information is collected, and from this information a main idea emerges. Study this paragraph on vitamin C:

> Eight mice with tumors were injected with massive doses of vitamin C, and their physical appearance as well as their behavior were monitored. Within 48 hours, the tumors in four of the mice had decreased in size by 50 percent. Further, the body hair in these four mice was fuller, and they became more active. It thus appears that vitamin C given in large doses can shrink the size of growths and promote health, at least among some mice.

Did you note the specific details in the first three sentences? Did you also notice how these details led to the main-idea sentence at the end? This statement, like an umbrella, organized the information into a general statement that explained the details. Main-idea sentences, such as the ones in the paragraphs on stars and mice, should stay with you long after you have forgotten many of the details.

This same pattern may occur in lectures. The speaker presents several details at the beginning of the lecture, and the main idea, or induction, is presented last. So you may need to leave your I. blank temporarily while you jot down the details (A., B., C.) of the lecture. Then, when the speaker presents the main idea, you can go back to fill in the I.

Sometimes when you are writing a paragraph, you are not quite sure how to phrase your main idea, although you can easily express the details. Again, you can return to rephrase your main-idea sentence once you have written the rest of the paragraph.

Seeing and Hearing Main Ideas in Longer Sections of Writing and Speech.   You can also look for main ideas in the beginnings and endings of essays and lectures. In these longer pieces, the main idea can usually be found in the first paragraph of an essay or the first section of a lecture, called the *introduction*. In these longer works, the main idea may be stated in more than one sentence.

In the paragraphs or sections that follow the introduction, often called the *body*, details are usually presented to support this main idea. The last paragraph or section—the *conclusion*—is usually as general as the introduction. It either summarizes the main ideas of the essay or presents new conclusions that logically follow from the details. So when looking for main ideas in most essays, it is wise to read through the first and last paragraphs and then write out the main ideas in your own words.

This outline should help you better understand the relationship between main ideas and details in longer works:

I. Introduction: expresses main ideas; details are introduced here.

A.
B. } Body: a series of paragraphs or sections explaining the
C. details more thoroughly.

II. Conclusion: either summarizes the main ideas or presents a new main idea that follows from the details in A., B., and C.

Signal Words.   There are several *signal words* that can introduce main ideas. You will find these words or phrases most often in the introduction or conclusion of an essay or lecture. Become familiar with these words and phrases: *in general, generally, above all, of great importance, the main idea is, the main point is, the main feature is, the key point is, the truth is.*

Look at how the following paragraph incorporates signal words into its sentences:

> *In general,* a solid math background is useful in becoming a computer programmer. *The main feature* of a successful computer program is its clear logic. *Of great importance* in math courses as well is for students to use math rules efficiently. Let's look at some examples of how math and computer programming can work together.

Do you see how these signal words introduce the key points that this author intends to cover?

Now study the following words and phrases, which signal main ideas in conclusions: *in conclusion, to conclude, to summarize, therefore, thus, consequently, as a consequence, as a result, so, it can be seen that, it is suggested that, it follows that, from the above reasons, it is safe to say.* Let these words be signals for you to locate concluding main-idea sentences in your reading and in lectures. Authors frequently use these words and phrases to introduce a general statement that they want you to remember. Also, you need to start using these signal words when writing conclusions of your own.

Paragraphs Without Stated Main Ideas.   The preceding suggestions about first and last sentences as main ideas in paragraphs and in lectures cover most of what you will read and hear. In some material, though, you will not find a main idea explicitly stated. In these cases, you need to infer a main idea from the details. You will frequently find paragraphs without main ideas in descriptive writing, especially in short stories and novels where the author is creating a mood or recreating an experience. Descriptive writing, therefore, does not follow the "main idea followed by details" pattern.

Read the following description and infer a main idea:

The armed policeman forcefully opened the downtown hotel room door. He noticed that the window facing the highway was open, and cigarette smoke was trailing out the window. Looking more carefully, the young officer found a cigarette butt burned almost to the filter resting in an ashtray on the bedstand. The light from the bathroom slipped through a tightly shut door, and the officer could hear the trickling of water droplets as they fell slowly into the washbasin drain.

Nowhere does the excerpt say that the officer is looking for someone who is most likely a criminal, but do you see that all the details in this excerpt lead you to infer this? The officer is armed and forcefully opens the door, so he is clearly looking for a dangerous person. The window is open, a cigarette is still lit, a light is on in the bathroom, and water is dripping—all details suggesting that someone is still in the room or has just left. The author wants to create suspense for the reader, and a main-idea sentence would destroy the suspense. With descriptive writing, you must play detective and piece together your evidence to create a main idea. Thus, in the excerpt, your main idea would probably be that someone, probably dangerous, is lurking in that room or has just escaped from the window.

Applying Main-Idea Rules to Writing

Learning and using signal words and knowing how essays are organized will help you both to read and listen for main ideas and write organized essays. You will frequently be asked to write essays, testing your understanding of reading and lecture material.

Consider these three suggestions when beginning a writing assignment. First, the I., A., B., C. organization will help you jot down notes before you begin writing. Second, you can use some of the previously listed signal words to introduce your main ideas, inserting them in your introductions and conclusions for emphasis. Concluding, for example, with "John Donne was a gifted poet" is not as emphatic as saying, "To conclude, it is safe to say that John Donne was a gifted poet." Finally, note that most of your essays should have several well-developed paragraphs: an introduction, paragraphs giving details, and a conclusion summarizing or synthesizing what you have said. You will learn more about the extended essay in Chapter 15.

Are you beginning to see that reading, listening, and writing involve similar processes? The same organizational rules seem to apply to all three activities. The major difference is that when you read and listen, you take in information; when you write, you give out information. Good readers and listeners help make good writers. You will learn more about this reading-listening-writing connection throughout this book.

Summary

Determining the main idea of a paragraph and locating the main ideas in longer passages or in lectures are very important skills for students to learn. About half of the main ideas are found in the first sentence or sentences that one reads or hears. In fewer cases the main idea is in the last sentence or sentences that one reads or hears. Other main ideas are not stated at all but may be inferred from the details. Whether spoken or written, all main ideas fall into the outline pattern of:

I.

    A.
    B.
    C.

It is the dividing up of information into general and specific categories that you constantly perform when you read, listen, or write. In Chapter 4, you will study the A., B., C. of the outline form—the details. For now, apply what you have learned in this introduction to the following exercises.

Summary Box   *Main Ideas*

What are they?	Why do you need to use them?
The key statements made in writing or lecture, usually found at the beginning and end of material, and implied in most descriptions.	To make you understand the important points in what you read, hear, or write.
They are more specific than topics, less specific than details.	To serve as umbrellas for the details that support them.

Skills Practice

Exercise 3.1
Determining General
Classifications from
Lists

The following series of outlines contains details but no general classifications. Beneath each series of details you will find three or four choices. Write the letter of the most logical classification in the answer box.

1. I.

    A. noun
    B. verb
    C. adjective
    D. adverb

The general classification is:

    a. words
    b. parts of speech
    c. prepositions
    d. proper nouns

2. I.

    A. classical
    B. jazz
    C. rock and roll
    D. folk

The general classification is:

    a. kinds of music
    b. modern music
    c. folk rock
    d. baroque music

3. I.

    A. chancellor
    B. vice-chancellor
    C. deans of administration and instruction

The general classification is:

    a. professors
    b. chair of the English Department
    c. college administrative positions
    d. instructional positions

4. I.

    A. American Revolution
    B. Civil War
    C. Spanish-American War
    D. Vietnam War

The general classification is:

    a. wars
    b. World War I
    c. World War II
    d. American wars

5. I.

    A. sociology
    B. psychology
    C. anthropology
    D. political science

The general classification is:

    a. sciences
    b. philosophy
    c. social sciences
    d. history

The following series of outlines has details but no general classifications. Read all of the choices, and make a general classification of your own. Write this word or phrase in the answer box.

6. I.

    A. Colonial American literature
    B. literature of the American Renaissance
    C. American Literature of the Gilded Age
    D. modern American literature

7. I.

    A. Afro-American
    B. Asian-American
    C. Hispanic-American
    D. Irish-American

8. I.

    A. infancy
    B. childhood
    C. adolescence

9. I.

    A. fever
    B. chills
    C. nausea
    D. headache

10. I.

    A. topic
    B. main idea
    C. major details
    D. minor details

Exercise 3.2
Determining the
Stated or Implied
Main Idea

In the following paragraphs, the main idea may be found in the first sentence or the last sentence, or it may be implied. Locate the number of the main-idea sentence and place it next to the appropriate number in the answer box. If there is no main-idea sentence, write *implied* next to the number in the answer box.

1. _____

2. _____

3. _____

4. _____

5. _____

6. _____

7. _____

8. _____

9. _____

10. _____

70%

Ask instructor for answers.

1. (1) Karl Marx contributed both to the philosophy of his day and to the politics of his time. (2) He did much to reinterpret the works of the German philosopher Hegel. (3) His political writings include thorough studies of socialism and communism. (4) He saw communism as the logical progression in the governments and economic systems of Europe.

2. (1) For centuries, people raised children in order to have help on the family farm. (2) The young girls usually tended to the domestic work, and the boys learned the farming skills of the father. (3) In the 1800s in Europe, children, some as young as eight, worked in factories. (4) It is for these reasons that historians have considered children as the property of their family.

3. (1) The plasma membrane is the external part of all cells. (2) This membrane detects changes in the environment. (3) A second characteristic of all cells is the nucleus or nucleoid, which is responsible for the cell's development. (4) Between the plasma membrane and the nucleus is the third part of all cells, the cytoplasm, which is the cell's energy producer.

4. (1) Marie heard footsteps behind her as she began walking home from the library on a freezing Monday night. (2) The sidewalk was dimly lit, one street lamp about fifty feet ahead lighting the stop sign. (3) Hearing the quickening of these footsteps, she dared not look back, but with books, purse, and notebook clutched nervously in both arms, she began racing down the sidewalk. (4) Marie could feel her heart pounding and felt a tightening and throbbing in her throat.

5. (1) Buddhism emphasizes ethical behavior as the desired goal for all of its believers. (2) Buddhists believe that one's unkind actions today will bring sadness tomorrow. (3) However, one's kind actions will lead to enlightenment. (4) A kind person, therefore, is a wise person.

6. (1) Photosynthesis is an interesting energy-making process that occurs in two stages. (2) In stage one, the energy from the sun is absorbed into the chlorophyll. (3) In the chlorophyll, the energy goes through chemical changes. (4) In the second stage, these new chemicals work with carbon dioxide to form sugar, which serves as food for the plant.

7. (1) In mathematics, three kinds of angles can be made when two lines meet. (2) If these two lines meet to form a corner, a right angle is formed. (3) If these two lines meet to form a space that is smaller than a right angle, an acute angle is formed. (4) If the two lines meet to form a space that is larger than a right angle, an obtuse angle is formed.

8. (1) The Industrial Revolution had far-reaching effects on society. (2) For one, cities grew because more laborers were needed to work in the factories. (3) Because farmers now used machines to do some of their work, farms became larger, and many small farms went out of business. (4) Finally, craftsworkers were no longer in demand, because the machine could now make what the skilled worker once took pride in making.

9. (1) Word processors save writers much time because the writers' compositions can occur right on the screen rather than on paper. (2) Also, if writers want to edit their work, they can make their corrections on the screen rather than erasing their errors on paper. (3) Writers using word processors can move sentences and even paragraphs from one part of the screen to another. (4) Clearly, the word processor is a much more efficient writing tool than the typewriter.

10. (1) The cat licked its paw and then nestled next to the warm hearth's burning embers. (2) Gordon, sitting on the stuffed leather chair with eyes half closed, yawned and effortlessly tossed his slippers off his feet. (3) He lazily searched for his tumbler of brandy, polishing off the last thimbleful. (4) All Gordon wanted was to summon up enough courage to march from the comfort of the living room to the iciness of his bed sheets.

Exercise 3.3
Determining the
Topic and the
Main Idea

Read the following paragraphs carefully. You may need to reread some of them. As you read, ask the following questions: What is the topic? What is the main idea? Remember, the topic is more general; it is the subject of the paragraph usually phrased in two or three words. The main idea is the point of the paragraph—what all the sentences together are saying. Choose the letter of the correct topic and main idea and put each in the answer box next to the appropriate number.

Jean Piaget was a child psychologist known for his sensitive observations of children. From his research, Piaget developed several interesting psychological theories. One of his greatest contributions involves the concept of the ego in children. Piaget believed that children up to the age of five and sometimes later see themselves as the center of the universe. He conducted experiments with infants and toddlers and identified several developmental stages for children. In passing through these stages, children, Piaget found, give up part of their ego in order to understand and manipulate their environment better.

1. The topic concerns:

a. the life of Jean Piaget
b. Jean Piaget's contributions to child psychology

1. _____

2. _____

3. _____

4. _____

5. _____

6. _____

7. _____

8. _____

9. _____

10. _____

11. _____

12. _____

13. _____

14. _____

15. _____

16. _____

17. _____

18. _____

19. _____

20. _____

_____
75%

(Score = # correct ×
5)
Find answers on p.
307.

c. the perceptions of infants
d. the ego

2. The main idea concerns:

a. the amount of research done by Piaget
b. the conflicting psychological theories of Piaget
c. Piaget's concept of a child's environment
d. Piaget's emphasis on the child's ego in maturation

As a term, *prejudice* need not be associated just with people's negative attitudes toward others. It can also be seen as a neutral term and seen simply as a preconceived idea. For example, if you expect to fail an examination, you have a prejudice—a preconceived sense of failure. If on this same exam, you think that you will make the top score, you are equally prejudiced to see yourself favorably. In both cases, you are passing judgment on what has not actually happened. These are probably not the first associations that come to your mind when you think of prejudice.

3. The topic concerns:

a. a definition of prejudice
b. negative attitudes
c. positive attitudes
d. a definition of judgment

4. The main idea concerns:

a. a commonly accepted definition of prejudice
b. the dangers of prejudice
c. an unconventional definition of prejudice
d. the dangers of negative thinking

Psychologists are not sure what exactly happens when a person reads. They are now convinced that reading is more than decoding sounds or symbols and figuring out what each word or symbol means. Some theorists claim that readers get meaning from each sentence they decode, whereas other theorists see readers finding meaning in groups of sentences or paragraphs. Still other psychologists see reading as a process of skipping over what a reader already knows and concentrating on the parts he or she doesn't know.

5. The topic concerns:

a. various theories of reading
b. one major reading theory
c. the importance of the sentence in reading
d. the importance of the paragraph in reading

6. The main idea concerns:

    a. the agreement among theorists about what reading involves
    b. the difficulties of learning to read
    c. the often inconclusive theories regarding how readers read
    d. how reading cannot be formally taught

Weisman's Bookstore sat at the top of Newcastle Drive, the main street running through this historic Massachusetts town. A red brick façade and a rich oak door with an antique brass doorknob beckoned even the laziest readers to come in. Here, one found all books in excellent condition, organized neatly in rows along bookshelves that lined the walls from beamed ceilings to parquet floors. Most of the leatherbound books were over a hundred years old. Their gold-lettered titles—*Shakespeare's Complete Works, Plato's Dialogues, The Complete Works of Jane Austen*—seemed to have escaped the pain of the twentieth century. Even the uninterested passerby found it hard to leave these rooms for the noisy street outside.

7. The passage describes:

    a. Massachusetts
    b. old books
    c. a Massachusetts bookstore
    d. book lovers

8. The main idea concerns:

    a. the sadness of the twentieth century
    b. the peace and timeless feeling in an old New England bookstore
    c. the large numbers of books kept in a small bookstore
    d. the peaceful life in Massachusetts

Poetry is often divided into two types; knowing which type you are reading often helps you understand the poem. The first type is lyric poetry, which often describes the speaker's feelings. It does not tell a story. To read lyric poetry effectively, you need to visualize the images and be sensitive to the suggestiveness of the words. Narrative poetry, the second type, often tells a story. Although images and language are part of narrative poetry, the poem's story line is uppermost. As you read narrative poetry, you need to determine the significant events of the story line.

9. The topic concerns:

    a. narrative poetry
    b. lyric poetry
    c. two kinds of poetry—lyric and narrative
    d. poetry

10. The main idea concerns:

    a. how to read lyric poetry
    b. knowing the difference between lyric and narrative poetry
    c. the story line in narrative poetry
    d. the similarities between lyric and narrative poetry

Behavioral psychologists believe that learning is a simple process. The two key terms that behaviorists use to explain learning are *stimulus* and *response*. The stimulus is any element in the environment, whereas the response is how this element interacts with something else in the environment. Behaviorists believe that any human response, such as crying or laughing, can be traced to a particular stimulus. Many psychologists find behaviorism to be simplistic because it ignores the complexity of human thought.

11. The topic of the paragraph concerns:

    a. psychology
    b. stimuli and responses
    c. behaviorist psychology
    d. human learning

12. The main idea concerns:

    a. the popularity of behaviorism
    b. how stimuli affect responses
    c. the simplistic nature of behaviorism
    d. the complexity of the human brain

The open classroom became a popular teaching method in the sixties and seventies. The believers in the open classroom wanted to get away from the regimentation of large-group instruction, where an entire class does the same assignment at the same time. These open-classroom teachers wanted to reach the individual needs of each student. They designed learning centers in the classroom where students could complete various assignments when they were ready. If students chose to read in the reading center for two periods instead of one, that was permitted. In the open classroom, teachers respect the choices a student makes. Open-classroom teachers also believe that students who see the teacher as the sole authority do not develop their own leadership abilities.

13. The topic concerns:

    a. a typical open classroom
    b. large-group instruction
    c. individualized instruction
    d. schools in the sixties

14. The main idea concerns:

    a. the dangers of large-group instruction
    b. the failure of the open classroom
    c. the difficulties of teaching in the sixties and seventies
    d. the open classroom and its respect for the student's individual needs

Acid rain has become a serious problem in various parts of the world. This term refers to rainwater that reacts with sulphur and nitrogen in the atmosphere, forming sulphuric and nitric acid solutions. Acid rain has become a major concern in Northern Europe, Southeastern Canada, and the Northeastern United States. In these areas, acid rain has destroyed both forests and lakes. In some New York lakes, for example, acid rain has killed all the fish that used to thrive there.

15. The topic concerns:

    a. what acid rain is
    b. where acid rain is a problem
    c. the effects of acid rain
    d. all of these

16. The main idea concerns:

    a. the dangers of acid rain
    b. the number of fish killed by acid rain
    c. the harmlessness of acid rain
    d. the difficulty in defining what acid rain is

Idealists are philosophers who believe that thoughts rather than things define us. For them, human thought is more important than material things. Often idealists contend that every person and object has a spirit, and that this object or person simply is the house for the spirit. Ultimately, idealists have greater faith in the invisible than in the visible.

17. The topic concerns:

    a. what thought is
    b. people's belief in spirits
    c. how objects are different from thoughts
    d. a definition of an idealist

18. The main idea concerns:

    a. the idealist's emphasis on the spiritual over the material
    b. the idealist's emphasis on matter over the spirit
    c. how everyone is essentially a spirit
    d. the power of the invisible

The relationship between the diameter of a circle and its circumference is interesting. The *diameter* of a circle is any straight line that goes through the center of a circle, touching any two points on the circle. The *circumference* is the length around a circle. In every case, the diameter of a circle and its circumference have the same mathematical relationship. π (or approximately 3.1416) multiplied by the diameter always equals the circumference.

19. The topic concerns:

   a. π—its origins
   b. the definition of diameter
   c. the definition of circumference
   d. the relationship between the circumference and the diameter of a circle

20. The main idea concerns:

   a. the difficulty in determining the circumference of a circle
   b. the difficulty in determining π as a number
   c. the circle as a perfect shape
   d. the consistent relationship between the diameter and circumference of a circle

Exercise 3.4
Putting Topics and
Main Ideas into
Your Own Words

The following ten paragraphs deal with topics you would normally come across in college courses. After reading these paragraphs, write a topic and a main idea for each. Remember that the topic is normally expressed in a phrase and can serve as the title of the passage. The main idea expresses the passage's intent, often stated in the first or last sentence of the paragraph. For example, "Trout Fishing" can serve as the paragraph's topic, whereas "The Popularity of Trout Fishing" could serve as the main idea of the same paragraph. Writing out your own topics and main ideas is a big part of what you do when you take lecture and study notes.

Psychologists are currently studying the reasons why certain people in our society become criminals. Many psychologists are now saying that social and economic conditions are not the most important factors in the making of a criminal. They cite as evidence the majority of people who live in poor, violent environments who do not choose crime. Some psychologists are now suggesting that certain people become criminals because they choose to break the law. These theorists place much more responsibility on the individual in choosing a criminal lifestyle.

1. The topic concerns: _____

2. The main idea concerns: _____

Critical periods of development can be identified in both animals and humans. Small, newly hatched birds, for example, are sensitive to moving objects. The object is usually the mother, but experiments have shown that these fledglings can attach long-lasting importance to a moving object or even to a human being. Psychologists have likewise provided evidence to show that an enriched preschool program of activities in language and physical exercise can increase a child's intelligence potential. Early childhood seems to be a critical period for humans.

3. The topic concerns: _____

4. The main idea concerns: _____

The first digital computer, built in 1944 and called the Mark I, could generate mathematical tables. UNIVAC, built in 1951, was the first commercial computer and was able to store instructions. The computers in the IBM series, built in the early sixties, were smaller, less expensive, and more reliable. The 1970s and 1980s saw the development of microcomputers—small, powerful, and conducive to use in homes and small businesses.

5. The topic concerns: _____

6. The main idea concerns: _____

In the 1800s, the Abolitionists condemned slavery in America as immoral. They believed that slaveholders were criminals and should be punished. They were religious, referring to Biblical passages that condemned any form of servitude. The Abolitionists emerged in the early 1800s as the moral voice of America.

7. The topic concerns: _____

8. The main idea concerns: _____

Numbers can be used to express parts of a whole. When numbers are written as fractions, the top number (the numerator) is the part, the bottom number (the denominator) is the whole. In the fraction $\frac{3}{10}$, 10 is the whole, 3 the part. Decimals work similarly, so that the number to the right of the decimal (.3, for example) is the numerator, and 10 or a multiple of 10 is the understood denominator.

9. The topic concerns: _____

10. The main idea concerns: _____

Scientists have recently been using radioactive elements to date objects of scientific or historical interest. Radioactive elements have proven effective because they decay no matter what else happens around them. That is, a radioactive element will decay at exactly the same rate whether in a warm or cold climate. So artifacts that are very old can be accurately dated. Radioactive dating has proven effective in determining the age of skeletons and skeletal parts of human ancestors found in Africa and Asia.

11. The topic concerns: _____

12. The main idea concerns: _____

Hedonism is the belief that sensual pleasure is worth having for its own sake. The hedonist is seen as one who values only sensual pleasures. The hedonist cherishes those experiences that involve seeing, touching, tasting, smelling, and hearing. The pleasure that one gets from learning is intellectual and therefore not what the hedonist is seeking.

13. The topic concerns: _____

14. The main idea concerns: _____

It seems that everyone wants to learn to read and write better. The current literacy campaign in the United States is encouraging everyone who cannot read and write to seek help. Could it be, though, that there are drawbacks to being literate? Some literacy experts have suggested that learning to read and write tends to alienate the individual from family and community. The ideas gotten from books may go against accepted beliefs of the home and society. Further, experts note that reading is a solitary activity; rarely do adults gather to hear a story read to them.

15. The topic concerns: _____

16. The main idea concerns: _____

The Dred Scott decision of 1857 was a Supreme Court ruling that defined the slave as property to be transported at will by the master. This ruling gave to the slaveholder final control over the slave. Further, the ruling did not question the morality of slavery. The Dred Scott decision was applauded by the South and criticized by the North.

17. The topic concerns: _____

18. The main idea concerns: _____

Thomas was admired by all of his family because he was helpful and even-tempered. But Thomas knew a different person inside, one who resented doing his brother's chores. Because he was too shy to complain, his parents thought he liked the extra work. One day, Thomas simply had reached his limit, and decided to show them all by not coming home from school.

19. The topic concerns: _____

20. The main idea concerns: _____

70%

Ask instructor for answers.

Exercise 3.5
Determining the
Main Idea in a
Longer Passage

In determining the main idea of a passage, you can apply the same rules that you used in determining the main idea of a paragraph. Read the following extended essay on the Puritans, and follow these steps to determine the main idea:

1. Read the introductory paragraph to determine what the main idea of the entire passage is.

2. See how the three paragraphs that follow (the body) give the supporting details to the main idea. Locate a main-idea sentence for each of these paragraphs.

3. Read the last paragraph (the conclusion), which summarizes the main idea and the major details of the previous four paragraphs.

After you have followed these steps, answer the five questions that follow. You may look back.

The Puritans in America

(1) Who were the Puritans? To begin to understand these people, it is important to know why they came to the United States, to learn about the community they established, and to be introduced to their religious beliefs.

(2) The Puritans came from England and chose to settle in an uninhabited new world because they wanted to escape what they saw as tyranny and mistreatment in England. The first group of Puritans came to Plymouth, Massachusetts, in 1620. Soon other Puritans came and settled in various parts of New England. For about fifty years, these British immigrants were allowed to live without direct British control.

(3) The kind of government that the Puritans established was known as a theocracy. As a theocracy, they saw themselves as a community governed by God. Their priests therefore had much power, because the Puritans saw them as God's representatives. Although the Puritans left England because they were mistreated as nonconformists, they themselves discouraged new ideas and allowed only Puritans to reside in their communities, expelling those who had different religious beliefs.

(4) The Puritans had strict religious beliefs. They believed that everyone's life was directed by God. They saw human beings as es-

sentially sinful, saved only by God's grace. And the Puritans learned of God's plan by a careful reading of the Bible. Those who could not prove their beliefs with reference to the Bible were considered heretics.

(5)   The Puritans in America saw the human being as essentially corrupt. God was all good, but since the fall of Adam and Eve, the human being was born with sin. It was only through God's grace that the sinner could be forgiven. These first European Americans were not optimistic about human nature.

---

1. _____

2. _____

3. _____

4. _____

5. _____

_____
80%

Find answers on p. 307.

---

1. The main idea of paragraph 1 is:

   a. no one knows why the Puritans settled in the United States
   b. no on knows where the Puritans came from
   c. to understand the Puritans, it is important to know what they believed
   d. to understand the Puritans, it is necessary to know their history in England and America and to know something about their religion

2. The main idea of paragraph 2 concerns:

   a. the mistreatment of the Puritans by the British
   b. the reasons why the Puritans came to America
   c. the mistreatment of the Puritans in England and their settling in various areas in New England
   d. the first fifty years that the Puritans spent in America

3. The main idea of paragraph 3 concerns:

   a. the Puritans' rejection of theocracy
   b. Puritan theocracy, which centered around the interpretation of God's will
   c. the open-minded character of Puritan society
   d. how the Puritans expelled those they disliked

4. The main idea of paragraph 4 concerns:

   a. the open-minded attitude of the Puritans
   b. the strict religious beliefs of the Puritans
   c. when the Puritans read the Bible
   d. how the Puritans expelled people from their communities

5. The main idea of the last paragraph concerns:

   a. the Puritans' pessimistic attitude toward human beings
   b. the Puritans' optimistic attitude toward human beings
   c. the Puritans' belief in God's goodness
   d. the Puritans' interpretation of the Adam and Eve story in the Bible

Exercise 3.6
Writing Your Own
Paragraph from
Main Ideas

The excerpt on the Puritans that you just read can be easily outlined in the following way:

I. = the main idea of the passage, expressed in the introduction (paragraph 1)

A.
B. } = the main ideas of each of these paragraphs become the
C.   supporting details for the main idea of the passage

If you are still unclear what the main idea of each paragraph is, review the correct answers to questions 1–4 in the previous exercise.

Review the previous passage. Then, in a phrase, state the main idea of each of the four paragraphs on the following outline.

I. _____

A. _____

B. _____

C. _____

70%

Ask instructor for answers.

With this outline to guide you, answer the following essay question in a paragraph of four sentences, having one main-idea sentence and three supporting sentences.

Essay Question: In one paragraph, discuss where the Puritans came from and where they settled, what kind of government they established, and what their religious beliefs were.

Exercise 3.7
Determining the
Main Ideas in a
Textbook Excerpt

A. The following excerpt is from a textbook chapter on economic systems. Read through it quickly to get a sense of the topic. Then go back and read it slowly. The only term in the excerpt that might be new to you is *opportunity cost*, which refers to an economic opportunity that is lost when one chooses between two options.

When you finish rereading, answer the following five questions. You may return to the excerpt in deciding on your answers.

The message of Chapter 1 was that scarcity forces us to measure the inevitable costs and hoped-for benefits of every decision. This chapter describes the different routes societies take in making those decisions. After some preliminaries, most of the chapter is devoted to describing our kind of economic system, its history, and some of its successes and failures. The chapter is divided into four sections: (1) the three questions every economic system must answer, (2) three different ways of answering those questions, (3) a brief history of our market-price system, and (4) an evaluation of our market-price system.

The Three Questions Every Economic System Must Answer

(1) First, what do we mean by **economic system**? An economic system is the particular body of laws, habits, ethics, and customs (religious or otherwise) that a group of people observe to satisfy their material wants.

(2) All systems, from primitive to advanced, face three fundamental questions: (1) What goods and services should be produced (and in what quantities)? (2) How should they be produced? (3) For whom should they be produced? Let's now examine each of these questions.

What Goods and Services Should Be Produced?

(3) Every economic system must decide, consciously or not, what goods (TV sets or stereos or bicycles) and services (medical care or legal advice or plumbing) are to be produced and in what quantities. These decisions require, of course, an evaluation of opportunity cost. If we decide to devote more of our resources to making cars, we will have fewer resources for building rapid transit systems. The opportunity cost of each new car is measured by the amount of rapid transit we could have provided but did not.

(4) This observation must be qualified. For example, if people are unemployed, we might be able to use some of them to build cars without having to divert people already employed in rapid transit. Also, if new technology (new machines, tools, or production methods) makes it easier to produce cars, that will release some people from automobile production to work on rapid transit. A surplus of workers and/or new technology enables us to have more of both products.

How Should the Goods and Services Be Produced?

(5) Every society must decide not only what products and services it wants (and in what quantities) but also *how* it should produce them. The question of how involves choosing some combination of machines and people. For example, should we use large numbers of people working with garden tools to cultivate potatoes or a much smaller number of people working with tractors?

(6) Either way, we have to consider the opportunity costs of employing the machines and people in growing potatoes. We have to measure this cost in terms of the lost production of something else.

(7) But the problem is more complex than that. Let's take a very simple example. A potato farmer is understandably tired of cultivating his fields by hand. He wants to purchase a "machine"—in his case, a horse and plow. To buy the horse and plow, he will have to sell some of his potatoes. Consequently, the opportunity cost of the horse and plow is measured by the sacrifice the farmer and his family have to make in not consuming some of their potatoes. In some cases, this opportunity cost may be severe—the family may not get enough to eat. Of course, the decision to buy the horse and plow is made with

the expectation that future benefits will make up for these present costs.

(8) In poor countries, this kind of trade-off is an excruciating problem. If the government in one of these countries decides to build a hydroelectric dam, many hundreds of people may have to be taken away from food-producing activities. The opportunity cost of the dam may be further starvation of the people. Thus, the question of *how* may involve some very difficult decisions.

For Whom Should the Goods and Services Be Produced?

(9) Every society must decide who receives the products and services produced, which is another way of saying that a society must decide how income will be distributed among its people. Needless to say, whether by design or circumstance, the world's production and income are very unequally distributed. About 60 percent of the world's population receives only about 10 percent of total income, whereas 10 percent of the people receive about 50 percent of total world income.

(10) In the United States, the lowest 20 percent of families receive only 5 percent of total income, while the highest 20 percent of families receive over 40 percent of the total. And, roughly 25 million people in the U.S. are classified as poverty-stricken. More on the distribution of income in Chapter 11.

(11) Part of the "for whom?" question involves deciding which generation, present or future, should receive the goods and services produced. Decisions to use resources for long-term projects like the Tennessee Valley Authority or cancer research often mean a sacrifice for today's generation in favor of some expected benefit for tomorrow's. Most of the working population pays Social Security taxes for the benefit of older people. Research expenditures on power from hydrogen fusion are expected to be $1 billion per year for twenty years; commercial use of hydrogen fusion is not expected until the year 2015. Again, we must measure opportunity cost.[1]

1. _____

2. _____

3. _____

4. _____

5. _____

1. The topic of this excerpt concerns:

    a. what one should buy
    b. what one should sell
    c. from whom one should buy
    d. what, how, and for whom goods and services should be produced

2. The main idea of paragraph 4 is:

    a. the unemployed should be allowed to work
    b. technology makes production easier

---

[1] Philip C. Starr. *Economics: Principles in Action.* 4th ed. (Belmont, Calif.: Wadsworth, 1984), pp. 18–19. Used by permission.

    c. both additional workers and better technology are needed to produce more of the desired product

    d. new technology equals new machines

3. The main idea in paragraph 5 is:

    a. a society must determine what it needs and how these needs will be met

    b. machines and people make up society

    c. garden tools are necessary in raising potatoes

    d. farmers are often unemployed

4. The main idea in paragraph 8 is that poor countries:

    a. cannot feed their people

    b. often purchase technology at the expense of having some of their people starve

    c. often cannot build dams without help from other countries

    d. should not build dams

5. In paragraph 11, the main idea is:

    a. long-term projects often do not get completed

    b. social security is meant for older people's use

    c. power plants are expensive

    d. the people of a country generally must do without when the government of that country has undertaken long-term projects

B. Now go back and reread the excerpt. Then answer the following three questions in a short phrase or sentence without looking back at the excerpt.

1. Why is it that if a country produces more cars, it is often involved in fewer transportation projects? (1 point)

2. Why is it that the potato farmer who buys a horse and plow will have fewer potatoes for his family to eat? (2 points)

3. Why is it that current cancer research requires sacrifices for a society involved in this research? (2 points)

70%

Ask instructor for answers.

4

Locating Major and Minor Details

Explanation of Skills

Major Details

Now that you have practiced locating and writing main-idea sentences, you are ready to learn about major-detail sentences as they appear in your reading and lecture material and as you use them in your writing. Major details are the A., B., C. of the outline format I., A., B., C. They support the main idea, giving examples, steps, characteristics, causes, or effects. Major details often answer the who, what, where, when, why, which one(s), or what kind(s) of a sentence or passage. Also, remember that major details are usually found in the body of a paragraph, essay, or lecture.

Major Details That Give Examples. Main-idea sentences often express a point of view, as in the following: "America is known for its scenic national parks," or "Certain British kings were tyrants." In the major-detail sentences supporting these two points of view, you would be looking for examples. The examples for both sentences should answer the "which one(s)" question. Regarding the scenic parks sentence, you would be looking for names such as Yellowstone, or Bryce Canyon. In the sentence concerning British kings, you would expect to find names such as Richard III or Henry VIII.

Look at how a writer uses examples in the following paragraph:

ex

To be classified as a mammal, an animal must be warm blooded and nourish its young with milk. A *human being*, of course, is a mammal, since humans are warm blooded and nurse their young. Surprisingly, another mammal is a *whale*. Although whales live in the sea, they are warm blooded and regularly need to come up for air each day. Finally, though a *bat* flies, it is also a mammal. Nature has modified the forelimbs of the bat into wings.

Do you see how humans, whales, and bats become the examples that support the main idea—that a mammal must be warm blooded and nourish its young with milk?

When you come across the names of persons, places, or things, you have probably found details. The details become the support that you will need when defending a particular point of view. Start using the abbreviation *ex* in the margins to remind yourself that you are reading or listening to examples. Did you note that this abbreviation was used in the margin of the previous paragraph to signal the three examples?

Major Details That Give Steps. Details are sometimes laid out in sequence. For example, your instructor may be discussing the steps involved in using the scientific method, or you may be reading about the steps to follow in correctly using your computer. The main-idea sentence that comes before the steps usually alerts you to the number of steps involved. Steps are details that often answer the question "which ones?"

Consider this main-idea sentence: "There are five steps to remember in writing a research paper." The details that follow this sentence should include these five steps: researching, outlining, writing, revising, and typing. Be alert for the following signal words when you listen to or read for steps: *first, second, third, and so on; last, and finally.*

Look at how the details in the following excerpt on how a bill becomes a law provide steps:

steps   Passing a law in Congress is a complicated procedure. There are four steps. *First,* a member of Congress introduces a bill, and it is assigned to an appropriate committee for study. *Second,* the committee votes on whether to approve or reject it. *Third,* if the bill is accepted, it goes to the House and Senate. *Finally,* if both houses approve the bill, it is sent to the President for approval or rejection.

In this excerpt, the main-idea sentence introduces the number of steps necessary in passing a law. This sentence is general but is followed by specific information discussing the stages that a bill goes through. Did you note the signal words *first, second, third,* and *finally,* which led you through the four steps? Like examples, steps provide specific information. Unlike examples, steps are more closely interrelated. A writer cannot present step two before step one. A writer presenting examples is usually not concerned with correctly sequencing them; Bryce Canyon could have come before Yellowstone Park in the previously discussed set of examples. You will learn more about steps as details in Chapter 5, "Identifying Organizational Patterns."

Finally, did you note how the marginal note *steps* in the previous paragraph reminds you of the steps in the excerpt? Marginal notes such as *steps* or *ex* help direct your reading or listening.

Major Details That Present Characteristics.   Some major details are neither examples nor steps. Rather they are descriptive. Major details of characteristics frequently include adjectives or adverbs. Such details may be used to draw a character sketch, be the key points in a film or book review, or be used to define a word. Look at how the following main-idea sentences require characteristics to support their points of view: "Socrates demonstrated the characteristics of a great teacher" or "Alfred Hitchcock's film *Psycho* represents the best kind of horror film." In these main-idea sentences, examples or steps would not be the best kind of support. Saying that Socrates was Plato's teacher would not describe the greatness of Socrates's teaching, nor would mentioning another film by Hitchcock show how *Psycho* is successful as a horror film. Each of these main-idea statements needs details expressing qualities or feelings that answer "why" to the main-idea statement.

Look at how the following excerpt on John Keats, the British poet, effectively uses characteristics:

reasons why

John Keats is considered one of the greatest poets in the English language. The language of his poetry is *rich* and *sensuous.* Many of his descriptions appeal to all of the senses, not just to the eyes. Further, Keats's best poems are *concrete.* His poems treat objects in this world, not just ideas. Through the objects that he presents, Keats makes *profound* comments about life.

In this description, do you see that the author does not refer to specific poems or to specific lines of Keats's poetry? This paragraph, rather, emphasizes the qualities of Keats's poetry. See how the author uses the adjectives *rich, sensuous, concrete,* and *profound* to describe the nature of Keats's poetry. By placing the comment *reasons why* in the margin, you remind yourself that you are emphasizing the characteristics of Keats's poetry.

Major Details That Present Causes and Effects.   A great number of major-detail sentences are closely related to the main-idea sentence. They do not give examples or qualities to support the main idea, nor do they list steps that follow from the main-idea sentence. These sentences of cause and effect are either the reasons for or causes of what the main idea suggests, or they are the results, or effects, of what the main idea suggests. These sentences usually answer the "what" question suggested in the main-idea sentence. Words that signal causes are *cause, reason, factor source, influence;* and those suggesting effect are *effect, consequence, result,* or *outcome.*

Read the following paragraph and note how all major-detail sentences provide causes for social deviance, which is mentioned in the main-idea sentence:

causes
There are several *reasons* for antisocial, or deviant, behavior among people. For many sociologists, the *source* of deviant behavior is an unstable family. Other sociologists say that antisocial behavior *stems* from an uncaring society. Finally, Freudian psychologists say that all human beings can be antisocial and that this behavior is kept in check by the superego, or conscience.

Do you see how the words *reasons, source,* and *stems* signal causes? Do you note as well that these major-detail sentences provide specific information to support the main-idea sentence's point of view? Finally, note how the word *causes* in the margin reminds you of the kind of information found in this paragraph.

Now look at this paragraph, which deals with the effects of World War I:

effects
The results of World War I were staggering, both for the people and their governments. First, the war's cost had to be paid for in extra taxes imposed on the losing countries. *Consequently,* the standard of living in these countries declined. As a second *outcome* of the war, dictators emerged who promised to solve their countries' economic problems. Finally, over ten million deaths brought on by the war *resulted* in hatred among nations.

Do you see how the signal words *consequently, outcome,* and *resulted* suggest a paragraph of effect? Again, note how in the major-detail sentences, you are given specific information concerning the results of World War I. And the word *effects* in the margin becomes your signal that this paragraph is treating the results of World War I.

Major-detail sentences of cause and effect often provide important information. Like steps and examples, they are specific; but unlike examples, causes and effects require you to see relationships in time—how one occurrence leads to another. You will learn much more about how cause-and-effect details are used in lectures and textbooks in Chapter 5, "Identifying Organizational Patterns."

Remember that in your lecture or reading notes, you should mark major details as examples, steps, characteristics, causes, or effects, as you have seen done in the previous example paragraphs. Actively identifying details gives direction to your reading or listening, organizing and connecting information. By identifying details, you will also more easily review this study material for exams.

Signal Words in Major-Detail Sentences.   A number of words and phrases can be used to introduce any type of major detail. Once you become familiar with these words, you will have another way of locating major details in reading or in lecture.

for example	furthermore	again	last
for instance	moreover	another	of course
in addition	besides	specifically	
also	next	finally	

You should also begin using these words and phrases when you write essays. By using these signal words, you alert your reader to details that you consider important.

Minor Details

By now, you should be able to recognize the four types of major details. Thus it will be easy for you to locate minor details. You will find minor-detail sentences right after major-detail sentences, minor details providing you with more information about the major detail. When you come upon a minor detail, ask yourself whether or not you want to include it in your notes. Often, all you need to learn are the main ideas and the major details.

You will need to use minor details when you write paragraphs or essays. Adding a minor detail on an essay exam, for example, shows your instructor that you are well prepared. Often a minor-detail sentence picks up a word or phrase that was used in the preceding major-detail sentence.

Look at the following paragraph on family purchases, and note that the last sentence further explains the preceding sentences. It is therefore a minor-detail sentence.

> Children have been known to influence what their parents purchase. An infant, for example, has special food and clothing needs that the parent must consider. Children from ages five to ten influence what types of breakfast cereals their parents buy. Some parents allow their children to buy whatever cereal they have seen on television.

Do you see how this last sentence further explains how children influence their parents in buying breakfast cereals? This minor-detail sentence adds that children have seen these cereals advertised on television. Did you also note the word *cereal* is used in both sentences?

You can see more clearly what minor details are by looking at an outline of the previous paragraph. You will see that the minor detail is the material farthest to the right in this outline—the 1. under B.

I. Children's influence on purchasing

    A. Infants—special food and clothing needs

    B. Five- to ten-year-olds—influence parents' buying of breakfast cereals

        1. these cereals seen on television ads

Remember that it is the I. (main idea) and the A. and B. (major details) that you often need to write as lecture notes and remember on exams. You may use the 1. more effectively in your essays.

Signal Words for Minor Details. The following words and phrases are frequently used to introduce minor-detail sentences. You should use these words when you introduce minor details in essays, and you should look for these words to introduce minor details in lectures and in textbooks.

a minor point to be made	this is further clarified by	as an aside
incidentally	as further clarification	related to this issue
that is to say	another way of saying	a corollary to this
in other words	restated	issue
of less importance	namely	subordinate to this issue

Summary

Major details provide the information necessary to support main ideas. Major details may be examples, steps, characteristics, causes, or effects. They answer the questions "who," "what," "where," "when," "why," "which one(s)," or "what kind(s)." When you identify the types of major details that are in your reading or listening, you tend to understand the material better. Minor-detail sentences further explain a major-detail sentence that comes before it. It is not often necessary to include minor details in your reading and lecture notes, but you should use them in essays.

The following summary box should help you see how main ideas, major details, and minor details interrelate.

Summary Box   *Main Ideas, Major Details, and Minor Details*

What are they?	*Why do you use them?*
Main Ideas (I.): general statements in a paragraph or longer passage.	To read and listen more effectively for major and minor details.
Major Details (A., B., C.): support for the main ideas, presented as examples, steps, characteristics, causes, or effects.	To understand the main idea better. To see whether the main idea is based on sound evidence.
Minor Details (1., 2., 3.): further support for the major-detail sentence that comes before it.	To further explain a major detail. Used in essays, but often not necessary in reading and lecture notes.

Skills Practice

Exercise 4.1
Classifying Major
Details

The following outline forms contain a main idea and three major details. Your job is to choose from the lists that follow a major detail that best completes the outline. Remember that major details are less general than main ideas and more general than minor details. Place the letter of your answer next to the appropriate number in the answer box.

1. _____

2. _____

3. _____

4. _____

5. _____

6. _____

7. _____

8. _____

9. _____

10. _____

_____
70%

(Score = # correct ×
10)
Find answers on p.
308.

1. I. Kinds of communication

    A. Words
    B. Hand gestures
    C. Facial gestures
    D. _____

An appropriate major detail would be:

    a. Early human ancestors used gestures a lot
    b. Definition of communication
    c. Grunts and groans
    d. Southern Mediterraneans use hand gesturing

2. I. Pros and cons of competition

    A. Is ruthless at times
    B. May create a sense of inferiority
    C. Brings out future leaders of a community
    D. _____

An appropriate major detail would be:

    a. Brothers sometimes compared; often one brother feels inferior
    b. The nature of competition
    c. Competition most evident in athletes
    d. Can help you understand your strengths

3. I. Possible causes of criminal behavior

    A. All people have tendencies inside them
    B. Unstable or broken families
    C. An aggressive or violent personality type
    D. _____

An appropriate major detail would be:

    a. Freud believed in the criminal tendency inside us all
    b. Lack of schooling
    c. The characteristics of antisocial behavior
    d. Those who choose crime are often called sociopaths

4. I. Advantages of city life

    A. A variety of people
    B. Many different job opportunities
    C. Closer to large hospitals
    D. _____

An appropriate major detail would be:

    a. Higher crime
    b. Closer to government offices
    c. New York City has several museums
    d. The population density of Chicago

5. I. Early history of Charles Darwin

    A. Grandfather was a well-known philosopher in his day
    B. Father a physician
    C. Grandfather was also a physician
    D. _____

An appropriate major detail would be:

    a. Darwin's evolutionary theories
    b. Later years of Charles Darwin
    c. As a child, collected and studied sea shells
    d. Darwin's *On the Origin of Species*

6. I. Parts of a leaf

    A. Vein
    B. Lower epidermis
    C. Spongy mesophyll
    D. _____

An appropriate major detail would be:

    a. Upper epidermis
    b. Parts of a root
    c. Leaves have different structures
    d. Leaves of two kinds: simple and compound

7. I. Effect of lower death rate on world population

    A. Causes more births
    B. Causes greater percentage of older people
    C. Increases Social Security budget
    D. _____

An appropriate major detail would be:

    a. Effect of increased birth rates in the United States
    b. In parts of Africa, life expectancy only forty years

   c. Creates expanded health care needs

   d. A veterans' hospital in Washington, D.C., cares only for the elderly

8. I. Types of energy sources

   A. Solar
   B. Hydroelectric
   C. Natural gas
   D. _____

An appropriate major detail would be:

   a. Windmills
   b. Nuclear reactors
   c. Wind
   d. Solar panels

9. I. Possible causes of cancer

   A. Stress
   B. Environment
   C. Personality type
   D. _____

An appropriate major detail would be:

   a. Smog—a major environmental irritant
   b. Genetic tendency to develop cancer
   c. New cancer treatments
   d. Cancer often detected soon after one has gone through a stressful experience

10. I. Aspects of capitalism

   A. Few government controls
   B. Emphasis on individual success
   C. Opposite of communism
   D. _____

An appropriate major detail would be:

   a. Emphasizes a competitive market
   b. Conservative American politicians believe in few federal controls
   c. Definition of capitalism
   d. History of capitalism

Exercise 4.2
Locating Major
Details

Under each of the following ten main-idea sentences are five sentences, three of which support the main-idea sentence. The other two sentences are either minor details or main-idea sentences themselves that would introduce a new paragraph. Place the letters of the three major-detail sentences in the answer box.

<table>
<tr><td>1.</td><td>___ ___ ___</td></tr>
<tr><td>2.</td><td>___ ___ ___</td></tr>
<tr><td>3.</td><td>___ ___ ___</td></tr>
<tr><td>4.</td><td>___ ___ ___</td></tr>
<tr><td>5.</td><td>___ ___ ___</td></tr>
<tr><td>6.</td><td>___ ___ ___</td></tr>
<tr><td>7.</td><td>___ ___ ___</td></tr>
<tr><td>8.</td><td>___ ___ ___</td></tr>
<tr><td>9.</td><td>___ ___ ___</td></tr>
<tr><td>10.</td><td>___ ___ ___</td></tr>
</table>

___
70%

Ask instructor for answers.

1. Main-idea sentence: The earnings and employment status of blacks in America are consistently lower than the comparable earnings and employment status of whites.

    a. Unemployment for black adults is nearly double that of whites.

    b. Almost 40 percent of black teenagers are unemployed as opposed to 15 percent of white teenagers.

    c. These unemployed black teenagers are often high school dropouts.

    d. The economic plight of American Indians is worse than that of blacks.

    e. Black professionals tend to earn less than white professionals.[1]

2. Main-idea sentence: In the main, public education in the United States is free and mandatory, and most Americans take advantage of this opportunity.

    a. Almost all states require children to be in school for at least eight years.

    b. Today almost 70 percent of all students complete high school.

    c. In 1940, only about 25 percent of American students completed high school.

    d. Many more community colleges and state universities have been built in the past twenty-five years to accommodate the increasing number of college-bound students.

    e. A corollary to this issue is that since 1950 California and New York have greatly expanded their community college and state university programs.[2]

3. Main-idea sentence: Existentialism is a philosophy that contends that one creates one's own meaning in life.

    a. Existentialists believe that people are born without meaning or essence.

    b. Existentialists believe that all one is born with is existence, which is not ordered or directed by God.

    c. A person's actions therefore create one's essence.

    d. Phenomenology helped shape some of the ideas of existentialism.

    e. Incidentally, for the philosopher Sartre, bad faith is a special kind of inaction that makes life meaningless.

___

[1] From Earl R. Babbie, *Sociology: An Introduction* (Belmont, Calif.: Wadsworth, 1980), pp. 275–276. Used by permission.

[2] From Babbie, *Sociology*, pp. 378–379. Used by permission.

4. Main-idea sentence: The ancestors of most Americans are Europeans.

   a. In the 1600s, British settlers began settling in America.
   b. These people came from England to America to escape persecution.
   c. In the 1800s, immigrants from Germany and Ireland began coming to America.
   d. Many of these immigrants faced prejudice from those already in America, who were afraid of losing their jobs to these new arrivals.
   e. At the end of the nineteenth century and into the twentieth century, immigrants from southern and eastern Europe began immigrating to the United States.

5. Main-idea sentence: The nucleus of a living cell contains three identifiable divisions.

   a. The central section of the nucleus is the nucleolus, which is more dense than its surroundings.
   b. During cell division, the nucleolus temporarily breaks apart.
   c. Around the nucleus is another division containing DNA and protein.
   d. The outer section of the nucleolus is called the nuclear envelope.
   e. Much research is currently being conducted to determine the chemical composition of chromosomes.

6. Main-idea sentence: The scientific method is a system of discovery that is based upon certain well-defined procedures.

   a. The first step requires making careful and accurate observations.
   b. From the data derived from observation, the researcher then forms a problem.
   c. Then the researcher attempts to solve the problem; this attempted solution is known as the hypothesis.
   d. Incidentally, a hypothesis is a theory, not a statement of fact.
   e. The scientific method is what scientists use in several disciplines.

7. Main-idea sentence: In the Cenozoic period of geologic history, the Earth went through several physical changes.

   a. First, there was tremendous volcanic activity during this period, which altered the surface of much of the Earth.
   b. This volcanic activity occurred in North America, Europe, and Africa.
   c. In each continent, the volcanic material came up through faults and fissures.

    d. Second, glaciers extended from the polar caps and scarred large sections of North America.

    e. Third, crustal plates collided, creating new mountain ranges.

8. Main-idea sentence: All human cells require minerals to maintain health.

    a. Calcium and magnesium are necessary to ensure the proper functioning of enzymes in cells.

    b. Sodium and potassium are needed to maintain the cell's ion balances.

    c. Sodium and potassium, incidentally, are also required to maintain the health of muscles.

    d. Iron is used by blood cells to carry oxygen throughout the body.

    e. Vitamins are also needed by the human body in order to stay healthy.

9. Main-idea sentence: Aristotle was an ancient Greek philosopher interested in observing his world.

    a. Aristotle collected data from his observations.

    b. Aristotle was also one of the first great drama theorists.

    c. Aristotle tried to find patterns among the facts that he collected.

    d. From his keen observation, Aristotle helped create the study of biology.

    e. Each discipline, or study, is founded on data organized into systems.

10. Main-idea sentence: In the 1940s and 1950s, Alfred Kinsey published some startling discoveries regarding American sexual practices.

    a. In the 1960s, Masters and Johnson provided some valuable data concerning the physiology of sex among humans.

    b. Kinsey found that sexual attitudes were closely tied to social stratification.

    c. His data indicated that American women had strong sexual desires.

    d. He suggested that male and female homosexuality was more prevalent than many Americans had thought it to be.

    e. In the last half of the twentieth century, premarital sex in America has become more common.

Exercise 4.3
Identifying Types of
Major Details

The following paragraphs present different kinds of details to support their main-idea sentences. Your job is to read each paragraph and identify the kind of detail that is used. Write in the answer box: A if the details are examples; B if the details are steps, C if the details are characteristics, D if the details are causes, and E if the details are effects. The signal words used in some of the paragraphs should help you recognize the kinds of details that the paragraph uses.

1. _____

2. _____

3. _____

4. _____

5. _____

6. _____

7. _____

8. _____

9. _____

10. _____

80%

(Score = # correct ×
10)

Find answers on p.
308.

1. St. Thomas Aquinas presents a series of related arguments to prove God's existence. First, he notes that objects in the universe are in a constant state of motion. Second, he postulates that every event has a cause. Third, he concludes that this movement must originate in God, who is motionless and without cause.

2. Pablo Picasso's *Guernica* is an exciting work of art. The composition includes a screaming horse, a grieving mother holding onto a dead child, and several agonized faces. All of these faces are abstract, with the pained feelings of each emphasized. Through these pained expressions, Picasso makes a moving statement about the horrors of war.

3. Many artists consciously or unconsciously use mathematical and scientific principles in their work. Musicians playing a major chord, for example, are blending three sounds to the frequency ratio of $5:5:6$. Sculptors creating metal works must know much about the physical properties of that metal to complete their compositions. Finally, photographers need to know something about the physical properties of those chemicals they use to create color and shade in their photographs.

4. Children from infancy to three years of age acquire a tremendous amount of language ability in a short time. In the first stage infants go through, they produce several sounds; some they hear, others they make up. In the second stage, children begin to understand oral communication—from words spoken by their parents to more complicated phrases and sentences. Perhaps the most interesting stage is the last one, in which children begin to speak, often using a complicated sentence structure by age three.

5. Three significant factors led to the Great Depression of the 1930s in the United States. For one, banks made unsound loans, and this miscalculation led to the loss of personal savings for many Americans. Also, many Americans speculated wildly in real estate and lost. Finally, Presidents Harding, Coolidge, and Hoover were against government involvement in economic matters, so they took no measures to prevent the country's economic collapse.

6. How does city life affect people accustomed to life in farm or rural areas? The first major change that rural people feel is the increased pace of life in the cities. Also, people in large cities tend to have daily contact with greater numbers of people, because cities are more densely populated than rural areas. Yet in spite of population density, rural inhabitants who have moved to the city

tend to feel lonely. Alienation is a major complaint rural inhabitants have when they move to the city.

7. Jay Gatsby, the central character in F. Scott Fitzgerald's *The Great Gatsby,* is complex. For most of the novel, Fitzgerald portrays him as idealistic and industrious. Gatsby believes that hard work will allow him to realize his goals. More important, he is a fated romantic who wrongly sees the jaded Daisy, his only love, as both innocent and shy.

8. The twentieth-century novel has become the vehicle for technical experimentation. The American novelist Henry James, for example, concentrated on developing an elegant prose style. Each novel that he wrote displayed a more intricate sentence structure. In France at the turn of the century, Marcel Proust developed a style known as stream of consciousness, which tried to mirror the complex way the mind perceives the world. Finally, James Joyce, the twentieth-century Irish novelist, became so experimental with style and story line that his last work, *Finnegans Wake,* is unintelligible to the untrained reader.

9. Phenomenology is a school of modern philosophy that focuses on individual perception. It is a philosophy of consciousness that claims that the real is what one perceives. As a philosophy, it does not depend on an understanding of the external world of the senses. Rather, the focus of phenomenology is on the internal reality of each individual. Ultimately, it is a philosophy that gives value to the mind's workings, not to the study of the external or to those objects that are in the world and outside the mind.

10. There are several theories regarding the major causes of inflation. Many economists cite the government's irresponsible printing of money as the major factor causing inflation. Others blame the unions, which regularly demand salary increases for their workers. Finally, some economists look at the American family's inability to save money as the main source of inflation.

*Exercise 4.4
Identifying Main
Ideas, Major
Details, and Minor
Details*

The following paragraphs contain main-idea sentences, major-detail sentences, and minor-detail sentences. Read each paragraph carefully. Then, next to the appropriate number in the answer box, write A for a main-idea sentence, B for a major-detail sentence, and C for a minor-detail sentence.

(1) In economics, the term *capital* refers to an object that one purchases to increase production. (2) In early days, a tool was capital. (3) Axes and plows were the key tools that farmers used to increase production. (4) Today, capital includes machines such as tractors and harvesters.

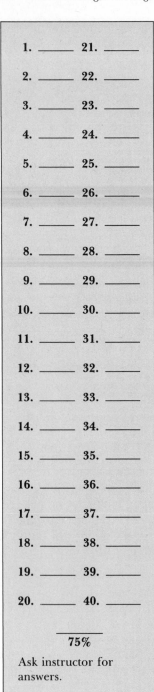

1. _____ 21. _____

2. _____ 22. _____

3. _____ 23. _____

4. _____ 24. _____

5. _____ 25. _____

6. _____ 26. _____

7. _____ 27. _____

8. _____ 28. _____

9. _____ 29. _____

10. _____ 30. _____

11. _____ 31. _____

12. _____ 32. _____

13. _____ 33. _____

14. _____ 34. _____

15. _____ 35. _____

16. _____ 36. _____

17. _____ 37. _____

18. _____ 38. _____

19. _____ 39. _____

20. _____ 40. _____

_____
75%

Ask instructor for answers.

(5) The law of demand states that, as the price of an item decreases, the number of items purchased increases, and from this law come three observations. (6) People buy more of an item if its price falls, because they can afford to. (7) As the quantity of a product increases, the consumer is unwilling to pay as much for each additional item. (8) Finally, if the price of a product continues to fall, the consumer will use this extra money to buy other products.

(9) Thomas Malthus was a famous nineteenth-century economist who shocked the world with his theory that population would decrease if humans were left alone to destroy themselves. (10) Malthus believed that famine and disease were nature's check on overpopulation. (11) This pessimistic theory was rejected on moral grounds by many religious leaders in England and throughout Europe. (12) That is to say, religious groups refused to see people dying in the streets of hunger as part of nature's or God's plan.

(13) James Joyce's masterpiece *Ulysses* is a novel dealing with life in Dublin on just one day: June 16, 1904. (14) Joyce's emphasis is on the lives of three people and on how they affect one another's experiences on that day. (15) Much of the novel is in an experimental stream-of-consciousness style. (16) This style—stream of consciousness—is one of the most studied aspects of this complex work.

(17) After a person buys a car, he or she tries to find as much evidence as possible to support the purchase of this new automobile. (18) Any evidence that this consumer hears that goes against choosing this automobile will cause internal conflict. (19) Further, if the consumer's friend does not support the purchase of the car, the consumer will feel even greater conflict. (20) Each of these situations is an example of cognitive dissonance—a theory in consumer behavior that deals with the psychology of buying.

(21) *Culture* can be defined as behavior that is learned and transmitted to members of a group. (22) A child learns a behavior through observation and through positive and negative reinforcement from family and peers. (23) A minor point to remember is that this feedback can be either overt or covert. (24) Much covert feedback involves nonverbal cues that an outsider to that culture would not understand.

(25) B. F. Skinner is a Harvard psychologist who developed the concept of positive and negative reinforcement in learning theory. (26) Positive reinforcement is a reward given to the learner who performs correctly. (27) Negative reinforcement is punishment given if the learner does not perform as expected. (28) In the case of teaching rats in a laboratory setting, this negative reinforcement often includes a mild electric shock.

(29) Knowing how to use percentages is helpful in the business world. (30) Real estate agents need to know what the current interest rate is and how it affects their clients. (31) Corporate executives must know what the percentage reports regarding company profits and

losses mean. (32) Even shopkeepers must use percentages to calculate sales and inventory taxes.

(33) I. P. Pavlov, a Russian physiologist, conducted learning experiments with dogs that revealed some basic learning laws. (34) He demonstrated that a secondary stimulus would cause a dog to salivate even without the presence of the primary stimulus. (35) Incidentally, the primary stimulus for Pavlov's dogs was usually meat, while the secondary stimulus was often the sound of a bell. (36) Pavlov showed that one could condition a dog's hunger response so that the sound of the bell, without the presence of the meat, would still cause the dog to salivate.

(37) Values are ethical beliefs that a person brings into the making of daily decisions. (38) Values change from one culture to another. (39) People use their value systems to help them select their friends, to find a marriage partner, and to raise their children. (40) Subordinate to this issue is the fact that people are often unaware that they are using their value system to make everyday decisions.

Exercise 4.5
Writing Effective
Topic Sentences

In composition textbooks, main-idea sentences are often called topic sentences. **Topic sentences** are general statements usually found at the beginning of a paragraph. Like main-idea statements, topic sentences direct the reader to what the paragraph will say.

Effective topic sentences are neither too specific nor too general. They should direct the reader to the details of support and not become details of support themselves.

Look at the following ineffective topic sentences and their revisions.

1. War does not solve problems. (too general)
   World War I did not solve the political problems of Europe. (acceptable)

   Note that the first sentence neither identifies the war, nor does it specify the problem the war created. Effective topic sentences clearly identify the "who" and the "what" of an issue.

2. *Star Wars* is an excellent film. (too general)
   George Lucas's *Star Wars* is an excellent film because of its imaginative special effects. (acceptable)

   Note how the revised sentence answers the "who" (George Lucas), and it also answers the "why" (imaginative special effects). You would assume that this paragraph would proceed to give examples of the film's memorable special effects.

3. Almost 30 percent of the children were stricken with the flu. (too specific)
   Many students at Larchmont School have contracted the Hong Kong flu. (acceptable)

Do you see that the figure (30 percent) would be better used as a supporting detail and after the topic sentence? It is important that you learn to write workable topic sentences that give necessary direction to your essays. Your job is to determine whether the following ten topic sentences are too general or too specific. Write in the answer box "general" or "specific." Then revise the topic sentences, making them more effective. Your revised topic sentences do not have to be factually accurate; in fact, be as imaginative as you want with your revisions.

1. _____

2. _____

3. _____

4. _____

5. _____

6. _____

7. _____

8. _____

9. _____

10. _____

_____
80%
(Score = # correct ×
10)
Find answers on p.
308.

1. Cigarette smoking is hazardous.

   Revision: _____

2. Forty percent of the fish in Lake April contain traces of lead.

   Revision: _____

3. Twenty-five of the thirty students in Miss Jackson's class were absent with the Asian flu.

   Revision: _____

4. Charles Dickens is a great novelist.

   Revision: _____

5. The first of the five steps in the study system involves surveying the textbook chapter.

   Revision: _____

6. Abraham Lincoln was a great American president.

   Revision: _____

7. The working budget for Haven College was about $45 million in 1986.

   Revision: _____

8. On five occasions the film gave incorrect historical information.

   Revision: _____

9. Crime is a problem.

   Revision: _____

10. The voting machines incorrectly tabulated 3 percent of the votes.

    Revision: _____

Exercise 4.6
Locating Major and
Minor Details in a
Longer Passage

In this exercise, you will be reading a longer passage, similar to ones you will find in college textbooks. Your job is to read for main ideas, major details, and minor details. After you have read the passage, answer the ten multiple-choice questions. If necessary, you may return to the passage when you answer the questions. Write all your answers in the answer box.

Human Nutritional Requirements

(1) Every human being burns energy to survive. Food is the source of energy for humans, and the unit for measuring this energy is the kilocalorie. Adult males need about 2700 kilocalories daily, adult females about 2000, and teenagers roughly 2400–2800. The three essential types of food the body makes into energy are: (1) carbohydrates and lipids, (2) proteins, and (3) vitamins and minerals. A healthy individual needs a combination of all three of these nutritional requirements each day.

(2) In the United States, the average person takes in 250–800 grams of carbohydrates each day, while the daily intake of lipids ranges from 25–60 grams. Starches and sugars are the food sources of carbohydrates. Once the body takes in carbohydrates, it breaks them up into glucose. A minor point to be made regarding glucose is that it can either be used immediately by the body or it can be stored in the liver. Lipids, which are found in the fats we eat, are used by the body in the form of triglycerides.

(3) Protein is a second important nutrient that the body must take in daily. For men, about 43 grams are required each day, and for women about 35 grams. Protein is an essential nutrient because it helps build body cells. So protein deficiency is a serious matter, especially for children, who grow rapidly. Protein requirements are especially necessary for the fetus of a pregnant woman; without adequate amounts of protein, the fetus may develop deficiencies. One of the most common fetal deficiencies resulting from low protein intake by a pregnant mother is mental retardation.

(4) Vitamins and minerals are additional substances that the body needs for many of its processes. The mineral iron, for example, is needed by the blood in building its cells. Luckily, almost all vitamins and minerals are found in the food one normally eats in a well-balanced diet. So, taking large amounts of vitamins and minerals is not necessary, since the body will excrete the excess. Vitamins A and D, incidentally, can be dangerous if taken in large amounts.

(5) To summarize, the essential nutrients for the body include carbohydrates, lipids, proteins, vitamins, and minerals. What the scientific research has consistently suggested is that the body needs all of these substances in moderate amounts. The excessive eating of protein or the intake of enormous quantities of vitamins can be dangerous to your health. The body seems to maintain an interesting chemical balance among the substances that it breaks down. Many

fad diets or alleged wonder cures from vitamins destroy this delicate balance.[3]

```
1. _____
2. _____
3. _____
4. _____
5. _____
6. _____
7. _____
8. _____
9. _____
10. _____

      80%
Ask instructor for
answers.
```

1. The topic of this passage concerns:

   a. energy
   b. human energy
   c. vitamins and minerals
   d. the substances the human body needs to take in daily

2. The main idea of paragraph 2 concerns:

   a. the dangers of lipids
   b. the required intake of carbohydrates and lipids and their use by the body
   c. the amount of lipids and carbohydrates required by the body
   d. how starches and sugars are used by the body.

3. A major detail presented in paragraph 2 is:

   a. carbohydrates become glucose in the body
   b. the need to eat carbohydrates
   c. the use of lipids by the body
   d. Americans eat improperly

4. The specific details in paragraph 3 include:

   a. men need 43 grams of protein a day
   b. protein deficiency can cause retardation in infants
   c. women need about 35 grams of protein a day
   d. all of these

5. The last sentence in paragraph 3 is:

   a. a major-detail sentence
   b. a minor-detail sentence
   c. a main-idea sentence
   d. a topic sentence

6. The first sentence in paragraph 4 is:

   a. a major-detail sentence
   b. a minor-detail sentence
   c. a main-idea sentence
   d. the topic of the passage

7. A signal word that introduces a minor detail in paragraph 4 is:

   a. many
   b. for example

---

[3] Adapted from Cecie Starr and Ralph Taggart, *Biology: The Unity and Diversity of Life,* 4th ed. (Belmont, Calif.: Wadsworth, 1987), pp. 443–444.

   c. incidentally

   d. so

8. The first sentence in the concluding paragraph is a:

   a. major-detail sentence

   b. minor-detail sentence

   c. main-idea sentence

   d. none of these

9. The last sentence of paragraph 5 is saying:

   a. fad diets should be used only under a doctor's care

   b. fad diets go against the natural metabolism of the body

   c. fad diets are a recent craze

   d. fad diets seem to agree with the natural metabolism of the body

10. The conclusion to this passage, stated in the last sentence of paragraph 5:

   a. restates the main points of the passage

   b. introduces a new topic (fad diets and wonder cures) not treated in the passage

   c. seems to contradict the details of the passage

   d. none of these

Exercise 4.7
Writing Your Own
Paragraph from
Main Ideas and
Major Details

Now go back to the passage on nutrition and locate its main idea, found in paragraph 1; the three major details found in paragraphs 2, 3, and 4; and the minor detail in paragraph 4. Jot this information down in the following outline.

I. _____

   A. _____

   B. _____

   C. _____

      1. _____

70%

Ask instructor for answers.

From this outline, answer the following essay question. Use only the outline to answer this question.

Essay Question: Identify the three important nutrients the body needs. Then discuss the consequences of ingesting large amounts of certain vitamins.

Exercise 4.8
Determining Main
Ideas and Major
Details in a Text
Excerpt

A. The following is an excerpt from a music history chapter on the Renaissance. Read through it quickly to get a sense of its topic. Then go back and read it slowly.

When you finish rereading, answer the following five questions. You may return to the excerpt in deciding on your answers.

Renaissance Music

(1) The word "renaissance" literally means "rebirth." Historically it referred to a revival of interest in the philosophy and arts of ancient Greece and Rome, although there was much more to it than just an admiration of a previous civilization. Music, however, had no ancient Greek roots to go back to. So the concept of rebirth in regard to music has little direct significance. In music it refers only to the style that predominated from about 1450 until 1600.

(2) The intense interest of Renaissance artists and scholars in ancient Greek civilization led to a curious mixture of Greek and Christian belief. Michelangelo expressed this union of the pagan and Christian by decorating the ceiling of the Sistine Chapel with alternating figures of prophets and sibyls. Erasmus, the great philosopher, regarded Socrates as a pre-Christian saint, and once wrote, "St. Socrates, pray for us."

(3) The Renaissance developed a number of intellectual outlooks that have become standard for our culture today. Among them are optimism, worldliness, hedonism (the importance of pleasure, especially physical pleasure, for its own sake), naturalism, and individualism. But most important is humanism: the glorification of the human and natural as opposed to the otherworldly or divine. Pride, considered to be a sin in the Middle Ages, was elevated to a virtue.

(4) The results of humanism are well illustrated by the two treatments of the human body shown in this chapter. One is a piece of Gothic sculpture found on the cathedral at Chartres. Notice that this figure has a spiritual, otherworldly quality about it. The attitude of the head and eyes is serene, and the position of the body is formal. The proportions of the figure are distorted through exaggerated length, giving the body an emaciated look. The feet seem to dangle from the robes as though they are merely attached. Michelangelo's *David,* on the other hand, looks like a magnificent Greek god. (The figure of David stands over thirteen and a half feet in height.) The work suggests confidence and an admiration of the human body. David looks natural, almost casual and free. The body emerges from the withered state given it by medieval beliefs to the idealized status accorded it by Renaissance attitudes.

(5) With the increasing interest in the value of worldly life, there was a corresponding interest in the fine arts. A beautiful painting or piece of music began to have value for its own sake; it was no longer regarded only as a means to religious devotion. As a result of this change of outlook, the list of great Renaissance sculptors and painters is long—Botticelli, da Vinci, Michelangelo, Dürer, Raphael, Titian, Bruegel, Tintoretto. Botticelli's *The Adoration of the Magi* can be seen in plate 3.

(6) Not only were works of art being enjoyed in a new climate of acceptance. The increasing affluence, especially in the cities of northern Italy and the Netherlands, meant that money was available with which to hire artists and musicians. The Church sought rich adornment for its buildings, one of several practices that led to the reform movement started by Martin Luther in 1517. An example of the art of this era is Dürer's *Portrait of a Clergyman*, plate 4. The effect of the Reformation on the world of music did not show its full impact until after 1600, but the seeds of change had been planted.

(7) An event that reached into every area of human endeavor—education, religion, commerce—was Gutenberg's invention of printing from movable type. Printing made possible the wide dissemination of music, beginning with the appearance of the first printed music books in 1501.

(8) The spirit of the times was one of optimism and discovery. The voyages of Columbus, Cabot, Balboa, and Magellan took place during the Renaissance. Copernicus was announcing his new discoveries about the universe. Rabelais, Machiavelli, Boccaccio, Montaigne, Thomas More, Francis Bacon, and Erasmus were exploring new ideas in literature and philosophy. However, no person embodied the ideal of the "Renaissance man" more abundantly than did Leonardo da Vinci.[4]

1. _____

2. _____

3. _____

4. _____

5. _____

1. In paragraph 3, the Renaissance is explained. What kinds of details does the author use to describe it?

   a. examples
   b. steps
   c. causes
   d. characteristics

2. In paragraph 4, the Renaissance concept of the human body is treated. What kinds of details are used to describe it?

   a. examples
   b. steps
   c. causes
   d. characteristics

3. The main idea of paragraph 5 is:

   a. the Renaissance valued the physical life
   b. the Renaissance valued the fine arts
   c. Michelangelo was a famous Renaissance artist
   d. both a and b

---

[4] Charles R. Hoffer, *The Understanding of Music*, 5th ed. (Belmont, Calif.: Wadsworth, 1985), pp. 124–126. Used by permission.

4. What kinds of details does paragraph 6 use?

   a. characteristics
   b. examples
   c. causes
   d. effects

5. The main idea of paragraph 7 is:

   a. Leonardo da Vinci was a great Renaissance painter
   b. Columbus and Balboa made many profitable voyages
   c. the Renaissance was a period of optimism and exploration
   d. literature and philosophy reached new heights in the Renaissance

B. Now go back to reread the excerpt. Then, without looking back at the excerpt, answer the following three questions in a short phrase or sentence.

1. List three characteristics of the Renaissance. (3 points)

2. Describe the statue "David" by Michelangelo. Note three characteristics. (1 point)

3. List one effect of Gutenberg's invention of printing. (1 point)

70%

Ask instructor for answers.

5

Identifying Organizational Patterns

Explanation of Skills

Information that you hear is frequently presented in organizational patterns that have identifiable qualities. Each organizational pattern helps explain the author's material by suggesting a pattern to look for as you read or listen to lectures. The most common organizational patterns used in textbooks and lectures are: (1) cause-effect, (2) definition, (3) sequence of events, (4) spatial geographic, (5) thesis-support, (6) comparison-contrast, and (7) description. If you can identify the organizational pattern or patterns used in a lecture or textbook, you will likely understand the material better. You will be able to tie the important main ideas and details to the structure of the organizational pattern. Read over the descriptions of these seven organizational patterns; then apply what you have learned to the exercises that follow.

The Cause-Effect Pattern

Cause-effect is perhaps the most common organizational pattern that you will come across. You learned something about cause-effect in the previous chapter on major details. You will now study it as a pattern that can organize an entire chapter or lecture. You will find this pattern in almost every subject you study, but it is most often evident in the sciences and the social sciences. Cause-effect sentences, paragraphs, or essays have two parts: (1) the cause, or the source of the change and (2) the effect, or the result of the change.

Cause-effect relationships can be either direct or indirect. If cause-effect statements are *direct*, they are always true. Look at the following cause-effect statement from chemistry: "When water is lowered to 32 degrees Fahrenheit, it freezes." Do you see that lowering the water's temperature to 32 degrees is the cause, and that the water freezing at this temperature is the effect? This relationship is direct because water always freezes at this temperature (at least under normal physical circumstances). In your notes you can show this relationship by using an arrow ($\rightarrow$): "Lowering temperature of water to 32 degrees F. $\rightarrow$ water freezing."

An *indirect* cause-effect relationship is one whose effect is caused by several factors. Indirect causes are also called *contributory causes*. Indirect cause-effect relationships are often found in the social sciences and humanities. Consider the following statement from literature: "It seems that the seventeenth-century poetry of John Donne had an effect on the poetic style of T. S. Eliot." Here, the indirect cause is Donne's poetry, the effect the poetry of T. S. Eliot. The term of qualification "it seems" suggests that this relationship is indirect. Donne may have been one of several influences on Eliot's poetic style. One frequently finds contributory causes in relationships dealing with people and events, and often these relationships are worded with qualifying terms.

The following terms of qualifications are often associated with indirect cause-effect relationships:

it appears	perhaps	one can safely say
it seems	probably	one can say with reservation
apparently	likely	there seems to be a link
one can assume	contributing to	there seems to be a relationship

(For a more thorough list of terms of qualification, see the sections in Chapter 6 on "Words and Phrases That Express a Little Doubt" and "Words and Phrases That Express Some Doubt" (pp. 105–106).

There are also transitions suggesting results that you need to recognize, often designated by the words *consequently, therefore, so, as a result, as a consequence.*

How should you note cause-effect relationships? If you find them in your reading, you should separate cause from effect in the margins. For the previous example dealing with Donne and Eliot, you could write:

cause:
  Donne's poetry   It seems that the seventeenth-century poetry of John Donne had a
effect: powerful effect on the poetic style of T. S. Eliot, a modern poet.
  Eliot's poetic style

You could also note whether the cause is direct or indirect. You can follow the same pattern when you take lecture notes.

The Definition Pattern

You will find definitions in the lecture and textbook material of every course you take. Definitions make up a large part of examination questions, so you should listen and read carefully when you come upon a definition. Definitions are often expressed concisely, so you should write down every word of a definition. In your lecture and reading notes, you should use the abbreviation *def* as your signal that a definition follows. Look at the following example from data processing:

def: A terminal is a device usually equipped with a keyboard and some
terminal kind of display capable of sending and receiving information over a communication channel.[1]

Another successful technique to use when you are learning definitions is to list the general categories of the term first, then to give examples or features of the term. You may want to divide the term up into the following three parts:

Term	*General Category*	*Specific Features*

See how the following definition of the cerebrum can be neatly divided up into these categories: "The cerebrum is the part of the brain that controls all aspects of the nervous system."

Term	*General Category*	*Specific Features*
cerebrum	brain	controls actions of the nervous system

This method of categorizing will help you remember, because you are classifying information into general and specific parts, or into main ideas and details. Also, this chart helps you visualize each part of the definition.

When you come upon a definition, you should listen or read more actively. At first, you may have difficulty remembering all parts of a definition, because each part is written concisely. Definitions are the foundations for any course that you take; they are especially important in your understanding of introductory courses. More will be said about how to remember definitions in Chapter 12 "The SQ3R Study System" and Chapters 14 and 15, on exam strategies.

The Sequence-of-Events Pattern

You will find the sequence-of-events pattern in all subjects, but you will often see it in history material, in which dates are presented chronologically. You will also find the sequence-of-events pattern in vocational material, in which you must follow steps to make or repair an object or to work a machine such as a computer. You were introduced to this pattern in the previous chapter, where it was presented

---

[1] Perry Edwards and Bruce Broadwell, *Data Processing*, 2nd ed. (Belmont, Calif.: Wadsworth, 1982), p. 578. Used by permission.

as a type of major detail. Now you will see it as a structure that can organize a textbook chapter or a lecture. The sequence-of-events pattern presents events in chronological order or lists the steps in a procedure.

The following signal words often introduce a sequence-of-events pattern: *first, second, third,* and so on; *last, now, later, before, often, soon, finally, next.*

When you listen to or read material in a sequence-of-events pattern, you should number the order of events or steps. The numbers should stand out so that in reviewing your notes, you make a picture of the sequence in your mind. Look at how information is sequenced in the list that follows this paragraph on the Presidential Succession Act:

> The Presidential Succession Act of 1947 provided for the following order of events if the President and Vice-President of the United States were to die. First to replace the Vice-President is the Speaker of the House of Representatives. Second in succession is the President Pro Tempore of the Senate. The President's Cabinet members would follow. Third in line from the Vice-President would be the Secretary of State, and fourth the Secretary of the Treasury.

Presidential Succession Act of 1947

1. Vice-President
2. Speaker of the House
3. President Pro Tempore of the Senate
4. Secretary of State
5. Secretary of the Treasury

By placing this information vertically, you have a picture of these names that should help you remember the Presidential Succession Act.

The Spatial Geographic Pattern

The spatial geographic pattern is frequently used in biology and geography courses. In this pattern, you must visualize the various parts of an organism or the relative location of countries, states, or cities on a map.

In biology courses, the following signal words are used to direct you to various parts of an organism:

above	between	inward	anterior	distal
below	upper	external	posterior	
next to	lower	dorsal	medial	
behind	outward	ventral	lateral	

In a biology lecture, your instructor will use these terms along with a diagram or slide. Start associating these terms with what you see. If you can sketch, make rough copies of the organism during the lecture. In biology textbooks, organs and organ parts are often mentioned in conjunction with a diagram. As you read, refer to the diagram. After you have read the material and studied the diagram, close your book and draw the organ or organism from memory. Your biology instructor may well ask you to label an organism on an exam. On such an exam, your spatial geographic skills will assist you.

In geography courses, the same spatial skills are necessary. Your geography instructor may present maps in lecture and ask you to remember the correct location of various parts. Here are some signal words found in geography readings and lectures:

north	bordering	down
south	adjacent	opposite to
east	next to	
west	up	

Let these signal words help you to visualize the parts of a city, state, country, or continent. If you can, copy any maps that you see in lectures and important maps that you find in your reading. If you cannot draw well, be sure to use correct signal words as you take notes. "Southeastern," for example, should be the key word that you hear in the statement "Arizona touches California's southeastern border."

The Thesis-Support Pattern

The thesis-support pattern is used in all disciplines; its organization is similar to that of the multiple-paragraph essay discussed on p. 269. A *thesis* is a point of view made by a speaker or writer. You find the thesis most always in the first paragraph of an essay or at the beginning of a lecture. When you have located the thesis, write *thesis* in the margin; then summarize it. For example, if your history instructor beings a lecture with the statement "The French Revolution was the most significant war in European history," you could write something like:

Thesis: French Revolution most significant European war.

Underline the term thesis so that in your review, you will remember to reread this material. On exams, you are expected to know well the thesis of a lecture or an article.

Be certain that you can distinguish between a thesis and a fact. Somewhat like a main idea, a thesis expresses an opinion that needs support. Like a detail, a *fact* may support the thesis. Unlike the thesis, a fact does not ask you to question it. Determine which of the following two statements is the thesis and which is a fact that supports it: "Abraham Lincoln was a gifted writer who wrote simply and eloquently." "Abraham Lincoln wrote "The Gettysburg Address." Do you see that in the second statement, the writer is not presenting an argument, merely a fact? But in the first statement, you want to know what evidence this writer has that shows Lincoln's gifted writing style.

Once you have found the thesis, you need to analyze its details. Remember that a thesis is only as good as its details. Some details are well-chosen; others are not. Start training yourself to look for the well-chosen details. Make marginal comments in your textbook or when taking lecture notes, stating whether the details support the thesis well. If a professor were to say that James Joyce wrote several novels, you would be correct in wanting to know what is meant by "several." A more specific statement would be: "James Joyce wrote three novels." In your notes, you should identify important details with the abbreviation *det.*

Here are some signal words that introduce a thesis-support pattern:

the thesis is	for example	especially
it is theorized that	for instance	one example is
the hypothesis is	specifically	the idea is supported by
it is my belief that	in particular	proof is found in

Also, remember that you can use these same signal words in writing your own thesis-support essay.

You may find that details used to support a thesis are causes, effects, spatial or geographic words, or descriptions. Begin to see this thesis-support pattern as the most general of the seven. This pattern may include within it other organizational patterns.

The Comparison-Contrast Pattern

The comparison-contrast pattern is used in all disciplines. Like the thesis-support pattern, the comparison-contrast pattern may be made up of several paragraphs, and it may include other organizational patterns. The comparison-contrast pattern asks you to find similarities or differences in what you read or hear.

Here are the most common signal words for the comparison-contrast pattern:

Contrast

but	on the one hand	although	opposed
however	on the other hand	while	opposing
yet	contrary	different from	conversely
nevertheless	on the contrary	differently	whereas
at variance	in contrast	oppositely	
otherwise	rather	opposite	

Comparison

and	similar	as	parallel to	exactly like
also	similarly	just as	much the same	analogous
like	as if	resembling	comparable	analogously

You should use these signal words not only to recognize comparison-contrast patterns but also to write essays that show comparison or contrast. By using these signal words, you will highlight the similarities and differences that you present in your writing.

When you take reading and lecture notes that show comparison or contrast, you can best show these similarities or differences in a chart like this one:

	Topic	*Topic*
Similarity or	1.	1.
difference	2.	2.
	3.	3.

In this chart, you can neatly place similarities or differences side by side and thus more easily see how the various pieces of information relate.

Look at the following information taken from an economics lecture; then see how a chart can be used to explain the material.

> Capitalism and socialism begin with different ideologies. While capitalism believes in private ownership, socialism assumes state ownership of certain property. Capitalism allows its people to pursue economic gain; socialism controls the economic gains of its people.

Capitalism	*Socialism*
Differences:	
1. Private ownership of property	1. State ownership of most property
2. Economic freedom for its people	2. Economic control of its people

Do you see how this chart highlights the differences between socialism and capitalism?

A lecturer or the author of a textbook may present similarities and differences by using such a chart. If you come upon comparison-contrast patterns and the information is presented in paragraph form, you may want to create your own chart. These charts often allow you to remember comparison-contrast information more easily.

The Descriptive Pattern

The descriptive pattern is different from the other organizational patterns. You find the descriptive pattern most often in literature—in short stories, novels, poems, and plays. Descriptive patterns re-create experiences through the suggestiveness of language. Your job is to see how description awakens your senses. In your comments in textbooks and lectures, you should note how well the description re-creates an experience. The descriptive pattern often uses characteristics as details.

Read this excerpt from *The Picture of Dorian Gray* by Oscar Wilde and see whether your senses of smell and hearing are awakened:

vivid images of smell and sound

The studio was filled with the *rich odor of roses,* and when the *light summer wind stirred* amidst the trees of the garden, there came through the open door *the heavy scent of lilac,* of the more delicate perfume of the pink flowering thorn.

Do you almost smell the roses? Do you hear the "light summer wind"? Do you smell the lilac with its "heavy scent"? Wilde was known for his sensuous descriptions. If you were reading this novel, a marginal comment such as "vivid images of smell and sound" would be helpful.

In any literature course that you take, you will come across the descriptive pattern. Your literature instructor will probably give you reading strategies to use in analyzing descriptions. When you read any descriptive passage, remember to study the words and what they suggest rather than analyzing the thesis and details of support.

Summary

Organizational patterns are used by speakers and writers to present their ideas more clearly and to show the structure of their arguments. By recognizing which organizational pattern is used and by knowing how that pattern works, you will better understand the material. Organizational patterns often overlap; that is, several structures may be used by a lecturer or writer. Don't expect each paragraph you read or each lecture you hear to use only one organizational pattern. The seven most common organizational patterns are: (1) cause-effect, (2) definition, (3) sequence of events, (4) spatial geographic, (5) thesis-support, (6) comparison-contrast, and (7) descriptive. Each organizational pattern has its own logic and signal words that show you how the material is organized. Being familiar with these seven organizational patterns will make your reading and lecture notes clearer and will improve your writing.

Summary Box *Organizational Patterns*

What are they?	Why are they used?
Structures used in writing and speaking to explain ideas, describe experiences, or show the logic of an argument. Seven common patterns are: cause-effect, definition, sequence of events, spatial geographic, thesis-support, comparison-contrast, and descriptive.	To help a reader or listener (1) understand an argument better, and (2) take better reading and lecture notes To help a writer compose logical and organized essays

Skills Practice

Exercise 5.1
Identifying Thesis
Statements

A. Of the following ten statements, some express a point of view and would qualify as thesis statements; others are facts. In the answer box, write A for thesis statement and B for a statement of fact.

1. In economics, labor is defined as human effort that contributes to the production of a good or service.

2. The labor movement in the United States became a powerful political force in the 1930s.

3. In chemistry and physics, the mass number is the sum of protons and neutrons in the nucleus of an atom.

4. Splitting of the atom is perhaps one of the most controversial discoveries of physics.

5. In philosophy, innate ideas are defined as those that are inborn, or not learned through experience.

6. Herman Melville was born in 1819.

7. Melville's *Moby Dick* is perhaps the greatest American novel.

8. Joseph Conrad was born in Poland but wrote his novels in English.

9. The character Lord Jim in Conrad's *Lord Jim* is a mysterious figure throughout the novel.

10. Hydrogen has the smallest atomic number—one.

B. The following five paragraphs each have only one thesis statement. Write in the answer box the letter of the sentence that is the thesis sentence.

1. _____

2. _____

3. _____

4. _____

5. _____

6. _____

7. _____

8. _____

9. _____

10. _____

11. _____

12. _____

13. _____

14. _____

15. _____

(Score = # correct ×
5 [1–10] + number
correct × 10 [11–15])
Find answers on p.
308.

11. (A) Pesticides have proved unsuccessful in exterminating harmful insects. (B) A small number of an insect group will survive a pesticide application because they have a natural resistance to that poison. (C) The next generation of insects increases the number of those insects resistant to the pesticide. (D) As the number of resistant insects increases, heavier pesticides are introduced, but again a number of resistant insects develop.

12. (A) In 1964, President Lyndon Johnson established the Commission on Civil Rights. (B) In that same period, he established the Equal Opportunity Employment Commission. (C) In 1964 as well, the Civil Rights Act was passed by Congress, an act that gave blacks several voting rights. (D) Indeed, President Johnson did much to give blacks freedoms that had previously been denied them.

13. (A) Henry James was both a successful and prolific novelist. (B) In all, James wrote twenty novels. (C) The first, titled *Roderick Hudson,* was published in 1875. (D) Toward the end of his writing career, in 1904, James wrote *The Golden Bowl,* one of his most carefully plotted works.

14. (A) In industrialized countries, the average per capita food production has risen significantly over the past twenty years. (B) In developing nations, however, food production has increased only slightly in the same period. (C) Three-fourths of the world's population lives in these developing nations. (D) Thus, it is clear that food production and hunger are critical world problems.

15. (A) Many Americans often skip breakfast, lunch, or dinner. (B) Often when they do eat, they overeat or eat too fast. (C) Also, much of what they eat has a high sugar, salt, and cholesterol content. (D) It is safe to say that such eating habits among Americans can be linked to the high incidence of stomach and colon disease.

Exercise 5.2
Locating Steps in an
Argument

A. Read the following paragraphs; then return to them and list the steps that are presented in correct sequence. With the first four paragraphs, complete the charts that follow the paragraphs. With the last four paragraphs, you will need to create your own chart and title it.

1. Determining percentages from a fraction involves three simple steps. First, divide the denominator into the numerator. Then multiply your quotient by 100. Finally, add a percentage sign to the right of the last number.

Steps in Determining Percentages

    1.

    2.

    3.

2. Starting a car can sometimes be difficult. If your car won't start, do the following. On cars with an automatic choke, press the accelerator to the floor and then release it. Then, turn the key and start the engine. Finally, if the car starts, let the engine idle fast for one minute.

How to Start a Car

    1.

    2.

    3.

3. There are three stages writers should go through before they begin their rough drafts. First, knowing the question they want to answer, writers should do thorough research, taking complete and accurate notes. Then they should go through all of their notes, pulling out the information that they want to include in their paper. From this information, they can begin to structure a loose outline.

Prewriting Steps

    1.

    2.

    3.

4. When a young child gets the measles, the following sequence of symptoms occurs. First, the eyes become red and watery. This redness can be quite dark. Second, a dry cough develops that may last for days. Finally, a high fever and rash will develop. This rash will eventually cover the body and will usually develop on the fourth day.

Symptoms of Children's Measles

1.

2.

3.

B. Read the following four paragraphs, and look for the proper sequence of events in each. Before you list the steps, write an appropriate title.

5. What do you need to do to repair a leaky faucet? First, shut off the water by turning the valve under the sink. Then, loosen the packing nut, and remove the stem assembly. Replace the worn washer with a new one. Then, reassemble all the parts.

6. The negative effects of the American Civil War on the South were numerous. For one, Northerners known as carpetbaggers went south and created confusion, imposing unreasonable taxes and creating an unfair court system. A Southern white group known as the Ku Klux Klan emerged, which often harassed the blacks, sometimes burning their homes and even beating and lynching them. Southern contempt for the North finally led to the South's almost consistent voting for Democrats up to the first half of the twentieth century.

7. Life on Earth developed in certain identifiable stages. First, the gases in the atmosphere combined through the energy of the sun's rays and through contact with lightning to form organic molecules. Then these organic molecules dissolved in the oceans and formed more complex molecules, which finally became amino acids. Finally, these amino acids combined further to form primitive life forms resembling blue-green algae.

8. There were many events that preceded and foreshadowed the American Civil War. Three events stand out. In 1857, the Supreme Court handed down the Dred Scott decision, which stated that the slaves were property. This decision angered the North. In the fall of 1859, John Brown, an anti-slavery supporter, with his army of black and white sympathizers seized Harper's Ferry in Virginia. Brown's violent tactics aroused emotions on both sides of the slavery issue. Finally, in 1860 Senator John Crittenden proposed a compromise that would abolish slavery in new territory above the Missouri line but would continue to allow slavery in the South. The House voted for it, the Senate against it. So the compromise was not put into law, and anger grew on both sides.

80%

Ask instructor for answers.

Exercise 5.3
Understanding
Definitions

In the following ten definitions, you will be asked to separate the definition into its general category and its examples. Place all of your information in the chart that follows the definitions. Be brief. Use the following definition of a bird as a model. Definition: A bird (aves) is a class of vertebrates; eagles and vultures are birds.

Term	General Category	Examples
Aves (bird)	class of vertebrates	eagles and vultures

1. In economics, a depression is a severe decline in economic activity. The most famous American depression is the Great Depression of the 1930s.

2. Organizing complex procedures into specific tasks is known as mass production. The assembling of an intricate product such as the automobile is an example of mass production.

3. A monopoly is defined as exclusive control of an industry by one company. If there is only one doctor in a town, this doctor has a monopoly on medical care in this area.

4. A cartel is a group of businesses that produce the same product and agree on how much to produce and charge. An example of a cartel was the United States airlines, which were once controlled by the Civil Aeronautics Board.

5. A gland is an organ or cell that secretes a particular chemical. In human beings, the thyroid and pituitary are examples of glands.

6. A larva is an immature form of an animal that changes dramatically when it becomes an adult. A caterpillar is a larva that turns into a butterfly as an adult.

7. A herbivore is an animal that feeds mainly on plants. Cattle are herbivorous animals.

8. A conglomerate, such as International Telephone and Telegraph, is a combination of companies under one management.

9. A post hoc error in logic is made when one assumes that the first event in a series is the cause of the second. An example of a post hoc error is believing that eating potato salad caused your stomachache because right after you ate the salad, your stomach began to hurt.

10. Ethics is a branch of philosophy that attempts to determine what is right conduct. Biomedical ethics, for example, examines the rights of the patient as well as the moral obligations of the doctor and the patient's family.

Term	General Category	Examples
1.		
2.		
3.		
4.		
5.		
6.		
7.		
8.		
9.		
10.		

80%

(Score = # correct × 5)

Find answers on p. 308.

***Exercise 5.4
Identifying
Comparisons and
Contrasts***

A. The following ten statements each compares or contrasts an issue. In a one-sentence explanation of each statement, identify the issue that is compared or contrasted. Be sure that you use the word *compare* or *contrast* in your explanation. Assume that each of these statements introduces a discussion of the issue.

Example: Ralph Waldo Emerson and Henry David Thoreau, American poets, essayists, and philosophers, had a similar understanding of nature.

Explanation: This statement compares Emerson's and Thoreau's attitudes toward nature.

1. The metallic elements cadmium and lead are harmful to a human's health.

   Explanation: _____

2. Empiricism and idealism are philosophies opposite in their views of how humans perceive the world.

   Explanation: _____

3. Vertebrates and invertebrates are life forms that differ mainly in their body structure; vertebrates have a backbone and invertebrates do not.

   Explanation: _____

4. The British poet Gerard Manley Hopkins and the Welsh poet Dylan Thomas shared a similar poetic style.

   Explanation: _____

5. Presidents Jimmy Carter and Ronald Reagan express different economic philosophies.

   Explanation: _____

6. Romanian and Italian are languages with a similar history, both having descended from Latin.

   Explanation: _____

7. Microcomputers and minicomputers have different designs.

   Explanation: _____

8. British prime ministers are elected by a different procedure than that used to elect American presidents.

   Explanation: _____

9. South Africa and South America are geographically similar in that they both have large stretches of grasslands.

   Explanation: _____

10. The gaseous composition of the atmospheres of Mars and Earth are different.

    Explanation: _____

B. The following five paragraphs present either comparisons or contrasts. Read the paragraphs over carefully. Then complete the comparison or contrast chart that follows each paragraph.

11. There are three differences between a liberal and conservative political position in the United States today. Whereas liberals favor federal aid to education, health, and social security, conservatives work toward cutting funding in these areas. Conservatives, on the one hand, believe in building defense. Liberals, on the other hand, see military spending as too large, and they want to cut it. Finally, conservatives favor

military aid to foreign countries. In contrast, liberals fear that military aid to a foreign country might lead to American involvement in war.

	Liberal		*Conservative*
Different beliefs			
1.		1.	
2.		2.	
3.		3.	

12. James Joyce's *Ulysses* and Virginia Woolf's *Mrs. Dalloway* are novels that have certain similarities. Both are written in an experimental style known as stream of consciousness. *Mrs. Dalloway* is written almost completely in stream of consciousness, while several episodes of *Ulysses* are in the stream-of-consciousness style. Both novels portray characters who are alienated from society—locked inside themselves. Clarissa Dalloway in *Mrs. Dalloway* and Leopold Bloom in *Ulysses* are the two major alienated characters. Finally, both works suggest that although communication is difficult, there is some spiritual force in the universe. Joyce's characters often think similar thoughts even though they are separated from each other, while Woolf consistently uses the sound of Big Ben (a huge clock in London), whose gong several characters hear at the same time.

	Ulysses		*Mrs. Dalloway*
Novels' similarities			
1.		1.	
2.		2.	
3.		3.	

13. Classicism and romanticism, two literary and artistic movements in England, were founded on different beliefs. In poetry, the classicists of the eighteenth century believed that poets should follow established rules, whereas the romanticists of the nineteenth century wanted to break the old rules and create new ones. Second, the romanticists saw nature as a mysterious and powerful teacher. In contrast, the classicists saw nature as a backdrop for human beings, who were their own best teachers. Finally, the classical mind saw human beings as social, while the romanticists emphasized the solitary nature of human beings.

	Classicism	*Romanticism*
Differences		
1.		1.
2.		2.
3.		3.

14. Reading and writing are in some sense similar activities. Readers look for general categories and supporting details related to this category, while writers often begin with a general statement and provide details of support in the body of their writing. While reading, readers often come upon an idea that they write down; when they write, they often use ideas they have read. Readers often go back to reread what they did not completely understand, and writers need to revise what they have written to improve on what they have said.

	Reading	*Writing*
Similarities		
1.		1.
2.		2.
3.		3.

15. The parts of an atom are similar in their arrangement to the arrangements of the planets in the solar system. The nucleus of an atom is at its center, just as the sun is at the center of the solar system. The electrons orbit around the nucleus of an atom in the same manner that the planets orbit the sun. Finally, the particles in an atom maintain an electrical attraction to each other that is similar to the force of gravity, which attracts the planets and the sun to each other.

	Parts of an Atom	*Planets in the Solar System*
Similarity of parts		
1.		1.
2.		2.
3.		3.

70%

Ask instructor for answers.

*Exercise 5.5
Identifying
Organizational
Patterns*

The following ten paragraphs are structured according to particular organizational patterns. Read each paragraph; then identify the organizational pattern that describes it. Some paragraphs may use more than one organizational pattern; in this case, choose the one pattern that seems to dominate the paragraph. Place the appropriate letter in the answer box: A = cause-effect, B = definition, C = comparison-contrast, and D = sequence of events.

1. _____

2. _____

3. _____

4. _____

5. _____

6. _____

7. _____

8. _____

9. _____

10. _____

_____
80%

(Score = # correct ×
10)
Find answers on p.
309.

1. Radioactivity is defined as radiation, or energy, released from changes in the structure of the atom. These changes are frequently caused by nuclear reactions made by people. When the atomic structure is changed, radioactive particles may be released. Radiation also comes from outer space in the form of cosmic rays. Radiation thus comes from both artificial and natural sources.

2. Heart disease is the number-one killer in the United States. Cigarette smoking is a significant factor contributing to heart disease. Having a high cholesterol count and being overweight are two other likely causes of heart disease. A family history of heart disease and a lack of exercise are still other factors that contribute to heart conditions.

3. Preparing an effective speech requires intelligent planning. You must first select a topic; brainstorming often helps you to focus on what you want to say. Then you need to study who your audience will be to determine how you want to present your material. Then, once you have determined a topic and analyzed your audience, you are ready to do careful research on this topic.

4. Determinism and free will are two opposite points of view regarding human behavior. A determinist does not believe that a person freely chooses a lifestyle, whereas the believer in free will contends that one is free to change one's lifestyle at any time. A determinist sees biological and social forces determining one's decisions. Conversely, a proponent of free will discounts the influence of these forces in shaping one's life. Determinism can be a pessimistic philosophy, free will a hopeful one.

5. Edgar Allan Poe was born in 1809, the child of traveling actors. From 1815 to 1820, Poe was sent to schools in England. In 1825 he returned to the United States, entering the University of Virginia. In 1830, this great short story writer was accepted to West Point, an appointment that lasted only eight months.

6. Tropical rain forests are forests found in equatorial regions where rainfall is heavy and humidity is high. Here, vegetation is dense; mosses grow even on the large-leaved trees. On these leaves, one finds insects and spiders that live in the water that collects there. Several animal species thrive on the branches of these trees and on the ground of these lush forests.

7. Evaporation is an interesting natural process. The sun causes water to evaporate into the atmosphere. In the atmosphere, the water vapor cools. This cooling results in water forming again. The collected water is then expelled as rain, which restarts the evaporation process.

8. Gamma rays are high-energy electromagnetic waves. These waves have short wavelengths and are produced through radioactivity. X-rays are the most well-known example of gamma rays. Gamma rays are so strong that they can penetrate into the human body.

9. Sexually transmitted diseases have reached epidemic proportions in many parts of the world. Gonorrhea is a sexually communicable disease caused by bacteria that infect the genital tract. Syphilis is another sexually transmitted disease caused by bacteria that create sores on several parts of the body. Perhaps the most dreaded sexually induced disease to date is AIDS, whose cause is unknown, though researchers speculate that AIDS is induced by a virus.

10. In theory, a totalitarian form of government is different from a democracy. In a totalitarian government, all power resides with the state, and dissent is not permitted. If there are elections, almost all candidates belong to the same party. The voters in a totalitarian state have little or no choice in electing their leaders. In contrast, a democracy derives its authority from its people. Dissent is encouraged, to express the will of the people. Elections occur among candidates of different political beliefs.

Exercise 5.6
Identifying More
Organizational
Patterns

The following ten paragraphs have various organizational patterns. Your job is to identify the organizational pattern that best describes the paragraph. If more than one pattern seems to describe the paragraph, choose the pattern that more thoroughly fits the paragraph's structure. Place the appropriate letter in the answer box: A = spatial geographic, B = thesis-support, C = descriptive, and D = cause-effect.

1. Commercials may sell products, but they generally give little consumer information. Seeing a beautiful girl sipping a soft drink tells you nothing about the soda's content. Or showing a famous baseball player shaving with a name-brand razor does not tell the customer the cost or quality of the razor blade. Commercials sell wish fulfillments and sexual fantasies. They are rarely educational.

2. Humans breathe in air through their nose and their nasal cavity. The air then passes down from the nose to the larynx and the trachea. The trachea branches laterally into the bronchi, which lead directly to the lungs.

3. Emphysema is a respiratory disease in which walking, running, and exhaling are difficult. Some researchers suggest that the environment plays an important role in developing this disease. A young child who eats a poor diet and who catches many colds may

1. _____
2. _____
3. _____
4. _____
5. _____
6. _____
7. _____
8. _____
9. _____
10. _____

80%

(Score = # correct × 10)
Ask instructor for answers.

be a prime target for emphysema later on in life. Other researchers have pointed to certain hereditary deficiencies in people who develop emphysema. Cigarette smoking will also trigger emphysema in those people whose environment and heredity encourage this disease.

4. Families can be nurturing social structures. Parents can encourage in their children constructive behavior and discourage destructive actions. Brothers and sisters can develop lasting relationships. Both children and parents in a family unit can learn the value of giving and sharing.

5. The sudden rise in real estate prices has forced some young couples out of the home-buying market. Because houses cost more, fewer young couples can afford a home. If a couple buys a home, often both husband and wife must work to pay the monthly mortgage. Consequently, the once easy transaction of buying a home has become a privilege reserved mainly for the wealthy.

6. Hospitals need to be concerned both with curing the sick and caring for the dying. Every hospital should have a complete hospice facility where the dying are provided with a loving, homelike setting. Hospitals should also provide dying patients with pain-killing drugs so that their last days will be pain free. The philosophy of all hospitals should be that the last days of a dying patient need to be as meaningful and as pain free as possible

7. Greece is a country that is at the crossroads of three continents. It is the easternmost and southernmost country of Europe, just west of Asia and north of Africa. Presently, Greece is mainly bordered by communist countries, so it is at the crossroads of political differences as well. Albania and Yugoslavia border the northwestern section of Greece, and Bulgaria borders Greece on the northeast. Greece also borders Turkey on the east.

8. Being able to write effectively is a skill that one can use in almost all aspects of one's life. Writing certainly serves students very well in the courses they take—in completing exams and writing essays. But in life as well, being able to put into words what one is thinking gives individuals a better understanding of their lives. To be able to write down what they feel gives people a keener insight into themselves and allows them to plan ways to deal with their problems. Many composition teachers say, "If you can't put it into words, you don't know it." What they say makes sense.

9. She stopped for a moment on this placid spring afternoon to enjoy the lake, which was just minutes from her cottage. The sun was setting, and the water from the lake was glistening in silver-pink hues. She watched as a handful of geese bobbed up and down in the water in front of her. Soon, it seemed they had melted into the sunset. Other geese—loners, she thought—lined the boggy edges of the lake. She inhaled the fresh spring evening air, took one last long look, and made for the road pointing home.

10. Evan beheld for the first time on this crisp fall morning the university that would be his home for the next four years and that would remain in his memory for the rest of his life. Alternating red and brick circles emanated from the center of the plaza, around which the campus buildings stood guard. Standing in the plaza's center, he looked up at these medieval buildings, five stories high with rows of small, recessed windows. And as his eyes scanned this scene, he wondered which rooms would welcome him into the intellectual world he was so eager to join.

Exercise 5.7
Recognizing
Organizational
Patterns in a Longer
Passage

Read the following passage on the greenhouse effect carefully. Make marginal notes on the cause-effect patterns that are presented as well as the definitions that are given. Then answer the ten questions that follow. You may go back to the passage in answering the questions. Place all answers in the answer box.

The Greenhouse Effect

(1) Of the Sun's rays that reach the Earth, 70 percent are absorbed by the land, sea, and air, while 30 percent are reflected back into the atmosphere. Once the Earth's environment cools, the Sun's heat absorbed by the land, sea, and air is released in the form of infrared rays, or heat. Some of this energy escapes into space, and some of it is absorbed by water vapor and carbon dioxide in the atmosphere. The carbon dioxide and water vapor then repeat the cycle, returning some of this energy into the atmosphere and giving some back to the Earth.

(2) This returning to Earth of heat originally absorbed by the carbon dioxide and water of the atmosphere is called the greenhouse effect. Because of the greenhouse effect, the Earth's temperature has increased about 10 degrees Centigrade, or 18 degrees Fahrenheit, from what it would be without water vapor and carbon dioxide in the atmosphere.

(3) This natural cycle is being altered by the burning of coal as a fuel. Coal burning increases the amount of carbon dioxide and water in the atmosphere. This increase then allows for more heat to be returned to the Earth because of the greenhouse effect.

(4) What might happen if the greenhouse effect causes average temperatures to rise worldwide? Scientists speculate that an increase in temperature will cause rainfall patterns to shift and crop growing patterns to change. For example, the wheat belt in the United States might shift northward to Canada, where the soil is not as rich. Ultimately, the greenhouse effect might be responsible for less food production.

(5) A second result of an increase in temperature would be a melting of the polar ice caps. This melting would increase the water level in the oceans of the world. Scientists now speculate that the sea-level increase would be gradual, probably taking place over hundreds of years.

(6) But despite its potential to flood the land, the greenhouse effect seems to pose greater potential danger to the Earth's food-producing capacity. If there is less food in the next fifty years, there might be an increased hunger problem worldwide, for in the same fifty-year period, the world's population is expected to double.[2]

1. _____

2. _____

3. _____

4. _____

5. _____

6. _____

7. _____

8. _____

9. _____

10. _____

80%

(Score = # correct × 10)

Find answers on p. 309.

1. Most of the sentences in paragraph 1 are:

   a. main ideas
   b. topics
   c. minor details
   d. major details

2. The major organizational pattern of paragraph 1 is:

   a. definition
   b. spatial geographic
   c. comparison-contrast
   d. cause-effect

3. The major organizational pattern of paragraph 2 is:

   a. cause-effect
   b. spatial geographic
   c. comparison-contrast
   d. none of these

4. The main idea in paragraph 3 is:

   a. humans are using coal in increasing amounts
   b. coal use does not contribute to the greenhouse effect
   c. coal use causes more carbon dioxide and water to stay in the atmosphere
   d. coal use is on the decline

5. The major result of the greenhouse effect is:

   a. more rainfall
   b. a decrease in temperature
   c. an increase in temperature
   d. more snowfall

---

[2] Adapted from G. Tyler Miller, Jr., *Living in the Environment*, 4th ed. (Belmont, Calif.: Wadsworth, 1985), pp. E20–24.

6. The greenhouse effect can possibly:

   a. decrease the average temperature on the Earth
   b. reduce food production
   c. increase water levels in oceans worldwide
   d. both b and c

7. The melting of the polar ice caps would occur:

   a. quickly
   b. within weeks
   c. over several thousand years
   d. slowly

8. The major organizational pattern of paragraph 5 is:

   a. cause-effect
   b. comparison-contrast
   c. definition
   d. spatial geographic

9. Land flooding seems to be a major result of the greenhouse effect.

   a. true
   b. false

10. The major organizational pattern of paragraph 6 is:

   a. sequence of events
   b. comparison-contrast
   c. thesis-support
   d. definition

Exercise 5.8
Writing an Effective
Paragraph Using
Organizational
Patterns

Now that you have read the longer selection on the greenhouse effect, go back to reread the sections dealing with the causes and effects of the greenhouse effect. Your marginal notes should help you. As you review this material, complete the following two lists:

Definition of *the Greenhouse Effect*	*Possible Results of* *the Greenhouse Effect*
1.	1.
	2.

Refer only to these lists in answering the following essay question.

Essay Question: In one paragraph, define the greenhouse effect. Then discuss the two possible results of the greenhouse effect on our planet.

<u>70%</u>

Ask instructor for answers.

*Exercise 5.9
Determining Main
Ideas, Major
Details, and
Organizational
Patterns in a Text
Excerpt*

The following is an excerpt from a biology textbook on fossil fuels. The only two terms that may be new to you are *phytoplankton*, which are microorganisms found in fresh or salt water, and *carcinogens*, which are agents capable of promoting cancer.

Read through the excerpt quickly to get a sense of its organization. Then go back and read it slowly. When you finish, answer the five questions that follow. You may refer to the excerpt in deciding on your answers.

Fossil Fuels

(1) Fossil fuels are legacies from primary producers that lived hundreds of millions of years ago. Over time, immense coastal forests were submerged and the remains of countless populations of phytoplankton accumulated on ocean floors. They became buried and compressed in sediments; over time, these carbon-containing remains were transformed into coal, oil, and natural gas.

(2) Fossil fuels have been used as energy sources for many generations. Yet more fossil fuel has been used up during the past three decades than in all of the preceding years combined. Even with stringent conservation efforts, known fossil fuel reserves may be depleted early in the next century.

(3) In addition to petroleum reserves, there are vast deposits of oil shale in Colorado, Utah, and Wyoming. **Oil shale** is buried rock that contains kerogen, a hydrocarbon compound that can be converted to oil. The deposits in the western states probably contain more oil than does the entire Middle East. However, collecting, concentrating, heating, and converting kerogen to shale oil may cost so much that the net energy yield would be negligible, if not nonexistent. Also, the extraction process would disfigure the land, increase water and air pollution, and tax existing water supplies in regions already facing water shortages. Another problem is that a product of the extraction process is benzopyrene, a known carcinogen. Benzopyrene would be produced by the ton, even though there is no known way to use it or dispose of it safely. Finally, oil shale processing produces 12 percent more solid waste than the space the original

rock formation occupied. (It is something like popping unpopped corn.) Where do the leftovers go? Some have suggested that controlled atomic blasts deep in the rock formations might distill the kerogen in place. It would take six blasts a day to meet 10 percent of our current demands for energy. No one has determined what six blasts a day would do to the ecological and geological stability of the surrounding regions.

(4) What about **coal**? One-fourth of the world's known coal reserves occur in the United States. In principle, the reserves are enough to meet the energy needs of the entire population for at least several centuries. The problem is that coal burning has been the largest single source of air pollution. Most coal reserves contain low-quality, high-sulfur material. Unless sulfur is removed from coal before it is burned or removed afterward (from the gases in smokestacks), this fuel burning produces high levels of sulfur oxides in the air.

(5) In addition, coal mining carries its own risks. More than a billion dollars a year is being paid in benefits to coal miners afflicted with black-lung disease. Modern air-quality standards in mines minimize but do not eliminate this affliction, an outcome of breathing coal dust. Also, mine explosions, collapsed mine shafts, and the release of poisonous gases are still frequent.

(6) Pressure is on to permit widespread **strip mining**. Some coal reserves are close enough to the surface to be gouged out of the earth. How many millions of acres should be opened to mining companies? Strip mining renders the land useless for agriculture until it is restored. However, who will pay for restoration, and will restoration be complete?[3]

A. 1. The main idea of the entire passage is:

    a. fossil fuels are plentiful

    b. fossil fuels come from organisms that died millions of years ago

    c. fossil fuels have been used for energy for many years

    d. the technology necessary to extract fossils from the earth will lead to several negative effects on the environment

2. The main idea of paragraph 2 is:

    a. fossil fuels may not last through the twenty-first century

    b. fossil fuels have been used for years

    c. fossil fuels have steadily increased in use

    d. fossil fuel is a poor energy choice

1. _____
2. _____
3. _____
4. _____
5. _____

[3] Cecie Starr and Ralph Taggart, *Biology: The Unity and Diversity of Life*, 3rd ed. (Belmont, Calif.: Wadsworth, 1984), p. 675. Used by permission.

3. The major organizational pattern of paragraph 3 is:

   a. cause-effect
   b. spatial geographic
   c. thesis-support
   d. comparison-contrast

4. The major organizational pattern of paragraph 4 is:

   a. cause-effect
   b. spatial geographic
   c. thesis-support
   d. comparison-contrast

5. The major organizational pattern for the entire passage seems to be:

   a. comparison-contrast
   b. description
   c. cause-effect
   d. spatial geographic

B. Now go back and reread the excerpt. Then answer the following three questions in a phrase or sentence without looking back at the excerpt.

1. What are two effects of extracting oil from oil shale? (2 points)

2. What are two effects of coal mining on the environment and its people? (2 points)

3. What is the effect of strip mining on the land? (1 point)

70%

Ask instructor for answers.

6

Reading and Listening for Inferences

Explanation of Skills

Now that you have begun to identify various organizational patterns in writing and speech, you are on your way to reading and listening more critically. But sometimes knowing the organizational patterns is not enough. Books and lectures often leave much unsaid, and you must "read between the lines." Making judgments and drawing conclusions about what is suggested is called *making inferences*. The efficient student is an efficient inference maker, gleaning important points from what is suggested. It is the correct inference that instructors are looking for on exams and essays.

You can make inferences about most material by looking for: (1) the terms of qualification in a sentence, (2) the author's or speaker's word choice, and (3) the kinds of details used by a writer or speaker.

Terms of Qualification

A single word or phrase can change the message of a sentence. Terms of qualification can give strong support for a statement, or they can add doubt. A *term of qualification* is a word or phrase that limits the truth of a statement. In most cases, the speaker or writer will not tell you the degree of certainty intended in a statement; you need to infer this certainty from the term of qualification.

Terms of qualification can be divided into four categories: (1) terms expressing no doubt, (2) terms expressing little doubt, (3) terms expressing some doubt, and (4) terms expressing much doubt. Study the terms under each category.

Words and Phrases That Express No Doubt

all	surely	assuredly	there is no doubt
none	conclusively	undoubtedly	without reservation
never	clearly	absolutely	without hesitation
always	unequivocally	constantly	it is a proven fact
certainly	precisely	undeniably	it is undeniable
definitely	plainly	without a doubt	without question

Let these words and phrases become signals to you that what you are reading or listening to carries certainty. You can also use them when you write particularly strong statements.

See how the use of the word *absolutely* adds conviction to the following statement: "John Kennedy was absolutely the wisest presidential choice for the sixties, an era of youth and hope." The author evidently has positive feelings for Kennedy and uses "absolutely" to help establish these positive feelings. Sometimes, when you find such strong terms of qualification, you may want to underline them and make a marginal note such as "strong statement."

Now consider some terms that express a small degree of doubt.

Words and Phrases That Express a Little Doubt

most	seldom	there is little	it is believed
mostly	rarely	doubt	almost never
usually	slightly	with little	almost always
consistently	one can safely say	reservation	the consistent pattern

When you find such words and phrases in your reading and listening, you should ask yourself what the exceptions to the statement might be. These exceptions are often not discussed by the author. By failing to notice the term of qualification, you might wrongly conclude that the statement had no exceptions.

Consider how in the following statement the word *usually* plants a question in your mind: "If a ring forms in the subject's urine, you can usually conclude that the subject is pregnant." If the author does not discuss the exceptions, it be wise for you to underline the term of qualification and write in the margin something like: "When do these rings not suggest pregnancy?" You should begin using these terms in your own writing when you want to show a little doubt.

Now look at this list of terms expressing some doubt. If these terms are used, you need to consider the exceptions, which are often not elaborated upon by the writer.

Words and Phrases That Express Some Doubt

many	ostensibly	it seems
frequently	apparently	one can infer
often	somewhat	one can say with some
may	likely	reservation
might	this might mean	the hypothesis is
one would assume	this could mean	the theory is
the assumption is	the results imply	it is possible that
one would infer	possibly	it is probable that
it is suggested that	at times	
seemingly	it appears	
generally		

Let's look at the following sentence, which uses the term of qualification *it appears*. How does this term alter the meaning of the statement "It appears from this experiment that too much aspirin can lead to stomach problems"? Because the writer includes *it appears* in this statement, you cannot conclude that aspirin automatically leads to stomach problems. This experiment does not show a direct cause-effect relationship between aspirin and stomach ailments. In a marginal comment, you might ask what elements in the experiment add some doubt to the conclusion. You can also start using these terms in your own writing when your statements are not definite.

Finally, consider the following words, which suggest much doubt. When you see or hear these words, you should suspect the truth of these statements.

Words and Phrases That Suggest Much Doubt

supposedly	it is suspected that
it is guessed that	it is rumored that
it is conjectured that	

Note how the phrase "it is rumored that" makes the following statement questionable: "It is rumored that President Carter was forced to seek a second term as president in 1980." Because this statement is rumor, you cannot include it in any serious discussion of the 1980 presidential election. Many irresponsible speakers and publications use rumor as the basis for their arguments. You should never cite these speakers or publications as sources in a serious essay or speech.

Word Choice

You can make many inferences by noting the kinds of words a speaker or author uses. **Connotations** are the suggested meanings of words, telling you whether an author or speaker has a positive, neutral, or negative attitude toward the topic. Authors or speakers often do not directly tell you their attitude toward their topic, because they do not want to be accused of being biased. But you can infer these attitudes through the connotations of their words.

Look at the following sentence on former President Herbert Hoover and see if you can locate the word with the strong negative connotation: "Herbert Hoover remained blind to the economic depression of his country." Do you see that *blind* is a negative word, suggesting that Hoover could not see the problems of his country? Someone who is blind is also handicapped. Perhaps being handicapped is another negative suggestion the author wants you to associate with Hoover. Finally, blind is also a synonym for stubborn. It is likely that all three of these negative connotations are part of the author's attitude toward Hoover. In a marginal note about this sentence, you could ask: "Is the author suggesting that Hoover is blind, handicapped, and stubborn?"

Now look at the use of "no-nonsense" to see how it gives positive associations to the sentence about Harry Truman, another American president: "This was just one of many of Harry Truman's no-nonsense replies." Do you see that "no-nonsense" suggests common sense and straightforwardness? Although the author does not directly show an appreciation for Truman, this approval is suggested in the connotations of "no-nonsense." By making a marginal comment noting the connotations of this word, you would better understand the author's intent.

Note how this third statement uses neutral language: "In 1988, President Reagan completed his third term of office." Do you see that the author uses no words that suggest that the president was either competent or incompetent? Here the author may be purposely using neutral language so as not to offend either supporters or opponents of the president.

Details of Support

In longer written passages or in longer lectures, you can infer something about the author or speaker by the details that are presented. If the details are presented logically, you can infer that the speaker or author is in command of the material. But if the details are disorganized, you can infer that the speaker or author is poorly prepared. You can also infer something about the speaker or writer by studying the sources used in the work. If known publications or experts are cited, you will be more likely to value the argument. If the speaker or author does not mention sources, you would be justified in questioning the thesis. Again, the author or speaker will probably not comment on the nature of the details; it is up to you to determine the value of the work from the nature of the details. Look at the following paragraph on Vietnam. What do the details say about the competence of the writer?

Vietnam was a frustrating and senseless struggle. Many political leaders warned President Johnson and President Nixon that this war could never be won. Someone once said that guerilla fighters cannot be subdued by modern armaments. Many thousands of American soldiers died senselessly at the hands of these guerillas hiding in the bushes and jungles of their country.

Even if you agree with the thesis of the excerpt, the evidence is vague. The author does not name the political leaders who warned the presidents. The author does not mention who first said that guerillas cannot be destroyed by modern technology. Because these details are vague, you can infer that the writer, though logical, is not well prepared and therefore not convincing.

Study the details of this second passage on William Shakespeare, and infer something about the author:

William Shakespeare has been critically appreciated for three centuries, and in each century he has been appreciated for different reasons. In the eighteenth century, Samuel Johnson praised Shakespeare for his believable characters. In the nineteenth century, Samuel Taylor Coleridge was impressed with the complexity of Hamlet's character. Finally, in the twentieth century, Andrew Bradley was amazed at the sophisticated structure of Shakespeare's tragedies.

Note that the author of this excerpt has researched the subject; specific critics are named, and their praise of Shakespeare is discussed. You will likely read this writer carefully because the material is both logical and well documented.

When you write your own critical essays, be sure to cite your sources and present accurate details. If you do, your reader will read your work more carefully. You will learn more about effective essay writing in Chapter 15.

Summary

An inference is an insight that a reader has that is not stated directly in the text. By making correct inferences, you better understand your material. You make inferences by noting: (1) terms of qualification, (2) word choice, and (3) the nature of the details. You should make marginal comments on your inferences.

The more you read and listen, the more sophisticated your inferences will become. You will begin comparing past knowledge with what you are currently learning. And your learning will be that much more rewarding.

Summary Box   *Inferences*

What are they?	*How do you make them?*	*Why do you need them?*
Insights or deductions made by a reader or listener but not directly stated.	By studying terms of qualification, word choice, and details.	To give more meaning to your reading and listening. To become more questioning of what you read and hear.

Skills Practice

Exercise 6.1
Making Inferences
from Details

You can make inferences from the examples an author uses. The examples may be accurate, and you can infer that the author is credible; the examples may be inaccurate, and you can infer that the writer is unprepared. Read the following paragraphs carefully, and determine whether the speaker is being detailed or vague. Write A in the answer box if the paragraph is detailed and B if the paragraph is vague.

1. According to the 1975 *Statistical Abstract of the United States,* membership in American unions increased steadily from 1940–1970. In 1940, only 8.7 million workers were union members; by 1970, the numbers had more than doubled. The percentage of workers belonging to unions sheds a different light on these figures. In 1940, 15.5 percent of the total labor force belonged to unions; in 1970, the percentage of union workers had increased slightly to 22.6 percent.[1]

2. A federal study on single people was recently completed. The results showed that poor adult males were more likely to be single than wealthy adult males. The results for females were the opposite. Wealthy women were much more likely to be single than poor women.

3. How much of the Sun's energy is absorbed by the Earth? Surprisingly, only about one-half of one-billionth of the Sun's emitted energy is caught by the Earth. This energy travels to the Earth at

---

[1] From Philip C. Starr, *Economics: Principles in Action,* 2nd ed. (Belmont, Calif.: Wadsworth, 1978), p. 139. Used by permission.

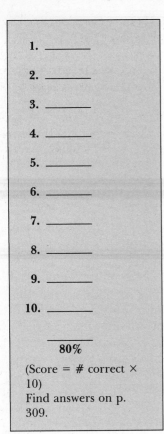

1. _____

2. _____

3. _____

4. _____

5. _____

6. _____

7. _____

8. _____

9. _____

10. _____

80%

(Score = # correct ×
10)
Find answers on p.
309.

186,000 miles per second. This voyage from the Sun to the Earth takes roughly eight minutes—a voyage of 93 million miles.

4. A federal report recently revealed an increase in violent and property crimes in the United States over the past years. Murder has gone up nationwide; so has forcible rape. Burglaries have increased even more than rapes. No crime category, in fact, has shown a decline.

5. The causes of the American Civil War are numerous, but very few historians agree about the most significant causes. Many cite economic differences between the North and South. Others say that the North and South really were different cultures with different histories. Of course, other historians emphasize the issue of slavery as the major cause of the Civil War.

6. The national debt has been steadily increasing over the past fifty years. In 1930, the national debt amounted to $18 billion. By 1950, the debt had risen to $257 billion. In 1982, the debt had increased to sixty times the debt of 1930—to $1 trillion, 142 billion. Economists do not know when or if this debt will begin to come down.

7. In a recent publication, it was noted that men and women have increased their average weekly earnings over the past years. The average dollar earnings are still higher for men than for women. An interesting finding was that black men and women also showed higher earnings. Black men still earned more than black women, on an average.

8. Charles Dickens is respected by several critics for his abilities as a novelist. Humphry House sees him as a great writer who was in step with the ideas and feelings of the English people during the mid-1800s. George Santayana regards Dickens as a gifted creator of character, especially in rendering the eccentricities of people. Even F. R. Leavis sees Dickens as a great artist able to entertain readers fully.

9. Two thousand years before Copernicus, an ancient Greek named Aristarchus of Samos believed that the Earth revolved around the Sun. This belief was rejected by Aristotle, the more respected philosopher of the time, and for nearly 2000 years Aristarchus's theories were ignored. In 1530, Copernicus in his *Commentariolus* once again supported the theories of Aristarchus. Kepler further refined the ideas of Copernicus in his 1609 publication titled *Aetological Astronomy*, in which he showed that the planets do move around the Sun, but in an ellipse.

10. A recent article discusses the increase in crime over the past few years. This article suggests that the denser the population, the

greater the incidence of crime. That is, crime in a rural area is a less serious problem than in a large city. This article concludes that people living closer together tend to develop animosity for each other—this animosity sometimes is expressed in crime.

Exercise 6.2
Locating and
Analyzing Terms of
Qualification

A. The following five statements on the effects of television viewing on children all contain terms of qualification. First, underline the term of qualification; then write a one-sentence comment explaining how the term alters the meaning of the statement. Comment on whether the term makes the statement stronger or casts doubt on the statement. You may want to refer to pp. 105–106 for the lists of terms of qualification.

Example: <u>In most instances,</u> when the supply of a product goes down, the demand goes up.

Explanation: The statement is weakened by "in most instances"; we need to know which instances violate this law of supply and demand.

1. It appears that watching too much television dulls a child's imagination.

   Explanation: _____

2. Without a doubt, what children used to work hard to imagine in books and on radio now flashes before their eyes on the television screen.

   Explanation: _____

3. There is little doubt that habitual television watching also discourages a child from reading and writing regularly.

   Explanation: _____

4. Many parents have dealt with this problem of their children watching too much television by closely monitoring what they watch.

   Explanation: _____

5. Closely monitoring what children watch seems to be an intelligent response to television in the household.

   Explanation: _____

B. Read the following paragraph on technology and education. In it you will find five terms of qualification. Locate them; then comment on how they alter the meaning of the sentence they are in.

The schools of tomorrow will likely make more use of technology, particularly computers. In the area of writing, word processors undoubtedly will replace typewriters in homes where parents can afford word processors. Perhaps in the future, students will not have to attend school for all of their courses; some of their instruction will be completed on video consoles at home. Educators also claim that possibly in the next generation elementary students will do their math drills on a computer that selects problems specific to the skill needs of each student. Clearly, the schools of tomorrow will be dependent upon technology to educate their students.

6. Term: _____

   Explanation: _____

7. Term: _____

   Explanation: _____

8. Term: _____

   Explanation: _____

9. Term: _____

   Explanation: _____

10. Term: _____

   Explanation: _____

80%
Ask instructor for answers.

**Exercise 6.3
Commenting on
Word Choice in
Sentences**

The writer of the following five sentences has a definite attitude toward imperialism. Read the five sentences; then reread each one, considering how the underlined word changes the meaning of the sentence. You may want to consult a dictionary or a thesaurus to determine the shades of meaning of the underlined word.

Example: Imperialism extended its underlined leprous hand across Africa.

Explanation: Leprosy is un unattractive disease of the skin that is sometimes fatal. By associating leprosy with imperialism, the writer is suggesting that like leprosy, imperialism brings disease and ugliness to those it controls.

A. 1. Imperialism is the desire of a powerful country to subjugate a less powerful country.

Explanation: _____

2. The <u>unquenchable</u> desire for power is the frequent goal of the more powerful country.

   Explanation: _____

3. Often the smaller, <u>defenseless</u> country has a resource that the larger country needs.

   Explanation: _____

4. All too often the people in the smaller nation are <u>sacrificed</u> for their natural resources.

   Explanation: _____

5. Sadly, all that imperialism often leaves to the subjugated country is evidence of human <u>greed</u>.

   Explanation: _____

B. In the following passage on Martin Luther King, Jr., there are five underlined words with strong connotations. Read the entire passage; then reread each sentence. Finally, comment on what the underlined word suggests and how it alters the meaning of the sentence.

In the 1950s and 1960s, Dr. Martin Luther King, Jr., was the most <u>influential</u> figure in America to expose the problems of black Americans to all Americans. King's personal heroes were Thoreau and Gandhi—both <u>enlightened</u> thinkers who preached nonviolence. The success Dr. King had in his nonviolent demonstrations in the South made him something of a <u>miracle</u> worker to blacks throughout the United States. King <u>graciously</u> accepted the respect of blacks and whites throughout the country for the strides he made in civil rights causes. King's successes were <u>senselessly</u> curtailed when he was assassinated in Memphis, Tennessee, in the spring of 1968.

6. Explanation: _____

7. Explanation: _____

8. Explanation: _____

9. Explanation: _____

10. Explanation: _____

70%

(Score = # correct ×
10)
Find answers on p.
309.

Exercise 6.4
Making Inferences
in a Longer Passage

In the following passage on education, you will be asked to make various inferences based upon details, word choice, and terms of qualification. Read the passage carefully. Then answer the questions that follow. You may refer to the passage when answering the questions. Place all answers in the answer box.

Schools Without Feeling

(1) A child's early education is critical to that child's development as a learner. The most enlightened instructional programs are those that respect the child's individual development and understand the learning stages a child passes through. All too often, unfortunately, young children are forced to conform to an education that dictates an instructional program that has little to do with the child's needs.

(2) All children by nature are inquisitive. From infancy, children want to learn whatever they can. They explore their world through crawling, then walking, and finally through talking—when they ask questions about their world.

(3) In humane school programs, this childlike questioning is fostered. Children are encouraged to help each other and to learn by doing individual research. Teachers in such schools often urge their students to choose their own reading books, while math and science topics are taught from the child's perspective. Children are not told simply to memorize hard and cold facts but are consistently shown how math operations and physical processes work as they do.

(4) Tragically, in many schools today, such an individual learning environment does not exist. Five- and six-year-olds are placed in classes of thirty students or more and are forced to complete the identical assignment. No attempt is made to see learning from the child's perspective; the child's individual learning needs are unjustly ignored. What often occurs is that students who do not fit into the average ability range are branded as learning disabled, when often these children are simply developing intellectually at a different rate from that of the average students in the class. Such large-group teaching pays little attention to each child's development and thus may damage a child's sense of self and ability to learn.

(5) Many schools today do not encourage children to be inquisitive. By ignoring the individual in favor of the group, many elementary schools make students dislike learning at an early age. School for these children becomes drudgery. In such unenlightened, large-group teaching environments, many potential Einsteins are carelessly discarded because their learning styles do not fit into the group's.

1. Read the first sentence in paragraph 1. Which word from this sentence has the strongest connotations?

   a. child's
   b. early
   c. education
   d. critical

1. _____

2. _____

3. _____

4. _____

5. _____

6. _____

7. _____

8. _____

9. _____

10. _____

80%

Ask instructor for answers.

2. In the last sentence of paragraph 1, "dictates" suggests:

    a. weakness
    b. stupidity
    c. a command
    d. intelligence

3. Locate the term of qualification in the first sentence of paragraph 2. It suggests:

    a. much doubt
    b. some doubt
    c. little doubt
    d. no doubt

4. In the first sentence of paragraph 3, there is a word with a strong positive connotation. It is:

    a. school
    b. humane
    c. programs
    d. continued

5. The "hard and cold facts" mentioned in paragraph 3 suggest:

    a. a lack of feeling
    b. a painful feeling
    c. an unkind feeling
    d. all of these

6. Read the last sentence in paragraph 3. The term of qualification in this sentence suggests:

    a. no doubt
    b. little doubt
    c. some doubt
    d. much doubt

7. In the first sentence in paragraph 4, which word has the most negative connotation?

    a. many
    b. tragically
    c. individualized
    d. exist

8. In paragraph 4, the author notes that the students' "individual learning needs are unjustly ignored." "Unjustly" suggests that these schools are:

    a. unethical
    b. legal
    c. cruel
    d. uncontrolled

9. In the first sentence of paragraph 5, the term of qualification suggests:

 a. little doubt
 b. some doubt
 c. much doubt
 d. none of these

10. In paragraph 5, two words with the strongest connotations are:

 a. natural, inquisitive
 b. ignoring, dislike
 c. drudgery, dreaded
 d. Einsteins, group

Exercise 6.5
Writing Your Own
Paragraph Using
Main Ideas and
Major Details

Your job is to go back to the passage on schools and reread the first paragraph (introduction) and the following three paragraphs (body). First, write down the main idea of the first paragraph. Then, jot down the major aspects of small-group instruction and the significant characteristics of large-group instruction that are mentioned. Place this information in the following outline. From the completed outline, answer the essay question in one paragraph.

I. _____

 A. Characteristics of small-group instruction:

 _____

 B. Characteristics of large-group instruction:

 _____

 Essay Question: What type of instruction does the author clearly favor? To support your choice, discuss three characteristics of large-group instruction that are mentioned, and three characteristics of small-group instruction that are treated.

70%
Ask instructor for
answers.

*Exercise 6.6
Determining Main
Ideas and Major
Details and Making
Inferences in a
Textbook Excerpt*

The following is an excerpt from a philosophy textbook on science and philosophy. Read through the excerpt quickly to get a sense of its organization. Then go back and read it slowly, paying particular attention to the definitions and its terms of qualification. When you finish, answer the following five questions. You may refer to the excerpt in deciding on your answers.

Challenges to Essentialist Views

Scientific Views

(1) Science's increasing impact has created a marked tendency to view the human "scientifically." However, what this means depends very much on what scientific perspective you take.

(2) For example, one strict scientific view claims that people can be explained by the natural sciences. True, humans are more complex than other entities, but ultimately they can be reduced to physical and chemical phenomena. There is no essential human nature in the classical or religious sense. There is no so-called mind or ability to love that makes us unique. The mind and thinking are simply the electrochemical activities of the brain.

(3) Those who maintain this view, that complex processes like life and thought can be explained wholly in terms of simpler physical and chemical processes, are often called *reductionists* or *mechanists*. Reductionism is the idea that a whole can be completely understood by analyzing its parts, or that a developing process can be explained as the result of earlier, simpler stages. Reductionists take something that is commonly thought to be real and reduce it to an appearance of something else. Thus, the strictly scientific view we've sketched holds that science reaches no further than objective facts. Human nature can be attributed or reduced to such facts.

(4) However, not all scientific views reduce human nature to a physiochemical process. Since the nineteenth century, a number of sciences have emerged that deal directly with human beings, society, and the relationships between them. These include anthropology, economics, political science, sociology, and psychology. These sciences have amassed an impressive collection of facts and material that describe people and human relationships. Social scientists do not study the human as a strictly physical object, as do the natural sciences; but nonetheless, many of them have advanced the theory that people can best be understood as an integrated system of responses resulting from genetics and environment; that individuals are basically passive objects—things that are acted upon and that really cannot help acting as they do. Even a cursory reading of social science literature discloses a widespread belief that humans are driven beings, moved by outer and inner needs or urges. Historically, debate has centered over what these needs are.

(5) Political philosopher Karl Marx (1818–1883) rejected the primacy of reason and the divine origins of humankind. Material forces, said Marx, produce both human nature and societal tendencies. What changes social structure is the production and reproduc-

tion of life; the primary need is survival. How we make a living is therefore of utmost importance, for the basic social characteristic that motivates humans is their productive capacity. We can influence our lives and history somewhat by altering our living conditions, but this capacity does not reside in our brains, wills, ideas, or desires. It exists mainly in the means of production and the class dynamics of society. Marx's view, then, is not strictly scientific but psychosocial.

(6) An example of the psychosocial approach in psychology is the work of Sigmund Freud. Freud held that nothing we do is haphazard or coincidental; everything results from mental causes, most of which we are unaware of. According to Freud, the mind is not only what is conscious or potentially conscious but also what is unconscious. This unconsciousness is a reservoir of human motivation comprised of instincts. In general, most of what we think, believe, and do is the result of unconscious urges, especially those developed in the first five years of life in response to traumatic experiences.

(7) While Marx and Freud both evidence some reductionism, they still seem to have supported the notion of a basic human nature. But as the social sciences have continued to grow and as the influence of the natural sciences has increased, the belief in an essential human nature has steadily declined. As a result, today there is a tendency to view humans in a more strictly scientific way. This view has received impetus from psychological **behaviorism**, a school of psychology that restricts the study of humans to what can be objectively observed—namely, human behavior.[2]

A. 1. The topic of the excerpt deals with a definition of:

    a. idealism
    b. reductionism
    c. behaviorism
    d. b and c

2. Which word in the following sentence from paragraph 4 has the strongest positive connotation? "These sciences have amassed an impressive collection of facts that describe people and human relationships."

    a. science
    b. amassed
    c. impressive
    d. collection

3. In paragraph 4, in regard to social scientists, the author notes: ". . . many of them have advanced the theory that people can best be understood as an integrated system of responses." The term of qualification used here suggests:

1. _____
2. _____
3. _____
4. _____
5. _____

[2] Vincent Barry, *Philosophy: A Text with Readings,* 2nd ed. (Belmont, Calif.: Wadsworth, 1983), pp. 51–52. Used by permission.

    a. no doubt
    b. little doubt
    c. some doubt
    d. much doubt

4. Reread paragraph 5. Marx believed that human behavior is mostly influenced by:

    a. physiology
    b. economics
    c. society
    d. b and c

5. In discussing Freudian theory in paragraph 6, the author says, ". . . nothing we do is haphazard or coincidental; everything results from mental causes." The tone of the statement expresses:

    a. no doubt
    b. little doubt
    c. some doubt
    d. much doubt

B. Now go back to reread the excerpt. Then, without looking back at the excerpt, answer the following three questions in a phrase or a sentence.

1. In your own words, define reductionism and behaviorism. (2 points)

2. For Marx, what were the basic causes for human behavior? (2 points)

3. For Freud, what were the basic causes for human behavior? (1 point)

70%

Ask instructor for answers.

7

Reading Graphs and Tables

Explanation of Skills

Reading graphs and tables is a necessary college skill. A graph is a visual representation of information; a table presents information compactly. If you learn more easily visually, graphs should help you learn. For each kind of graph, you need to use a specific strategy.

Circle Graphs

Circle graphs show how the whole is broken up into recognizable parts. The entire circle equals 100 percent, and the divided sections represent the parts. When you study circle graphs, you must first determine the subject. Then you should see how the various parts relate to this subject and then how the various parts relate to each other.

Look at the graph in Figure 7-1 on the various elements in the Earth's crust. Answer the following questions as you study this graph:

1. What does the whole circle represent?
2. How are the parts organized? Smallest percentage to largest? Largest percentage to smallest?
3. Can you remember the three most plentiful elements in the Earth's crust?

Having studied this circle graph, you should have noted that the entire circle represents the composition of the Earth's crust, or its ten most plentiful elements. You should have then noticed that as you move clockwise, the percentages become smaller, from the most plentiful element, oxygen, to the least plentiful, titanium. If on an ecology

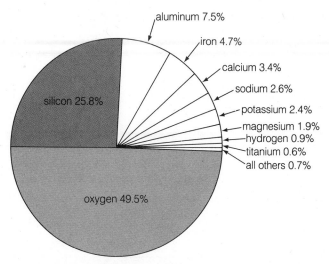

Figure 7-1   *Earth's crust. (From G. Tyler Miller, Jr.,* Living in the Environment, *4th ed. [Belmont, Calif.: Wadsworth, 1985], p. 235. Used by permission.)*

exam, for example, you had to remember the elements making up the Earth's crust, this circle graph would have helped you.

Bar Graphs

Bar graphs are usually a series of rectangles comparing the parts of a whole, much like circle graphs. Each rectangle represents 100 percent, and this rectangle is often divided up into parts of this 100 percent. You should ask the same questions that you would when studying a circle graph:

1. What is the subject?
2. How do the parts relate to this subject?
3. How do the parts relate to each other?

Look at the bar graph in Figure 7-2 on the use of natural resources in the United States. Determine the subject, the various parts of each rectangle, and how these parts relate to each other.

Having studied this material, did you determine that the first rectangle represents world population, the second bar the world use of petroleum, and the third the world use of nonfuel minerals, or metals and nonmetals? Did you determine that the shaded areas in each rectangle represent the proportion belonging to the United States?

This bar graph strikingly illustrates how the United States is a nation of overconsumers. The shaded 5 percent, the population of the United States relative to the rest of the world, uses one-third (33 percent) of the world's petroleum and over one-third (36 percent) of

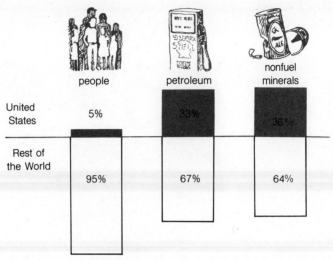

Figure 7-2   *Annual use of resources in the world. (Data from U.S. Bureau of Mines, Minerals Yearbook, 1975. From G. Tyler Miller, Jr., Living in the Environment, 2nd ed. [Belmont, Calif.: Wadsworth, 1979], p. 235. Used by permission.)*

the world's nonfuel minerals. This bar graph would be an effective study aid if you needed to remember this information for an exam.

Line Graphs

With line graphs, you may have a more difficult time than with circle or bar graphs. Line graphs are made up of three important parts: (1) the vertical axis, or the line going up and down; (2) the horizontal axis, or the line going from side to side; and (3) the diagonal line, or the line either going up, down, or parallel to the horizontal axis. Line graphs always illustrate relationships, usually cause-effect relationships. In business or economics material, the line graph often shows how the supply of a particular product affects its demand—how, for example, lowering the supply increases the demand. In biology material, the line graph often shows how a biological activity is affected by a particular variable or change—how, for instance, temperature (a variable) affects cell movement (a biological activity).

As with circle and bar graphs, you need first to determine the subject of the line graph and what the numbers on the vertical and horizontal axes mean. Unlike circle and bar graphs, you need to study the vertical and horizontal axes as well as the diagonal line to determine the nature of the relationship. Determining this relationship is crucial, because without it, you will not understand what the details of the line graph mean, and you will not understand the meaning of the diagonal's movement in going up, down, or staying parallel to the horizontal axis.

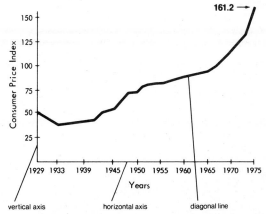

Figure 7-3   *The Consumer Price Index, for 1929–1975 (1967 = 100). (Source:* Economic Report of the President, 1976, *p. 220. From Philip C. Starr,* Economics: Principles in Action, *2nd ed. [Belmont, Calif.: Wadsworth, 1978], p. 295.)*

Look at the line graph in Figure 7-3 on the Consumer Price Index (CPI), which shows how prices fluctuated in the United States from 1929–1975. First, determine what the numbers on the vertical and horizontal axes represent. Then decide what the diagonal's upward movement suggests.

Having studied this graph, did you determine that the Consumer Price Index increased over this time span, that it doubled between 1929 and 1967, and more than tripled between 1929 and 1975?

With line graphs, you may have a problem in correctly estimating where the diagonal meets each axis. Using a small, six-inch ruler to locate a particular point on the diagonal will help your calculation. Use a ruler to find the CPI for 1950. Did it help you to calculate 70?

Sometimes line graphs get more complicated because there are two or more diagonals or variables for you to consider. And sometimes these diagonals intersect. No matter how complicated the line graph, though, your strategy should be the same as in reading a line graph with one diagonal: (1) determine the subject of the graph, (2) determine what the numbers on each axis represent, and (3) determine how the diagonals relate to each other.

Look at the line graph in Figure 7-4 on the use of crude oil in the United States. Determine the subject, what the numbers on each axis mean, and how the two diagonals relate to each other.

Having studied this more complex line graph, you should have determined that it compares the supply of domestic and imported crude oil in the United States. The vertical axis measures crude oil in billions of barrels, while the horizontal axis lists the years the United

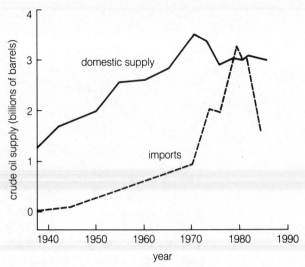

Figure 7-4   *Annual domestic extraction and imports of crude oil in the United States, 1940–1983. (Source: U.S. Bureau of Commerce. From G. Tyler Miller, Jr.,* Living in the Environment, *4th ed. [Belmont, Calif.: Wadsworth, 1985], p. 263. Used by permission.)*

States has purchased both domestic and imported crude from 1940 to 1983. The diagonal lines suggest that from roughly 1940 to 1970, the United States each year imported and produced more crude oil; then early in the seventies, the domestic supply began decreasing, while the imported crude began to rise suddenly. Finally, in the eighties, the supply of domestic crude leveled off, while the imports began to fall drastically. By carefully reading a line graph such as this one with two or more diagonals or variables, you can see that much information can be extracted.

Tables

Unlike graphs, tables are not visual. They simply present information concisely. Tables are especially helpful study aids because they present much information in a small space. When you read tables, as you did with graphs, first determine the subject; then establish what each category and subcategory represents. If you do not know what a particular part of a table means, you may not be able to use the table efficiently. Unlike a line graph, whose diagonal shows a trend (up, down, or staying the same), a table does not spell out these trends for you; you need to make these inferences from the data in the table. If you note a trend in a table, make a marginal note saying what that trend seems to be.

Table 7-1 *U.S. Import Dependence for Selected Key Nonfuel Minerals in 1982*

Mineral	Percentage Imported	Rank of Major Suppliers
Niobium	100	Brazil, Canada, Thailand
Manganese	98	South Africa, Gabon, Brazil, France
Tantalum	91	Thailand, Canada, Malaysia, Brazil
Cobalt	91	Zaire, Belgium-Luxembourg, Zambia, Finland
Chromium	90	South Africa, Philippines, Soviet Union, Turkey
Platinum	85	South Africa, Soviet Union, United Kingdom
Nickel	72	Canada, Norway, Botswana, Australia

Source: U.S. Bureau of Mines. From G. Tyler Miller, Jr., *Living in the Environment,* 4th ed. (Belmont, Calif.: Wadsworth, 1985), p. 251. Used by permission.

Look at Table 7-1 on minerals that the United States imports. Note the categories of the table, and note the order of each entry. What inferences can you draw from the data?

The table presents seven minerals, and lists them according to the relative need the United States has for each one. Niobium, the first mineral mentioned, is not found at all in the United States; nickel is the last entry because the United States depends upon imports for only 72 percent of its supply. Note that the category "Rank of Major Suppliers" presents the supplying countries in order of their ability to produce. South Africa seems to be rich in minerals because it is listed three times as the first major producer.

Do you see how densely packed with information this table is? Most tables that you will come across are equally informative. As you continue to read tables, you will be able to make more subtle inferences and determine more patterns that are suggested in the data. You will also find yourself relying on tables more for study purposes.

Summary

Graphs are visual, concise means of presenting information. There are three kinds of graphs: circle, bar, and line. Line graphs show relationships among two or more variables and are sometimes difficult to understand. Tables are not visual; rather, they present information in categories. In reading a table, you need to make inferences regarding the patterns that emerge from the data.

Graphs and tables are often effective study aids because much information is presented in a small amount of space. You may choose to create your own graphs and tables for study purposes when you want to condense the material you are studying.

Summary Box   *Graphs and Tables*

What are they?	Why use them?
Graph: a visual way to present information using circles, bars, or lines.	Graph: To present information visually and to help you learn material more easily.
Table: a concise way to relate information by setting up categories and subcategories.	Table: To present information concisely. To show relationships among facts and figures. To gain insights about the material you are studying. To help you remember information for exams.

Skills Practice

Exercise 7.1
Reading Graphs and Tables

Use the strategies you have just learned to answer the following questions concerning graphs and tables. Place all answers in the answer box.

1. The line graph in Figure 7-5 concerns:

    a. the increasing per capita income in the United States
    b. the increasing per capita income in India
    c. the number of years it has taken India to match the per capita income of the United States
    d. both a and b

2. At the twenty-year mark, the per capita income of the United States was about:

    a. $8,000
    b. $9,000
    c. $10,000
    d. $12,000

3. The per capita income of India over the twenty-four-year comparison:

    a. stayed the same
    b. doubled
    c. tripled
    d. none of these

4. The subject of the bar graph in Figure 7-6 (on p. 129) is:

    a. the amount in tons of sixteen metals
    b. the projected depletion rate of sixteen key metals
    c. the scarcity of gold and mercury
    d. the abundance of chromium

5. If reserves increase five times and consumption increases 2.5 percent annually, mercury will be depleted in:

    a. the year 2000
    b. about 1990
    c. about 2002
    d. about 2010

6. If present reserves are consumed with a 2.5 percent annual increase, iron will be depleted in the year:

    a. 2040
    b. 2060
    c. 2080
    d. 2090

7. If reserves increase five times and consumption increases 2.5 percent annually, the metal that will be available the longest is:

    a. chromium
    b. cobalt
    c. iron
    d. nickel

8. In Table 7-2, what form of energy does the federal government seem to support the most?

    a. fossil fuel
    b. nuclear
    c. wind
    d. breeder fission

9. About how many billions of dollars did the federal government spend on energy research in 1979?

    a. 3
    b. 4
    c. 4½
    d. 5

10. About how much does one nuclear-powered aircraft carrier cost?

    a. $3 billion
    b. over $2 billion
    c. over $1 billion
    d. $388 million

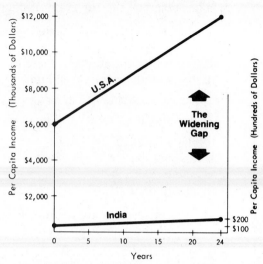

Figure 7-5 *Per capita income in both the United States and India doubled, but the income gap widened. (From Philip C. Starr,* Economics: Principles in Action, *2nd ed. [Belmont, Calif.: Wadsworth, 1978], p. 355.)*

Table 7-2 *Expenditures for Energy Research in 1979*

Program	(millions of dollars)	Total Energy Budget	Approximate Military Expenditure Equivalents
Nuclear energy	1,132	29	One missile-carrying submarine
Breeder fission	608	15	Two conventional submarines
Conventional fission	297	8	One conventional submarine
Fusion	227	6	Three long-range bombers
Conservation	792	20	One conventional aircraft carrier
Fossil fuel energy	577	15	Four destroyers
Basic energy research and technology development	338	9	Four long-range bombers
Solar energy	321	8.6	Three long-range bombers and one F-15 fighter plane
General science and research	307	8	Three B-1 bombers
Environmental research and development	186	5	Two long-range bombers
Geothermal energy	133	3	One destroyer
Wind energy	54	1.4	Four F-15 fighter planes
Biomass energy	24	0.5	Two F-15 fighter planes
Hydroelectric energy	23	0.5	Two F-15 fighter planes
Total	3,887	100	Three nuclear-powered aircraft carriers

Source: Staff report 1978h. From G. Tyler Miller, Jr., *Energy and Environment: The Four Energy Crises,* 2nd ed. (Belmont, Calif.: Wadsworth, 1980), p. 157. Used by permission.

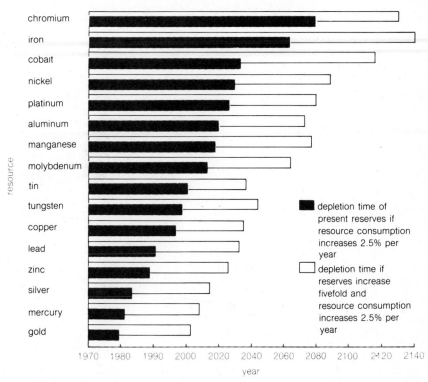

Figure 7-6 *Projected times for 80 percent depletion of world reserves of sixteen key metal resources, based on two sets of assumptions. Note that the time scale changes after the year 2000. (Data from U.S. Geological Survey 1973. From G. Tyler Miller, Jr.,* Living in the Environment, *2nd ed. [Belmont, Calif.: Wadsworth, 1979], p. 245. Used by permission.)*

**Exercise 7.2
Reading More
Graphs and Tables**

Here are two more graphs and another table, each followed by questions. Place your answers in the answer box.

1. From Figure 7-7, determine how many million kilocalories the developed nations used in 1900:

   a. 11
   b. 15
   c. 20
   d. 25

2. In 1980, about how many million kilocalories did the developed nations use?

   a. 15
   b. 20
   c. 25
   d. 30

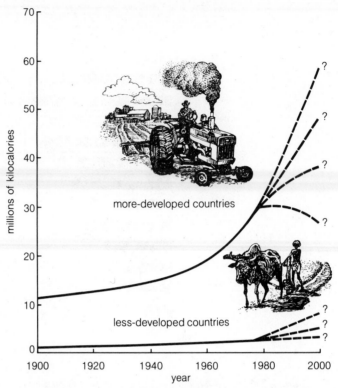

Figure 7-7 *Past (solid lines) and projected (dotted lines) average per capita annual energy consumption in the world. (Data from Keyfitz 1976, United Nations 1976. From G. Tyler Miller, Jr.,* Energy and Environment: The Four Energy Crises, *2nd ed. [Belmont, Calif.: Wadsworth, 1980] p. 6. Used by permission.)*

3. Developing nations from 1900 to 1980 have annually used:

   a. more than 5 million kilocalories
   b. more than 10 million kilocalories
   c. less than 5 million kilocalories
   d. graph does not say

4. The line graph in Figure 7-8 represents how many categories of working women?

   a. four
   b. three
   c. two
   d. one

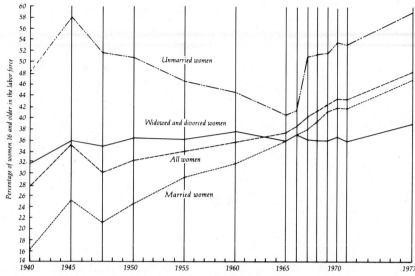

Figure 7-8 *Women in the American labor force, 1940–1977. (Source: U.S. Bureau of the Census,* Statistical Abstract of the United States, *1978, p. 404. From Earl R. Babbie,* Sociology: An Introduction *[Belmont, Calif.: Wadsworth, 1980], p. 311.)*

1. _____

2. _____

3. _____

4. _____

5. _____

6. _____

7. _____

8. _____

9. _____

10. _____

_____
80%

Ask instructor for answers.

5. The working women who seemed to have made the most consistent advances in increasing their numbers are:

   a. married women
   b. widowed and divorced women
   c. unmarried women
   d. all women

6. The working women who seem to have made the smallest advances in increasing their numbers are:

   a. married women
   b. widowed and divorced women
   c. unmarried women
   d. all women

7. A conclusion that can be reached regarding women in the labor force is that:

   a. their numbers did not increase significantly from 1940 to 1977
   b. their numbers decreased over the years 1940 to 1977
   c. their numbers increased about 10 percent over the years 1940 to 1977
   d. their numbers increased about 15 percent over the years 1940 to 1977

8. Table 7-3 analyzes noncollege and college youth's attitudes toward:

a. traditional American values
b. morally wrong activities
c. the value of education
d. both a and b

Table 7-3 *Personal and Social Values (By Total Noncollege Youth versus Total College Youth)*

	Total Noncollege Percentage	Total College Percentage
Belief in Traditional American Values		
Doing any job well is important	89	84
Business is entitled to make a profit	85	85
People should save money regularly	80	71
Commitment to a meaningful career is very important	79	81
Private property is sacred	74	67
A "strong" person can control own life	70	65
Competition encourages excellence	66	62
Duty before pleasure	66	54
Hard work will always pay off	56	44
People are basically good, but society corrupts	50	46
People who "accept" things are better off	31	15
Activities Thought to Be Morally Wrong		
Destroying private property	88	78
Taking things without paying for them	88	84
Collecting welfare when you could work	83	77
Paying for college by selling dope	80	64
Interchanging partners among couples	72	57
Using violence to achieve worthwhile results	72	66
Cheating big companies	66	50
Extramarital sexual relations	65	60
Having children without formal marriage	58	40
Living with a spouse you don't love	52	41
Having an abortion	48	32
Relations between consenting homosexuals	47	25
Casual premarital sexual relations	34	22

Source: *The Youth Study-1974,* (JDR Third Fund) Yankelovich, Skelly and White, Inc., New York. From Harold W. Berkman and Christopher G. Gibson, *Consumer Behavior,* p. 107. Copyright 1978. Reprinted by permission of Kent Publishing Co.

9. Of the following attitudes, which shows the greatest disagreement between noncollege and college youth?

   a. doing any job well is important
   b. private property is sacred
   c. destroying private property
   d. having children without formal marriage

10. The conclusion one can draw from this table is:

   a. noncollege youth tend to have more traditional American values than college youth
   b. college youth tend to have more traditional values than noncollege youth
   c. the values of college and noncollege youth are similar
   d. the information is contradictory; no conclusion can be drawn

Exercise 7.3
Writing a
Paragraph with a
Main Idea and
Supporting Details
from Information in
a Graph

In this writing exercise, you are to use only the information presented in the circle graphs in Figure 7-9 to answer the following essay question.

Essay Question: In an organized paragraph, discuss the four stages of energy consumption in the United States from 1850 to 1980. Where appropriate, give percentages of the energy use of oil in each era. Start with a topic sentence; then give supporting details.

Use the following outline to jot down notes you will use in your paragraph.

I. _____

   A. _____

   B. _____

80%
Ask instructor for answers.

   C. _____

   D. _____

Exercise 7.4
Determining Main
Ideas and Major
Details and
Interpreting a Table
in a Textbook
Excerpt

The following excerpt is from an economics text on Reaganomics, the economic policies of the Reagan Administration. Three terms that might be new to you are: (1) supply side, which refers to an economic theory contending that help to a lagging economy comes from tax cuts and reduced government regulation, (2) monetarist, which refers to one who believes in using monetary policies over fiscal policies to help the economy, and (3) Laffer Curve, a curve that suggests that low tax rates will increase the work incentive and thus tax revenues.

134

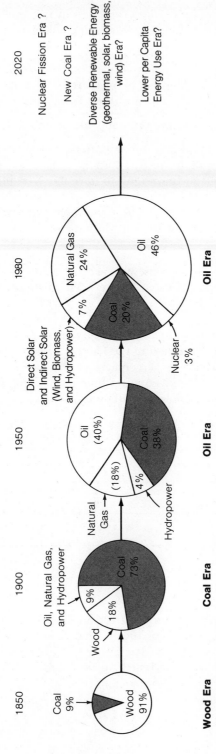

Figure 7-9 *Changing patterns in the use of energy resources in the United States. Circle size represents relative amount of total energy used. (Data from U.S. Bureau of the Census, Resources for the Future, and U.S. Federal Energy Administration. From G. Tyler Miller, Jr., Living in the Environment, 2nd ed. [Belmont, Calif.: Wadsworth, 1979], p. 254. Used by permission.)*

Read through the excerpt quickly to get a sense of its organization. Then go back and read it slowly, paying particular attention to the table and its relationship to the excerpt. When you finish, answer the five questions that follow. You may refer to the excerpt in deciding on your answers.

The Reagan Experience, 1981–1983

(1) The program initiated by President Reagan in 1981 was designed to please the conservatives of the country. Accordingly, his administration and his program embraced supply-side *and* monetarist policies, with emphasis on (1) the tax rate, (2) cuts in federal spending, and (3) efforts to control inflation. As it turned out, all three parts of the program developed problems.

The Tax Cut

(2) The tax cut, usually called the Kemp-Roth* Bill, was enacted in 1981. The bill was designed to cut personal income taxes by 25 percent over a period of three years. Additional tax breaks for depreciation and new investment were given corporations. The tax cut was adopted, in the spirit of the Laffer Curve, with the hope that lower tax rates would increase spending, saving, and investing, and at higher GNP levels, tax revenues would increase.

Almost immediately, the tax cut produced a furor. Analyses of the tax-cut bill indicated that it favored people with high incomes. Table 19-2 provides a sample.

(3) Table 19-2 clearly shows that the critics were right. The tax cut gave larger dollar savings to higher-income people; that was to be expected. But the tax saving as a percentage of income also rose—an indication that the tax cut was regressive. Another way to see the same point is to note that as income increases 10 times from $8,000 to

Table 19-2   *Federal Income Taxes in 1980 and 1984 Before and After the Kemp-Roth Tax Cut (For Married Individuals Filing Joint Returns)*

	Total Income Tax			Tax Saving as a Percentage of Taxable Income
Taxable Income	*1980*	*1984*	*Tax Saving*	
$ 8,000	$ 786	$ 693	$ 93	1.2%
15,000	1,823	1,581	242	1.6
30,000	5,607	4,762	845	2.8
60,000	17,705	15,168	2,537	4.2
80,000	29,989	26,104	3,885	4.9

Source: *1981 Prentice-Hall Federal Tax Guide,* August 1981.

* The official name was the Economic Recovery Tax Act of 1981.

$80,000, the tax saving increases 41.8 times from $93 to $3,885. One columnist commented: "It seems that when Reagan talks about lower taxes, he is not addressing the 96 percent of families making $50,000 or less." The same columnist suggested that supply side theory might be a smoke screen for cutting taxes at the very top. However, since 44 percent of U.S. families had incomes of $25,000 or more in 1981, many people did benefit from the cut. And personal savings—one goal of the cut—did increase to $140 billion in 1982 from $130.2 billion in 1981.

Cuts in Federal Spending

(4) The hoped-for reduction in the size of the federal government did not materialize. The Reagan administration *did* cut federal nondefense spending, but Reagan was also determined to increase defense spending under the theory that U.S. military strength was falling below that of the Russians. Given this rationale, the Reagan administration determined to increase military spending in *real terms* by more than 40 percent between 1980 and 1985. As a proportion of all federal spending, defense spending would rise from 23 percent in 1980 to 36 percent in 1985. And because of the increases in defense spending, the Congressional Budget Office estimated that defense spending as a percentage of GNP would increase from 22.6 percent in 1980 to 23.2 percent in 1985.

(5) The changes in the mix of federal spending from nondefense to defense generated more criticism: First, military spending is notoriously costly because there is little competition among suppliers. Second, increases in military spending tend to draw resources away from the private economy where they may be more productive. (A technician may benefit the average person more by making toasters than by making missiles.) Third, the opportunity cost of increases in military spending was measured by a decline in spending for the poor. Food stamps were cut by more than $2 billion in 1982; Medicaid was cut almost $2 billion; the school lunch program was cut by 30 percent; $1 billion (above 20 percent) was cut from aid to families with dependent children (AFDC), a program involving 4 million households.[1]

A. 1. The main idea of paragraph 1 suggests that:

    a. Reagan's policies were carefully thought out
    b. Reagan's economic policies did not succeed completely
    c. Reagan's economic policies favored the poor
    d. the cuts in federal spending were reasonable

---

[1] Philip C. Starr, *Economics: Principles in Action,* 4th ed. (Belmont, Calif.: Wadsworth, 1984), pp. 395–397. Used by permission.

1. _____

2. _____

3. _____

4. _____

5. _____

2. The main idea of paragraph 2 is that the Reagan Administration believed that a tax cut would cause:

    a. increased savings
    b. increased investing
    c. more tax resources
    d. all of these

3. In paragraph 3, the author states that one of the Reagan Administration's predictions came true:

    a. tax revenues decreased
    b. taxpayers saved less
    c. taxpayers saved more
    d. the poor received a tax cut

4. In Table 19-2, which category or earners received the biggest tax cut percentagewise?

    a. $30,000
    b. $60,000
    c. $80,000
    d. none of these

5. The table compares the difference in income tax paid within:

    a. a two-year period
    b. a four-year period
    c. a six-year period
    d. an eight-year period

B. Now go back and reread the excerpt. Then, without looking back at the excerpt, answer the following three questions in a phrase or sentence.

1. The author suggests that the rich profited from the Kemp-Roth Bill. List two details that the author uses that support this premise. (2 points)

2. Why does the author believe that military spending is so costly? (1 point)

3. Name two federal programs that were cut by the Reagan Administration in 1982. (2 points)

70%

Ask instructor for answers.

8

Summarizing and Paraphrasing

Explanation of Skills

Being able to summarize information from textbooks, lectures, and lecture notes is one of the most important skills to master. Organized summaries will provide helpful study sheets for exams. A **summary** is an accurate restatement of material, presented in condensed form. The key terms to remember are *accurate* and *condensed*. Inaccurate summaries are useless, and lengthy summaries are much like the original.

Summarizing, like note taking and critical reading, is a complex skill that improves with practice. So do not expect to be an expert summarizer right away.

How to Summarize

To be able to summarize efficiently, you need to identify main ideas and major details. In lectures and in reading textbooks, you need to focus both on the main ideas and the major details. As your summaries improve, you will be choosing the significant major details. In summaries, you rarely include minor details.

For now, follow these steps when you summarize textbooks and lecture material. Most of these hints apply to summarizing written material. You will learn more about how to summarize a lecture in Part Three.

1. In each paragraph of text or each page of lecture notes, locate the main idea, which is often the first sentence. You must include these main ideas in your summary.

   Underline the main idea twice or use a curved line. And underline the important parts of the sentence. Look at this example:

Algebra is a <u>mathematical language</u> employing both <u>letter and number symbols</u> to solve numerical and word problems.

2. Sometimes main ideas are implied, and often in textbooks two or three shorter paragraphs work like one big paragraph. If you read several paragraphs and cannot locate a main-idea sentence, write your own in the margin.

3. Underline one or two major details in each paragraph of text or section of lecture notes. Do not underline the entire sentence, just the important words. Underline these details once to differentiate them from main ideas. See how the major detail is highlighted in this sentence:

<u>Magnetic tape</u> used for computer memory comes in <u>various lengths</u> and is <u>wound</u> on a reel.

Which details should you include? This choice may be difficult at first, but just keep asking yourself: Which are the important details? Which most directly support the main idea? The layout of the textbook should help you. Main ideas and certain major details are often in boldface print or in italics. In lecture, listen for such comments as "I want you to remember that . . . ," "It is important to remember . . . ," or "I repeat . . . ." Also, note what the instructor writes on the blackboard. These are the instructors' clues that they are presenting key points.

4. When you have finished five or six paragraphs of textbook material and have underlined main ideas and major details, stop reading. Also, when you have marked a page or two of lecture notes, put your pen down. Then, write a summary of five or six sentences or phrases, either in outline form or in a short paragraph. It is often better to put your summaries in outline form because you can separate main ideas from major details.

Put this summary in your own words. By putting the information in your own words, you make it easier to learn. When you are copying from a textbook or from your lecture notes, you are not actively thinking, and you will probably not remember what you have copied. Only when you read or hear a definition should you copy. Here, the exact wording is necessary for you to understand the term. You will learn more about summarizing text material in Chapter 12, "The SQ3R Study System."

Read the following five-paragraph excerpt. Underline the main ideas and significant major details. Then place your summary in the outline skeleton that follows the excerpt. Use your own words wherever possible.

Law of Conservation of Matter: Everything Must Go Somewhere

(1) We always talk about consuming or using up matter resources, but actually we don't consume any matter. We only borrow some of the Earth's resources for a while—taking them from the Earth, carrying them to another part of the globe, processing them, using them, and then discarding, reusing, or recycling them. In the process of using matter, we may change it to another form, such as burning complex gasoline molecules and breaking them down into simpler molecules of water and carbon dioxide. But in every case we neither create nor destroy any measurable amount of matter. This results from the **law of conservation of matter**: In any ordinary physical or chemical change, matter is neither created nor destroyed but merely changed from one form to another.

(2) This law tells us that we can never really throw any matter away. In other words, there is no such thing as either a consumer or a "throwaway" society. *Everything we think we have thrown away is still here with us in some form or another.* Everything must go somewhere and all we can do is to recycle some of the matter we think we have thrown away.

(3) We can collect dust and soot from the smokestacks of industrial plants, but these solid wastes must then go somewhere. Cleaning up smoke is a misleading practice, because the invisible gaseous and very tiny particle pollutants left are often more damaging than the large solid particles that are removed. We can collect garbage and remove solid wastes from sewage, but they must either be burned (air pollution), dumped into rivers, lakes, and oceans (water pollution), or deposited on the land (soil pollution and water pollution if they wash away).

(4) We can reduce air pollution from the internal combustion engines in cars by using electric cars. But since electric car batteries must be recharged every day, we will have to build more electric power plants. If these are coal-fired plants, their smokestacks will add additional and even more dangerous air pollutants to the air; more land will be scarred from strip mining, and more water will be polluted from the acids that tend to leak out of coal mines. We could use nuclear power plants to produce the extra electricity needed. But then we risk greater heat or thermal pollution of rivers and other bodies of water used to cool such plants; further, we also risk releasing dangerous radioactive substances into the environment through plant or shipping accidents, highjacking of nuclear fuel to make atomic weapons, and leakage from permanent burial sites for radioactive wastes.

(5) Although we can certainly make the environment clearer, talk of "cleaning up the environment" and "pollution free" cars, products, or industries is a scientific absurdity. The law of conservation of matter tells us that we will always be faced with pollution of some sort. Thus, we are also faced with the problem of *trade-offs*. In turn, these frequently involve subjective and controversial scientific, political, economic, and ethical judgments about what is a dangerous pollutant level, to what degree a pollutant must be controlled, and

what amount of money we are willing to pay to reduce a pollutant to a harmless level.[1]

I. Law of Conservation of Matter

A. _____

B. _____

C. _____

D. _____

E. _____

F. _____

(Compare your underlining and summary with that on pp. 310–312.)

Now that you have completed your underlining and summary and checked it with the answer key, read the following comments about the excerpt.

1. In paragraph 1, you should have studied the boldface print, which directs you to the definition of the law of conservation of matter. You should also have noticed that the topic sentence, or main idea, of the first paragraph comes at the end rather than the beginning.

2. In paragraph 2, did you notice that the important detail is in italics? You should have underlined this sentence and made it the B. of your outline.

3. Paragraphs 3 and 4 do not have a topic sentence. The topic sentence of both is implied. This implied topic sentence would say something like "Here are examples of the law of conservation of matter." You could have underlined parts of any one of these examples; each illustrates this law. So, your C. and D. could be two of any of the examples in these paragraphs.

   Writing an implied topic sentence is a sophisticated skill, one that will develop with practice. For now, if you realized that the topic sentence was implied, you have some sophisticated summarizing skills already.

---

[1] G. Tyler Miller, Jr., *Living in the Environment*, 2nd ed. (Belmont, Calif.: Wadsworth, 1979), p. 32. Used by permission.

4. What you wrote for E. and F. should be similar to the answer key; both these statements are the key points of paragraph 5. Remember, choosing the best major details from several is a sophisticated skill. If you did not choose these two points in paragraph 5, go back and reread the paragraph. Do you see how the comment about "pollution-free" vehicles, products, and industry follows logically from the details in paragraphs 3 and 4? Did you also note that the phrase "scientific, political, economic, and ethical judgments" introduces a new topic about pollution?

As you continue working through this book, you will be completing several summaries. As you complete each summary, your skills will improve.

How to Paraphrase

Instead of dealing with several sentences, a *paraphrase* may focus on a single sentence. Often you cannot understand this sentence either because it is long or the vocabulary is difficult. When you paraphrase, you try to make sense of a difficult sentence. A **paraphrase** is an accurate restatement of a phrase, sentence, or sentences, worded simply. Unlike a summary, a paraphrase may be longer than the original statement.

Here are some steps that you need to follow when you paraphrase. Most of these suggestions apply to what you read:

1. Read the difficult sentence carefully. Reread the sentence that came before it, and read the sentence that comes after it. You do this to place the difficult sentence in its proper context.

2. If the sentence has difficult words, look them up in the dictionary or in the glossary of the textbook. Often your confusion leaves when you understand the terminology.

3. If the sentence or sentences are long, divide them up into their phrases or clauses. Phrases and clauses are usually divided up for you by commas, semicolons, colons, and dashes. If you are hearing a particularly long sentence in a lecture, listen for the pauses.

4. Determine the subject and verb or subjects and verbs of the sentence. The subject and verb should give you the core meaning of the sentence.

5. If the statement is written, reread these phrases and clauses; even read these parts aloud if you have to.

6. Write your paraphrase in the margins.

Look at the following sentence, and use these six steps to paraphrase it correctly: "In general, progress in the transportation technology of Africa has allowed for more extensive communication among its people, some of whom never traveled beyond their kraal."

Write your paraphrase here: _____

_____

   Having written your paraphrase, see whether you used some of the following strategies:

1. You looked up the words *kraal, technology,* and *extensive.* You discovered that a *kraal* is a small African village, that *technology* involves work done by machines, and that a synonym for *extensive* is *widespread.*

2. You note that two commas divide the sentence into three recognizable parts—one phrase and two clauses. The first phrase, "in general," suggests that the statement is qualified. The clause that follows is long: ". . . progress in the transportation technology of Africa has allowed for more extensive communication among its people." The second clause is shorter and easier to understand: ". . . some of whom never traveled beyond their kraal."

3. You note that the subject is *progress,* and the verb is *has allowed.* You then ask: "What did this progress allow?"

4. When you look back in the larger clause, you find the answer; transportation technology has helped create better communication. Having understood this concept, you can make sense of the last clause, which must refer to those Africans who never left their village.

   Having gone through these steps, you are ready to write your paraphrase, which should say something like: "In Africa, improvements in transportation have generally let people in one area know more people in other areas, and some of these people had never gone out of their village."

   Paraphrasing may seem tedious, but as you continue to paraphrase, you will find that your critical reading skills will improve. Most students who cannot paraphrase simply ignore difficult passages and thus have poorer comprehension of the material. As your paraphrasing skills improve, you will be able to determine whether your difficulty in comprehension is due to difficult words or to long and involved sentences. In this way, you will begin to analyze the author's style. In many cases, you will find that your paraphrase is a simple statement after all; that in the original passage, the author used big words and many words to cover up a simple idea. Finally, you will discover that the more you learn in a particular subject, the easier it will be for you to paraphrase difficult sentences in that field.

Summary

Summarizing and paraphrasing are necessary skills in reading textbooks, in listening to lectures, and in reviewing your notes. Both are sophisticated skills. In summarizing, you locate main ideas and important details. It is an active process of sorting out the important from the less important and the unimportant. When you paraphrase, you attempt to understand a difficult sentence or sentences. Paraphrasing involves seeing a sentence in its context, looking up new words, and dividing up the sentence into phrases and clauses. Finally, when you summarize and paraphrase, you are putting information into your own words and thus have a better chance of remembering it.

Did the summary of this introduction separate the significant from the less significant? Was it worded differently? Do you think it was a successful summary?

You are now ready to practice summarizing and paraphrasing in the following exercises and in Part Three on note-taking skills.

Summary Box   *Summarizing and Paraphrasing*

What are they?	How do you use them?	Why do you use them?
Summarizing: accurate restatement of material in fewer words.	Locate main ideas and significant details and put this information into your own words.	To remember more easily large chunks of information.
Paraphrasing: accurate restatement of difficult material that is put more simply.	Read sentence in its context; look up new words; divide up sentences into smaller chunks.	To understand difficult sentences that you would otherwise skip over.

Skills Practice

Exercise 8.1
Summarizing a
Longer Passage

The following excerpt from an ecology textbook explains various types of energy. Your job is to underline main ideas and major details. Then, from your underlining, complete the five questions that follow. Remember not to underline entire sentences, just the important parts.

First Law of Energy: You Can't Get Something for Nothing

(1) *Types of Energy*   You encounter energy in many forms: mechanical, chemical, electrical, nuclear, heat, and radiant (or light) energy. Doing work involves changing energy from one form to

another. In lifting this book, the chemical energy stored in chemicals obtained from your digested food is converted into the mechanical energy that is used to move your arm and the book upwards and some heat energy that is given off by your body.

(2) In an automobile engine the chemical energy stored in gasoline is converted into mechanical energy used to propel the car plus heat energy. A battery converts chemical energy into electrical energy plus heat energy. In an electric power plant, chemical energy from fossil fuels (coal, oil, or natural gas) or nuclear energy from nuclear fuels is converted into mechanical energy that is used to spin a turbine plus heat energy. The turbine then converts the mechanical energy into electrical energy and more heat. When this electrical energy passes through the filament wires in an ordinary light bulb, it is converted into light and still more heat. In all of the energy transformations discussed in this section, we see that some energy always ends up as heat energy that flows into the surrounding environment.

(3) Scientists have found that all forms of energy can be classified either as potential energy or kinetic energy. **Kinetic energy** is the energy that matter has because of its motion. Heat energy is a measure of the total kinetic energy of the molecules in a sample of matter. The amount of kinetic energy that a sample of matter has depends both in its mass and its velocity (speed). Because of its higher kinetic energy, a bullet fired at a high velocity from a rifle will do you more damage than the same bullet thrown by hand. Similarly, an artillery shell (with a larger mass) fired at the same velocity as the bullet will do you considerably more harm than the bullet.

(4) Stored energy that an object possesses by virtue of its position, condition, or composition is known as **potential energy**. A rock held in your hand has stored, or potential, energy that can be released and converted to kinetic energy (in the form of mechanical energy and heat) if the rock is dropped. Coal, oil, natural gas, wood, and other fuels have a form of stored or potential energy known as chemical energy. When the fuel is burned, this chemical potential energy is converted into a mixture of heat, light, and the kinetic energy of motion of the molecules in the air and other nearby materials.

(5) With this background on the types of energy, we are now prepared to look at the two scientific laws that govern what happens when energy is converted from one form to another.[2]

In answering these five questions, you may refer to the excerpt. Place all answers in the answer box.

1. The main idea of paragraph 1 is:

   a. chemical energy in the body is changed to mechanical energy
   b. the body gives off energy in the form of heat
   c. energy is found in many forms
   d. work does not necessarily involve energy

---

[2] Miller, *Living in the Environment*, p. 33. Used by permission.

2. Paragraph 2 presents information that:

   a. introduces a new main idea
   b. supports the main idea of paragraph 1
   c. supports the main idea of paragraph 3
   d. all of these

3. The main idea of paragraph 3 concerns:

   a. a definition of kinetic energy
   b. a definition of heat energy
   c. a discussion of potential energy
   d. both a and c

4. In paragraph 4, the sentence beginning "A rock held in your hand has stored, or potential, energy . . ." is:

   a. a main-idea sentence
   b. a major-detail sentence
   c. a minor-detail sentence
   d. none of these

5. Which of the following is not a main idea of this excerpt?

   a. energy is found in many forms
   b. automobiles convert chemical energy into mechanical energy
   c. kinetic energy is the energy of matter in motion
   d. potential energy is stored energy

Exercise 8.2
Summarizing a
Second Passage

The following is a second excerpt from an ecology textbook. It explains the first law of energy. As in the previous exercise, underline the main ideas and significant details in each paragraph. Underline only key sentence parts. From your underlinings, finish the partially completed outline that follows.

(1) *First Energy Law* What energy changes occur when you drop a rock from your hand to the floor? Because of its higher position, the rock in your hand has a higher potential energy than the same rock at rest on the floor. Has energy been lost, or used up, in this process? At first glance it seems so. But according to the *law of conservation of energy,* also known as the *first law of thermodynamics,* in any ordinary physical or chemical process, energy is neither created nor destroyed but merely changed from one form to another. The energy lost by a *system* or collection of matter under study (in this instance the rock) must equal the energy gained by the *surroundings,* or *environment* (in this instance the air).

(2) Let's look at what really happens. As the rock drops, its potential energy is changed into kinetic energy (energy of motion)—both its own kinetic energy and that of the air molecules through which it passes. This causes the air molecules to move faster so that their temperature rises. This means that some of the rock's original potential energy has been transferred to the air as heat energy. The

energy lost by the rock (system) is exactly equal to the energy gained by its surroundings. In studying hundreds of thousands of mechanical processes (such as the rock falling) and chemical processes (such as the burning of a fuel), scientists have found that no detectable amount of energy is created or destroyed.

(3) Although most of us know this first energy law, we sometimes forget that it means in terms of energy quantity we can't get something for nothing; at best we can only break even. In the words of environmentalist Barry Commoner, "There is no such thing as a free lunch." For example, we usually hear that we have so much energy available from oil, coal, natural gas, and nuclear fuels (such as uranium). The first law of thermodynamics, however, tells us that we really have much less energy available than these estimates indicate. *It takes energy to get energy.* We must use large amounts of energy to find, remove, and process these fuels. The only energy that really counts is the *net energy* available for use after we have subtracted from the total energy made available to us the energy used to obtain it.[3]

I. First Energy Law

   A. Law of conservation of energy, or first law of thermodynamics: "Energy is neither created nor destroyed, but merely changed from one form to another."

   B.

   C.

   D. We can't get something for nothing

   E.

   F.

   G. Net energy = total energy − energy needed to produce it

(Answers will vary.)
Ask instructor for sample underlinings and outline.

Exercise 8.3
Summarizing a
Third Passage

The following is a third excerpt from an ecology textbook. It explains the second law of energy. As with the previous two exercises, underline main ideas and significant details. Then complete an outline—this time without any help—summarizing the main ideas and major details.

Second Law of Energy: You Can't Break Even

(1) *Second Energy Law and Energy Quality*   Energy varies in its *quality* or ability to do useful work. The chemical potential energy concentrated in a lump of coal or liter of gasoline, and concentrated heat energy at a high temperature are forms of high-quality energy. Because they are concentrated, they have the ability to perform useful work in moving or changing matter. In contrast, dispersed heat energy at a low temperature is low-quality energy, with little if any ability to perform useful work. In investigating hundreds of thousands of different conversions of heat energy to useful work, scientists have found that some of the energy is always degraded to a more

[3] Miller, *Living in the Environment*, pp. 33–34. Used by permission.

dispersed and less useful form, usually heat energy given off at a low temperature to the surroundings, or environment. This is a statement of the *law of energy degradation,* also known as the *second law of thermodynamics.*

(2) Let's look at an example of the second energy law. In an internal-combustion automobile engine, the high-quality potential energy available in gasoline is converted into a combination of high-quality heat energy, which is converted to the mechanical work used to propel the car, and low-quality heat energy. Only about 20 percent of the energy available in the gasoline is converted to useful mechanical energy, with the remaining 80 percent released into the environment as degraded heat energy. In addition, about half of the mechanical energy produced is also degraded to low-quality heat energy through friction, so that 90 percent of the energy in gasoline is wasted and not used to move the car. Most of this loss is an energy quality tax automatically extracted as a result of the second law. Frequently the design of an engine or other heat-energy conversion device wastes more energy than that required by the second law. But the second law always ensures that there will be a certain waste or loss of energy quality.

(3) Another example of the degradation of energy involves the conversion of solar energy to chemical energy in food. Photosynthesis in plants converts radiant energy (light) from the sun into high-quality chemical energy (stored in the plant in the form of sugar molecules) plus low-quality heat energy. If you eat plants, such as spinach, the high-quality chemical energy is transformed within your body to high-quality mechanical energy, used to move your muscles and to perform other life processes, plus low-quality heat energy. In each of these energy conversions, some of the initial high-quality energy is degraded into low-quality heat energy that flows into the environment.

(4) The first energy law governs the *quantity* of energy available from an energy conversion process, whereas the second energy law governs the *quality* of energy available. In terms of the quantity of energy available from a heat-to-work conversion, we can get out no more energy than we put in. But according to the second law, the quality of the energy available from a heat-to-work conversion will always be lower than the initial energy quality. Not only can we not get something for nothing (the first law), we can't even break even in terms of energy quality (the second law). As Robert Morse put it, "The second law means that it is easier to get into trouble than to get out of it."

(5) The second energy law also tells us that high-grade energy can never be used over again. *We can recycle matter but we can never recycle energy.* Fuels and foods can be used only once to perform useful work. Once a piece of coal or a tank of gasoline is burned, its high-quality potential energy is lost forever. Similarly, the high-quality heat energy from the steam in an underground geothermal well is gone forever once it is dispersed and degraded to low-quality heat energy in the environment. This means that the net useful, or high-quality, energy available from coal, oil, natural gas, nuclear fuel,

geothermal, or any concentrated energy source is even less than that predicted by the first energy law.[4]

Write your outline of this passage here.

(Answers will vary.) Check your underlinings and outline with the sample underlinings and outline on pp. 313–315.

Exercise 8.4
Paraphrasing
Sentences in
Paragraphs

Two paragraphs on Shakespeare follow. In both paragraphs, you will be asked to paraphrase certain sentences. Apply the rules for paraphrasing to these sentences; then read through the four paraphrasing choices and select the paraphrase that is most like yours. Place all your answers in the answer box.

(1) Shakespeare has been considered by many scholars to be the most gifted author of all time. (2) Scholars tend to emphasize Shakespeare's facility with language and his tremendous understanding of human psychology. (3) Though essentially a playwright, Shakespeare wrote plays that read like lyric poetry, in that each of his sentences has several layers of meaning. (4) Moreover, the words Shakespeare chooses in his plays often fit into recognizable image patterns. (5) Scholars have also noted that his later plays demonstrate a more controlled, less self-conscious use of language. (6) The same can be said about Shakespeare's characters; the later plays demonstrate character complexity. (7) King Lear, for example, is seen by many scholars as the consummate character—complex and mysterious. (8) In all of Shakespeare's plays, he demonstrates the variety of human experience, so that comedy is interspersed in his tragedies and sadness is a part of his comedies.

1. An effective paraphrase for sentence 2 is:

    a. Shakespeare uses language well.
    b. Shakespeare understands character.

---

[4] Miller, *Living in the Environment*, p. 34. Used by permission.

1. _____

2. _____

3. _____

4. _____

5. _____

6. _____

7. _____

8. _____

9. _____

10. _____

70%

Ask instructor for answers.

    c. Shakespeare had both a gift for language and an understanding of human behavior.

    d. Shakespeare's gift for language surpasses his understanding of character.

2. An effective paraphrase for sentence 3 is:

    a. Shakespeare wrote poetry.

    b. Like poetry, the language of Shakespeare's plays has many interpretations.

    c. Shakespeare's language is difficult to understand, though pleasant to the ear.

    d. Shakespeare was both a poet and a playwright.

3. An effective paraphrase for sentence 5 is:

    a. Shakespeare's later plays show a more effective, natural style.

    b. Shakespeare's later plays are less complex and more interesting.

    c. Shakespeare's use of language is much more effective in his later plays.

    d. In his later plays, Shakespeare was less concerned about his style.

4. An effective paraphrase of sentence 7 is:

    a. Many scholars are satisfied with Lear.

    b. King Lear is an amazing character.

    c. King Lear is a very intricate, if often not completely understood, character.

    d. King Lear is too complicated a character for readers really to understand him.

5. An effective paraphrase of sentence 8 is:

    a. Shakespeare doesn't just write comedies.

    b. Shakespeare's tragedies are not entirely sad.

    c. Shakespeare often mistook comedy for tragedy, so it is hard to identify just what each play is.

    d. Shakespeare's plays are honest to human experience, so in his tragedies there is humor and is his comedies there is grief.

(9) *Hamlet* is a much debated Shakespearean tragedy. (10) Hamlet's motivation is the key question that recurs in reading or watching the play. (11) Hamlet soon learns that his uncle and mother have conspired to kill his father, so he must avenge his father's murder. (12) When he discovers that Claudius, his uncle, is the murderer of his father, Hamlet goes into a state of melancholy. (13) Though he has occasion to kill Claudius, Hamlet finds reasons for not killing him. (14) Many critics have attributed his indecision to his intellectual character. (15) In many instances, Hamlet demonstrates a very complicated mind—one that speculates on the nature of life and death.

(16) Yet many critics are dissatisfied with just seeing Hamlet as intellectual. (17) Some theorists see more complicated, subconscious reasons for Hamlet's inability to act at the appropriate moment.

6. An appropriate paraphrase for sentence 10 is:

    a. The major question one asks about Hamlet is why he acts the way he does.
    b. Reading *Hamlet* can be a confusing experience.
    c. Hamlet seems unable to cope with the problems presented to him.
    d. Readers and spectators present different interpretations regarding Hamlet's actions.

7. An appropriate paraphrase for sentence 13 is:

    a. Hamlet cannot muster the courage to kill his uncle.
    b. Hamlet seems afraid of his uncle's power.
    c. Although Hamlet could have killed his uncle, he chooses not to.
    d. Hamlet always finds reasons for not acting.

8. An appropriate paraphrase for sentence 14 is:

    a. Some have said that Hamlet does not act because he thinks too deeply.
    b. Hamlet is a genius and cannot live with the common people around him.
    c. Hamlet's intelligence makes him act stupidly.
    d. It is illogical to make Hamlet's intelligence a cause of his passivity.

9. An appropriate paraphrase for sentence 15 is:

    a. Hamlet shows that he is a deep thinker.
    b. Hamlet likes to consider questions that have no answers.
    c. Hamlet's intelligence leads him to depressing thoughts.
    d. Hamlet shows that he is a complex thinker by his questions about human existence.

10. An appropriate paraphrase for sentence 17 is:

    a. Hamlet is too complicated to be understood by anyone.
    b. Hamlet's indecision has been seen by some critics as caused by factors existing below his conscious thoughts.
    c. Hamlet's conscious thoughts do not adequately explain his character.
    d. Hamlet's subconscious thoughts reveal a very disturbed young mind.

Exercise 8.5
More Paraphrasing
of Sentences in
Paragraphs

The following two paragraphs deal with bilingual education. Read through the paragraphs; then, using your paraphrasing skills, write appropriate paraphrases for the numbered sentences that come after the paragraphs.

(1) Bilingual education has become a major topic of controversy in many parts of the United States, especially where there are large numbers of Spanish-speaking people. (2) The controversy centers on whether only English should be used in the public schools. (3) Proponents of bilingual education suggest that students who do not speak English become terrified of school if they hear only English spoken. (4) Those who are against bilingual education claim that using the child's native language in school only delays the child's learning of English. (5) This debate continues each year as state governments and the federal government consider whether they will continue to fund bilingual programs.

(6) Many educators contend that bilingual education varies tremendously among school districts and among states. (7) In some public schools, English is used along with the native language. (8) In other schools, only the native language is used. (9) For many educators, a successful bilingual program must establish a clearly defined schedule determining when children entering the school system will have mastered English and will be able to use it effectively to learn.

Paraphrase the following numbered sentences:

1. _____

3. _____

70%

(Score = # correct ×
20)
Find answers on p.
315.

---

4. _____

5. _____

9. _____

Exercise 8.6
Using Summarizing
and Paraphrasing
Skills in a Longer
Passage

The following passage contains several paragraphs on the learning theories of Jean Piaget. The underlined sentences will require paraphrasing either on a separate sheet of paper or in the margins. When you have completed your reading, answer the five questions that follow. In answering the questions, you may refer to the passage. Place all your answers in the answer box.

The Learning Theories of Jean Piaget

(1) Jean Piaget was one of the most gifted child psychologists of our century. His most interesting work involved understanding how children learn; that is, what mechanisms a child needs to develop thinking skills.

(2) The major premise on which Piaget based most of his research was that children want to control their environment. As they mature, children develop more complex mechanisms for controlling their environment. A key term for Piaget is autoregulation, or the ability of learners to regulate or control their world.

(3) Central to controlling the environment are two ongoing thinking processes that Piaget calls *assimilation* and *accommodation*. Assimilation is taking in stimuli from the environment; accommodation is adjusting these stimuli to fit the children's learning needs. For Piaget, the assimilation-accommodation process is the crux of learning. The infant, for example, sees a ball (assimilation) and attempts to crawl to grasp it (accommodation). For Piaget, most learning involves the assimilation-accommodation process.

(4) A third key term for Piaget is schemata, which he defines as inborn, organizing structures of the brain. These schemata impose order on the child's world and thus allow him or her to learn. In the example of the child crawling to the ball, Piaget would say that there is a schema of space in the child's mind—the child knows that going from point A to point B will be the route necessary to take in order to grasp the ball.

(5) These three terms—assimilation, accommodation, and schemata—are part of Piaget's larger psychological system, called constructivism. All three of these processes work together to help children construct a meaningful, controllable world.

1. _____

2. _____

3. _____

4. _____

5. _____

_____
80%
Ask instructor for answers.

1. The main idea of paragraph 1 is that:

   a. Piaget was a gifted psychologist
   b. Piaget's major contribution was in child learning
   c. Piaget used several terms to explain his psychology
   d. thinking skills are difficult to explain, even for psychologists

2. An appropriate paraphrase of the last sentence in paragraph 2 is:

   a. Autoregulation is an important term for Piaget.
   b. Autoregulation refers to children working on their own.
   c. Autoregulation refers to the way children order their world.
   d. Children must use autoregulation to survive.

3. An appropriate paraphrase of the second sentence in paragraph 3 is:

   a. Assimilation means bringing information in; accommodation is using this information to learn.
   b. Assimilation and accommodation are keys to understanding autoregulation.
   c. Assimilation stimulates the mind; accommodation dulls it.
   d. Assimilation and accommodation are essentially opposite skills.

4. An appropriate paraphrase of the first sentence of paragraph 4 is:

    a. Schemata are part of us at birth.
    b. Schemata are ways the human being structures the world.
    c. Schemata are brain processes that help structure what one sees.
    d. Schemata are clearly tied to learning.

5. A summary of paragraph 5 is:

    a. Constructivism is a vital force in human thinking.
    b. Constructivism is made up of three thinking processes.
    c. Constructivism is Piaget's term for how people use accommodation, assimilation, and schemata to organize what they see.
    d. Constructivism cannot be understood unless one understands schemata, assimilation, and accommodation.

Exercise 8.7
Writing a
Paragraph Using
Summarizing and
Paraphrasing Skills

Your job is to go back to the excerpt on Piaget and find the information to answer the following four questions. Most of this information is to be found in your paraphrases and your summary of the last paragraph. From your responses to these questions, answer the essay question that follows.

1. A definition of autoregulation: _____

2. A definition of assimilation: _____

3. A definition of accommodation: _____

4. A definition of constructivism: _____

> ——— 70% ———
> Ask instructor for answers.

Essay Question: In one paragraph, briefly discuss Piaget's contribution to child learning theory. In your discussion, define constructivism, autoregulation, assimilation, and accommodation.

Exercise 8.8
Using Summarizing
and Paraphrasing
Skills on a Textbook
Excerpt

A. The following is a music history textbook excerpt on artists in the twentieth century. Read through the excerpt quickly to get a sense of its organization. Then go back and read it slowly, paying particular attention to longer sentences that you may want to paraphrase. You also need to underline the main idea and the major details in paragraphs 1 and 4. When you finish, answer the five questions that follow and put your answers in the answer box. You may refer to the excerpt in deciding on your answers.

Contemporary Society and the Creative Artist

    (1) The twentieth-century world is increasingly shaped by technology. Just about every civilized human activity is involved in some way with technology. Not only does this fact have far-reaching eco-

nomic implications; it affects people's values and thinking as well. The vast array of goods made possible by technology and mass production in an affluent society has encouraged an attitude of materialism—the placing of primary value on material goods. Materialism usually means that nonmaterial items such as learning, truth, and beauty usually come out second to a vacation in the Caribbean and a sports car.

(2) Twentieth-century society is becoming increasingly urban in its orientation. More and more people live in metropolitan areas, and the comforts and conveniences of the city are also enjoyed by residents of the country. Existence no longer seems to depend directly upon an adequate rainfall or sunlight; fields can be irrigated and lights turned on by which to work.

(3) Any place in the world is accessible in a few hours by jet; communication via radio and television is instantaneous. Even the moon has been explored. These advances have made human beings think and act in international terms. Except in newly emerging nations, the ardor of nationalism has decreased somewhat. Many of the nations of Europe, which were at war with one another so frequently during the nineteenth century, have now joined into the European Common Market.

(4) The intellectual climate of the twentieth century is different, too. It is more objective and concerned with scientific inquiry. Evidence of this can be seen in paintings such as Mondrian's *Broadway Boogie-Woogie*. Intellectuals feel they have outgrown the slushy sentimentality and emotionalism of the Romantic period, although some second thoughts have surfaced recently about the emphasis on intellectual activity. Neither is the Romantic fascination with the unknown as common as it was in the nineteenth century. Scientists are exploring the outermost reaches of space and the inmost realms of the mind.

(5) However, despite material comforts and scientific achievements, people seem to be less clear about the meaning of life than were their predecessors; consequently, they seem no happier. Many old beliefs have been rejected, but new understandings and beliefs have not appeared. The result is often a feeling of confusion, a desire to escape from reality, or a sense of being hopelessly trapped in the tangle of life. Twentieth-century drama illustrates these points well. In Jeal-Paul Sartre's *No Exit* the three characters are trapped in their private hell, which is largely of their own making. In Samuel Beckett's *Waiting for Godot* two characters symbolize mankind waiting for Godot, who will take care of their problems. Godot never shows up.

(6) Coupled with the difficulty of finding meaning in life is the change that contemporary people see all about them. But change to what, and for what reason? Sometimes change seems to be valued for its own sake, yet a few of the older values persist. Some nineteenth-century ideas, specifically those of Thoreau (who in turn drew upon the ideas of Jean Jacques Rousseau), have received renewed attention in recent years. Some of the tenets of Renaissance humanism are still espoused, too. However, there is little consensus on what is really important in life or how life should be lived.

(7) The creative artists are especially sensitive to what they see about them. They often mirror the feelings of the times in which they live. They react to circumstances and give expression to prevailing attitudes. Creative artists do not, of course, all react alike. Some become cynical and discouraged; others withdraw along an escapist route that ignores society; others reflect the conflict and confusion of the times. Still others become "commercial," bowing to mass taste in order to get a fair share of society's material comforts.[5]

1. _____

2. _____

3. _____

4. _____

5. _____

1. An appropriate summary of paragraph 1 is:

   a. Technology pervades the twentieth century and makes most people prefer objects to nonmaterial things.
   b. The twentieth century is a scientific age run by the very educated.
   c. The twentieth century is characterized by interest in material things as well as religious ideas.
   d. The twentieth century allows people more time for vacations and less time for labor.

2. Paraphrase this sentence from paragraph 3: "Except in newly emerging nations, the ardor of nationalism has decreased somewhat."

   a. Pride in one's country has decreased today.
   b. There are many developing nations today.
   c. Patriotism is necessary for success in the twentieth century both in developed and developing countries.
   d. In developed countries one sees less concern and respect for one's country.

3. The main idea of paragraph 4 is:

   a. the twentieth century has rejected romanticism
   b. the twentieth century tends to be more scientific
   c. the twentieth century is a period of space exploration
   d. Mondrian was one of the last romantic painters

4. An appropriate paraphrase for the first sentence in paragraph 5 is:

   a. People in the twentieth century are confused.
   b. The twentieth century is known for its technology and scientific achievements.
   c. Twentieth-century people seem confused and sad even though they have succeeded in technology and science.
   d. Technology and science do not bring happiness, although people think they do.

[5] Charles R. Hoffer, *The Understanding of Music*, 4th ed. (Belmont, Calif.: Wadsworth, 1981), pp. 370–371. Used by permission.

5. In paragraph 6, the author suggests that twentieth-century society is returning to the ideas of:

    a. Thoreau
    b. Rousseau
    c. the Renaissance
    d. all of these

B. Now go back and reread the excerpt. Then answer the following three questions in a phrase or sentence without looking back at the excerpt.

1. How has technology changed twentieth-century society? (1 point)

2. How has science changed twentieth-century thinking? (1 point)

3. List three attitudes that twentieth-century artists reveal in their works. (3 points)

70%

Ask instructor for answers.

Taking Lecture and Study Notes

In this part, you will learn several note-taking skills that you can successfully use in listening to lectures and in study reading. You will find that when you take effective notes, you are using several of the reading and listening skills that you acquired in Part Two. When you master these note-taking techniques, your studying for exams will become both organized and worthwhile.

9

Characteristics of Lectures

Explanation of Skills

Lectures are a special kind of communication. A lecture is a dialogue between you and the speaker. Your response to the lecturer is often in the form of notes rather than oral comments. Accurate notes are important, for they are your only record of what your lecturer said. In this part of the book, you will learn how to write useful notes. Consider the following aspects of a lecture: (1) the lecturer's speaking style, (2) the subject of the lecture, and (3) your obligations as a listener.

The Speaker

Lecturers' speaking styles are as varied as writers' styles. Some lecturers speak loudly, others softly. It is up to you to adjust your listening strategies to the speaker's style. The average lecturer speaks at 125 words per minute, whereas the average reading rate is 250 words per minute. Some lecturers speak quickly, others slowly. With a lecturer who speaks quickly, you may have a difficult time getting down all of the information. With a lecturer who speaks slowly, your mind may wander and you may become bored. But whatever the lecturer's style, you need to focus on the main ideas and the major details of the material.

If a lecturer presents too much information, consult with classmates, who may have written down some of the information that you did not get. If a lecturer speaks slowly and presents too little information, you need to concentrate on the important points of the lecture.

Also, you should realize that most instructors are not professional speakers. Their delivery will usually not be polished and humorous. Lecturers are not entertainers; they are trained to impart information, not to be comedians. Some students have even commented that the entertaining lecturers are generally not the most informative.

Most instructors present organized lectures, so your focus must be on the instructor's organization, which often centers on general and specific bits of information. Instructors often use the same signal words in their lectures that you find in written material. In fact, good lecturers use these signal words to direct you to important information. Good lecturers also realize that students can reread what is in writing, but that "relistening" without a tape recorder is impossible. Successful lecturers also understand that lectures are not as formal as written discourse. So they repeat themselves and make obvious comments such as "This is important" or "Write this down."

Along with repeating themselves and using signal words, lecturers use visual and vocal signals to punctuate their speaking. A lecturer's most effective visual aid is the chalkboard. When an instructor writes a term on the board or draws a chart or map, be sure to write this material down. A lecturer may also list important steps on the board or say "There are three steps to remember." Jot these steps down. Third, a lecturer's tone of voice or rate of speech may change when an important point is made. If lecturers speak rapidly, their rate will probably slow down when they say something important. Or if lecturers normally speak softly, they may present a key point in a louder tone. Get acquainted with each lecturer's speaking style, and look for his or her verbal signals. Finally, lecturers may sometimes read directly from the textbook. You should write down the page number of these passages, because they are probably important points.

A few lecturers are disorganized in their presentation, making your note taking a difficult chore. They may not consistently present main ideas and major details in proper proportion, and they may digress often so that main ideas lose their focus. Unfortunately, you will need to compensate for this lack of organization by noting what information is missing. You will then need to rely more on your textbooks and on library material. You may also need to consult with classmates who may have understood more of the lecture.

The Subject of the Lecture

All of the skills you have learned so far in this book should be used when you take notes. Lecturers will organize their material around main ideas, major details, and minor details as well as the seven patterns of organization. Thus you should listen for the words that signal a particular organizational pattern. You will also use your paraphrasing skills when a lecturer speaks in difficult sentences, and you will need to make appropriate inferences when a lecturer is being indirect.

Although you will be using all of these skills when you listen to lectures, you also need to know how lectures are different from writing. Lecturers are often repetitive, whereas writing is not. Consider repetition in lecture as a kind of rereading; what a lecturer repeats is often important and difficult to understand the first time.

A lecturer may also digress, or get off the main point. A lecturer may occasionally relate a humorous anecdote that is related to the lecture. These digressions would not make sense if you were to read them. Because writing is often concise, digressions in writing are seen as flaws. When you hear digressions in lecture, you should see how they apply to the topic as well as enjoy them. See digressions as unique to speaking, a feature that makes speech more intimate than writing.

The subject matter of the lecture also dictates the kinds of notes you will take. You will often take notes using main ideas and major details in the arts and humanities, the social sciences, and in some biological sciences. In a history lecture, for example, you will often group your information around main ideas and details of support. On the other hand, in physical science and math courses, you will need to copy down solutions to problems and ignore the traditional note-taking format. The successful note taker in a math or science course accurately writes down the steps in a problem. Finally, in a foreign language course you will be responding orally, so your notes will be brief—a grammatical rule or a new vocabulary word. With each course, you need to be flexible and devise a note-taking style that most fits the subject matter.

Student Obligations

The key to successful listening of lectures finally rests on you. You must see listening to lectures as a concentrated activity. You must anticipate the instructor's comments and determine the structure of the lecture.

Here is a list of hints that should help you to become a more effective note taker. Some of these points have already been discussed in this chapter, but it will help if you see them put together.

1. Listen attentively for the topic, the main idea, and details of support. Train yourself to hear both general and detailed statements. Keep asking yourself: Is this the topic? The main point? What details relate to this main idea?

2. Listen for signal words that introduce a particular organizational pattern. When you identify the proper organizational pattern, you will better understand the logic of the lecture.

3. Look for visual cues and listen for auditory cues—what the lecturer puts on the board, and when and why the lecturer's tone of voice changes. These cues often suggest important points.

4. Familiarize yourself with the topic before you begin listening to the lecture. If an instructor assigns a chapter before she lectures on it, read the material even if you do not understand all of it. The more exposure students have to a topic, the less difficult they tend to

find the material. Going to lecture without having done the assigned reading is unwise.

5. Listen attentively during class discussions. Do not assume that because a student is speaking you do not need to listen. What students ask or say often are the same questions and answers that you have. Sometimes, even student comments are worthy of being placed in your notes. Also, listen to the instructor's response to student comments. You will learn a lot about your instructor by listening to his responses to students' ideas. You may find that a particular instructor likes original thinking, while another is looking for the conventional answer. These inferences can help you in studying for exams in these courses.

6. Try to see the lecture material from the instructor's point of view. You have every right to disagree with the instructor, but only after you have listened to what he or she has said. Students often tune instructors out when they do not agree with their point of view. By not listening to the several points of view of each topic, they are being unfair both to the material and to the instructor.

Mastering these hints may take some time. But once these suggestions become habit for you, you will be able to anticipate the direction of the lecture—knowing beforehand when the lecturer will introduce a new topic or main idea or what organizational pattern the instructor intends to use. When you are able to anticipate information and structure, you find that listening to lectures becomes both interesting and challenging.

Your other obligation is to assess the value that is assigned to lecture material in each of your courses. By the second or third week of the semester, you should have determined the value of notes in each of your courses. You should have determined whether the lectures are like or unlike the material in textbooks. And by the first examination, you should have determined how much of the exam came from your notes. You will find that some instructors rely on the textbook when making up an exam; others rely on their lecture notes. Most instructors divide up their exam questions evenly between textbook and lecture material. It is you who must resolve all of these issues, and you should do so early in the semester.

Some students think that attending lectures is a waste of their time—that they can learn everything from the textbook and from the notes of others. Except for the very bright student, not attending lectures is a bad idea. Even if most of the instructor's lectures follow the textbook, by attending lecture, you will develop an appreciation for the subject that you cannot get from your textbook. You will also get to know your instructors from their lectures—both their personality and their attitude toward the material. If your instructor loves the subject, some of this enthusiasm will rub off on you. From the very best lectures, you will learn details and hear anecdotes that you cannot find in textbooks. And it may be in a particularly exciting lecture that you will decide to major in that subject—a decision that can affect the rest of your life.

Summary

Lectures are dialogues between the instructor and you. When you attend lectures, you must remember that speech is different from writing. Instructors repeat themselves in lectures, and they may digress. You should use all of the reading skills that you have learned in order to listen to lectures effectively. Each course you take assumes a different listening and note-taking style that you must determine early on in the semester.

Attending lectures gives you an appreciation for a particular course that reading will not give you. If you listen critically to lectures, you will have another important educational tool at your disposal.

Summary Box   *Lecture Material*

What is it?	Why do you need it?
An oral means of transferring information from the speaker to you.	To gather information in a particular area.
A dialogue between the speaker and you.	To record the speaker's attitude toward a subject.
Information that is usually organized around main ideas and major details.	To appreciate a subject—something you cannot acquire just by reading your textbook.
Information that is not as concise as writing and that requires active listening.	

Skills Practice

Exercise 9.1
Inventory of a
Lecture

Choose an instructor whose lectures are difficult for you. Then complete the following inventory on one of his or her lectures. This inventory may help you understand why you are having difficulty taking notes on the lecture material.

1. Name of instructor: _____

2. Name of course: _____

3. Place a check next to those qualities that describe your instructor's lecture style:

_____ a. speaks rapidly

_____ b. speaks slowly

_____ c. speaks loudly

_____ d. speaks softly

_____ e. does not use the chalkboard

_____ f. is disorganized

_____ g. makes statements you do not agree with

_____ h. other: _____

The following are some suggestions for dealing with the characteristics that you checked in item 3.

a. If the instructor speaks too fast, you must try to keep up with the pace. Don't get upset if you cannot write down all of the important points. Just keep listening for main ideas and supporting details. Check classmates' notes to see what you may have missed.

b. If the instructor speaks too slowly, you may get bored, and your mind may wander. Keep listening for the lecture's focus—main ideas and details of support.

c. If the instructor speaks loudly, notice when his or her voice gets softer or even louder. A change in loudness may signal that an important point is going to be made.

d. If the instructor speaks softly, you need to listen more actively; try to find a desk nearer to the instructor. As in c, notice when his or her voice changes volume and see whether this change signals important information.

e. If your instructor doesn't use the chalkboard to highlight important points, see whether he or she uses any other cues. Does your instructor repeat key words and phrases or use hand gestures that signal important material?

f. If your instructor is disorganized, you will need to listen more carefully, jotting down those questions that your instructor leaves unanswered. In this case, you will need to rely more on your textbook, library material, and your classmates.

g. If your instructor makes remarks you disagree with, try to follow his or her train of thought. You are free to disagree with your instructor, but you need to follow his or her line of argument first.

h. Bring any other problems that you may have to your study skills instructor. You may even choose to present your complaint to the instructor who is giving you difficulty. State what your criticism is and what you would like to see changed. Some instructors will take your criticisms seriously and try to change their lecture style.

Exercise 9.2
Inventory of Your
Notes

Choose one course whose notes you are not entirely satisfied with. Then complete the following inventory.

1. Name of course: _____

2. Place a check next to those qualities that describe your note-taking style:

   _____ a. too brief

   _____ b. too wordy

   _____ c. disorganized

   _____ d. inaccurate

   _____ e. messy

   _____ f. any other problem: _____

   The following are some suggestions for dealing with the problems that you checked in item 2.

   a. If your notes are too brief, you need to listen for supporting details. You are probably concentrating too much on main ideas. Remember, you also need to recall supporting details. Keep in mind that supporting details may be examples, characteristics, steps, causes, or effects. So listen carefully for names, places, and numbers. Remember that in a foreign language course, brief notes are acceptable.

   b. If your notes are wordy, you are probably trying to write down everything. Remember that minor details usually do not need to be part of your notes. Wordy notes obscure main ideas and supporting details. Before writing, ask yourself: Is this statement significant? Will it give support to the main idea? Is this statement a restatement of something I've already written? Does this statement further elaborate on a previous detail? Approximately two to three written pages of notes in an hour's lecture is adequate.

   c. If your lecture notes are disorganized, you probably cannot differentiate well between main ideas and supporting details. You will learn more about this issue in the next chapter, "Traditional Note-taking Techniques." For now, remember that separating general from specific information is a key to learning and remembering. You may want to review Chapters 3 and 4, which treat main ideas and supporting details.

d. If your notes are inaccurate, you must start listening more carefully. Inaccurate notes are often caused by a daydreaming note taker. Inaccuracy is especially problematic in a math or science course, where the right number or correct sequence is essential to a correct solution. Leave your personal life outside of class, so you can listen to the lecture material with full concentration. Anyone can listen more attentively; it just takes discipline.

e. If your notes are messy, go over them soon after class is over and rewrite any words that are hard to read. If your handwriting is poor, you may need to write more slowly, even if you write less. Notes with less information are better than those that you cannot read.

f. If you have any other problems with your notes, speak with your study skills instructor.

10

Traditional Note-taking Techniques

Explanation of Skills

Now that you have made an inventory of your strengths and weaknesses as a note taker, you are ready to study the note-taking tips and techniques that have helped many students. The two most common techniques are the *numeral-letter format* and the *indenting format*. You will find that taking notes in math and science courses requires different note-taking strategies. In all three cases you can use abbreviations to save time.

Numeral-Letter Format

The numeral-letter format is the most commonly used note-taking system. You have already studied it in the beginning chapters on main ideas and major details. In this format, you identify main ideas with Roman numerals (I., II., III.) and place them farthest to the left of your margin. You identify major details with capital letters (A., B., C.) and indent them to the right of the Roman numerals. Look at the following example:

I. Two kinds of reproduction

    A. Sexual
    B. Asexual

In some cases you may want to include a minor detail. You identify minor details with Arabic numerals and place them to the right of your major details. Study the following example:

I. Shakespeare's most acclaimed plays

A. *Hamlet*

1. one of his most critically studied plays

There are many rules that go along with the numeral-letter format. In taking lecture notes, you do not need to know all of them. If you try to follow all of the rules, you may get confused. The main rule that you should follow is that main ideas should be placed to the left on your paper, major details indented to the right. By now, you should realize that main ideas and major details organize much of what you read and listen to. Main ideas must be attached to major details; both bits of information are meaningless unless you place them in a general and specific context. Knowing, for example, that Jimmy Carter served one term of office is meaningless unless you know that he was an American president and served from 1976 to 1980. Conversely, knowing that Carter served a term from 1976 to 1980 does not make sense unless you connect this detail to the more general statement that he was an American president.

You need to adhere to two minor procedures when you use the numeral-letter format. First, be sure to place a period after the numeral or letter (I. or A.). By using a period, you separate the number or letter from the words you write. The period thus shows that the numbers and letters are divisions and not part of your comments. Second, skip a line between Roman numerals (the main ideas). By separating main ideas, you give more emphasis to them, and you will be able to locate them more easily when you study your notes. Look at the following example:

I. Parts of an atom

A. Nucleus
B. Neutron
C. Proton
D. Electron

II. Nuclear fission

A. Atoms split up
B. Energy released

By creating a space between I. and II., you make "parts of an atom" a different chunk of information from "nuclear fission."

Don't expect to write all of the major details you hear. As with summarizing, only write down the significant details, or those that most directly support the main idea. If for some reason you miss a few major details in lecture, ask to see a classmate's notes.

Indenting Format

The indenting system is another popular format; this one does away with letters and numbers entirely. You simply place main ideas to the left, major details indented to the right, and minor details indented to the right of major details. You separate general from specific statements by their positioning on your paper. Here is an example:

Measuring sound

Decibel—measures sound power and sound pressure

Named after Alexander Graham Bell

As you can see, the information gets more specific as you move to the right. Many students prefer this format to the numeral-letter format because they do not have to remember the correct sequence of numerals and letters. They do not need to go back to their notes to see whether their previous main idea, for example, was a II. or a III. Some students also complain that the numerals and letters clutter their notes.

Remember that both formats rely on the same idea. The farther to the right you put information, the more specific this information is. Try both techniques to see which one fits your listening and writing style.

Taking Notes in Mathematics and Math-Related Courses

In math and science courses, you will often find that the numeral-letter and indenting formats are inappropriate note-taking forms. Math and science instructors often present solutions to problems on the board, writing each step in sequence. With these solutions, you cannot separate main ideas from major details. In a sense, every step to the solution is a main idea.

Consider the following hints for taking notes in math and science courses:

1. Listen carefully when your instructor presents laws, axioms, theorems, or properties. When possible, write down these statements word for word, as you would a definition. In the margin, identify the particular statement as a law, an axiom, a theorem, or a property. Look at the following example:

   associative property | $a + b = b + a$ $5 + 3 = 3 + 5$
   | $a \times b = b \times a$ $5 \times 3 = 3 \times 5$
   | Numbers may be added or multiplied in any sequence.

2. When an instructor solves a problem on the board, copy it down step by step. The problems an instructor writes on the board are probably important ones. These solutions will often be like home-

work problems and problems on exams. Number each step, and make comments after any step that is unclear to you. Put question marks next to those steps that you cannot follow. Try to answer your questions before you come to the next class. Look at this example:

	Problem #3 $2(5x + 5) + 4x = 80 - 20x$
	Solve for x.
Do operations in parentheses first.	(1) $10x + 10 + 4x = 80 - 2x$
	(2) $14x + 10 \quad\quad = 80 - 2x$
+2x balances both sides of the equation	(3) $16x = 80$
	(4) $x = 5$

3. Leave spaces next to those problems that you did not complete. When you review your notes, you should try to complete the solutions.

4. Leave extra spaces between problems or draw a line across your page of notes to show where one problem ends and another begins.

5. Reread your notes after every lecture. Math and science are disciplines that build upon information that you have previously learned. If you are unclear about Monday's solutions, Wednesday's will be even more confusing.

6. Use the numeral-letter and indenting formats whenever the instructor presents material that does not require problem solving.

Condensing Information

Learning to condense information will help you write down more information in a shorter period of time. When you summarize, you locate main ideas and major details from long passages. When you **condense**, you write the key elements in a sentence and delete unnecessary words and phrases. What you usually write down are the subject, verb, and object of a sentence. Often you reduce a complete sentence to a phrase. Look at the following sentence, and see how it is condensed: "Large numbers of rural poor in underdeveloped countries tend to flock to the cities, causing poverty and unemployment." "Rural poor flock to cities—cause unemployment and poverty." In condensing, you are often left with the "who" or "what" and the "what was one" of the sentence. In this sentence, the "who" is the rural poor, and the "what was done" is poverty and unemployment. In lecture, then, listen for names and for what these names did.

It is sometimes preferable to copy information exactly as it is stated. You have already seen the importance of copying down a mathematical or scientific law or theorem or of copying the steps in a solution. When you hear a definition, try to write it exactly as you hear it. Definitions are the tools for understanding a subject, so it's best to write down their exact meanings.

I. Primates

    A. Def: any mammal of the order Primates, including humans, apes, monkeys, lemurs, tarsiers, and marmosets.

With the exception of definitions and mathematical solutions and laws, you will often not be copying information exactly as you hear it. So condensing is a key skill to learn—as important as summarizing. You cannot write down everything that the instructor says unless you know shorthand. By condensing each sentence into the "who" or "what" and the "what was done," you uncover the significant elements of the lecture. You will have several opportunities to condense lecture and textbook material in the exercises in this chapter and in those that follow.

Note-taking Tips

Now that you have studied the numeral-letter, indenting, and math-science outlining formats and learned about condensing, you are ready for the following note-taking tips.

1. The notes that you take for each course should be written in a separate bound notebook or in a three-ring notebook with dividers for each class. Three-ring notebooks are especially useful because you can add supplementary material to your notes, you can take out material, and you can insert notes for a lecture that you may have missed. Also, you can keep all of your lecture notes in chronological order. You may think that all of this organization is a waste of time, but you will find that such preparation will pay off when you have to study for an exam. You do not want to be one of those students who have difficulty studying for the exam because lecture notes are missing or disorganized. Divide your notebook into two sections: one for your lecture notes and another for your study reading notes. More will be said about preparing reading notes in Chapter 12 "The SQ3R Study System."

2. Put the title of each day's lecture at the center of the top line of a clean sheet of paper. Put the date at the top right-hand corner of the same page. Look at the following title:

Nuclear Fission

5/24/88

3. Use a ball-point pen, a fountain pen, or a felt-tipped pen when you take notes in courses that use traditional outlining formats. For math and science courses, which require figuring and refiguring, use a pencil.

4. Write on only one side of the page. Draw a line (preferably red) 2½ inches from the left side of the page. Use this margin for extra comments that you make as you go over your notes. You can also use the reverse side of the page for any additional comments that you might make during the semester.

5. You can also use this left-hand margin during lectures to remind yourself of important due dates: a project due date, an examination date, and so on. In this margin, you can also ask a question about the lecture. Often you cannot interrupt a lecturer with your question. Look at how comments are incorporated into the following lecture notes on Benjamin Franklin:

	Benjamin Franklin
What does "man of letters" mean?	**I.** His contributions
	A. A man of letters
	B. A philanthropist
	C. Published scientific papers
First test 3/18	D. Member of many learned societies

6. Identify the kinds of details that you write in the margins, either during or after a lecture. The abbreviations that you will most commonly use are: *def,* for definition; *ex,* for example; *eff,* for effect; and *char,* for characteristic. *Cause* and *step* have no abbreviations. As you identify the details, you will better understand the lecture's organization. See how the abbreviation *ex* is used in the following lecture notes on the Vietnam War.

Vietnam War

   Many famous objectors

      Ex: Martin Luther King

7. Do not recopy your notes. Recopying does not require much thinking, and it takes time that you can better spend doing other assignments. You must edit your notes, though. After class or within twenty-four hours, reread your notes. Reviewing information right after it has been introduced helps you remember it. During your review, rewrite any words that are unclear, and answer those questions you posed in the left-hand margin (preferably in a different color ink). You may also use this margin to summarize the important points of the lecture or to make any insights that you come upon during your review. Look at the following example from a lecture excerpt on Benjamin Franklin:

Who is Bunyan?	Benjamin Franklin
17th-century British writer of <u>Pilgrim's Progress.</u>	**I.** His intellectual influences
<u>Essay on Human Understanding</u> revolutionized the way people perceived the world.	A. Bible B. John Bunyan C. <u>Essay on Human Understanding</u>

8. Write legibly, even if you write less; students lose time trying to decipher their handwriting.

Using Abbreviations

Now that you have learned various note-taking systems, you are ready to use abbreviations to save even more time when you take notes. You can use these abbreviations both for lecture and study notes. Like condensing, abbreviating reduces sentences to their essential meanings.

Abbreviation Symbols.   Here is a list of commonly used symbols that students use when taking notes; commit them to memory.

$=$	equals
$=\|y$	equally
$\neq$	does not equal
" "	repeat the same information
$\text{-----}\rangle$	causes
$\langle\text{-----}$	is caused by
$\text{-----}\rangle \quad \langle\text{-----}$	is both cause and effect
$>$	greater than
$<$	less than
$+$ or $\&$	and or more
$-$	less or minus
$\therefore$	therefore
$\supset$	implies or suggests
$\#$	number
$\%$	percent or percentage
$\P$	paragraph
$//$	parallel

See how the following sentence can be rephrased with abbreviations. "The percentage of those cured is greater than those not cured." "% cured > % not cured."

Words Commonly Abbreviated.   The following is a list of abbreviations for words and phrases that you will commonly see in textbooks and hear in lectures. Study these abbreviations; then commit them to memory.

yr(s) = year(s)
c = century
re = regarding
ft = foot
m = meter
yd = yard
in. = inch
cm = centimeter
mi = mile
km = kilometer
lb = pound
g = gram
1st, 2nd, 3rd, 4th =
   first, second, third, fourth
nec = necessary
wd = word
mn = main
ea = each
pt = point
prin = principal
usu = usually
genl = general(ly)
ie = that is, that is to say
s = singular
pl = plural
ant. = antonym
syn = synonym
def = definition
Am. = American
log. = logic(al)
inc = incomplete
sp = spelling
dept = department
incl = including
amt = amount

specif = specific(ally)
fem = feminine
masc = masculine
pos = positive
neg = negative
incr = increase
decr = decrease
maj = majority
min = minimum
max = maximum
sig = significant
imp't = important
sm = small
lg = large
mt = mountain
N = north
E = east
S = south
W = west
orig = original(ly)
co = company
cf = compare
w = with
w/o = without
vs = versus, or against
intro = introduction
concl = conclusion
cont'd = continued
thru = through
chpt = chapter
p = page
pp = pages
subj = subject
eg = for example

If you study this list carefully, you will find that four abbreviations end with a period (in., Am., ant., log.). You need to use a period after an abbreviation if the abbreviation spells out an actual word. The period corrects that confusion. For example, "ant" without a period could be mistaken for an insect rather than an antonym.

Once you have learned these abbreviations, you will be able to take down more information during lectures. Practice using abbreviations to write down the following statement concisely. "A large increase in defense spending results in higher taxes or major cuts in other areas." "lg incr defense spending → higher taxes or major cuts." Once you have memorized these abbreviations, they become easy to read, and they do not slow down your reading rate.

Rules to Follow When You Create Your Own Abbreviations.

1. If a word has only one syllable, write it out. It takes about as much time to write "tax" as it does "tx."

2. When you decide to leave out letters, leave out vowels rather than consonants. You recognize a word more easily if you see the consonants. You will probably recognize the abbreviation "bkgd" as "background" because you have kept the consonants.

3. Use the first syllable of a long word if that first syllable gives you enough information to identify the word. In your history class, for example, you might use "fam" for "famine" without getting confused. But "ty" does not easily equate with "tyranny," so write out two syllables, "tyran."

4. You can sometimes use an apostrophe to delete a syllable or syllables of a word. For example, "requirement" can be written as "requir't," or "unnecessary" can be abbreviated to "unnec'y."

5. To make an abbreviation plural, add an "s" to it as you would normally add to the entire word. For example, "wds" would be the plural for "words."

6. In general, use a number instead of writing it out. You can write "65" more quickly than "sixty-five." But "45 million" (or "45 mil") is easier to write than "45,000,000." In writing numbers, choose the method that will save you the most time.

7. You will often be writing down a key word or a phrase several times during a lecture. Early in the lecture, make up an abbreviation for that word or term. The first time you use the term, write your abbreviation and the complete word in the left-hand margin. For example, if you are studying learning disabilities in a

psychology lecture, you could abbreviate learning disability as LD. Then write "LD = learning disability" in the margin.

8. Quickly learn the symbols and abbreviations that your math and science instructors use. You will be regularly using these abbreviations and symbols when you read the textbook, take lecture notes, and solve problems.

9. When you edit your notes, be sure that you completely write out any abbreviated words that are not immediately clear to you. Edit your notes soon after the lecture. If you wait too long, you may not be able to decipher your abbreviations.

10. Use abbreviations even more when your lecturer speaks quickly or presents much information. In such lectures, you are pressed for time; using abbreviations will help you get down more information.

11. Do not overuse abbreviations. You do not want to begin reading over your notes only to find out that you do not know what the abbreviations stand for.

Summary

The two most common note-taking techniques—the numeral-letter technique and the indenting technique—are similarly organized; both have main ideas to the left of the margin and details to the right. Main ideas and major details are key elements to your notes. You should train your listening so that you automatically look for details when you hear a main idea. With practice, you should be able to balance main ideas properly with major details. Do not expect to write down all of the details, only the significant ones. Try to condense whatever you hear into the "who" and the "what" of each statement.

Notes in math and science courses are structured differently. In these courses, you do more copying, mainly of solutions to problems. You should comment on those steps to a solution that you do not fully understand.

Remember to review your notes daily, making comments and corrections. Because you will be using these notes all semester, they need to be legible.

You will find that using abbreviations helps you write down more information. Abbreviations are either symbols or shortened words. Memorize the most common abbreviation symbols and abbreviated words. In your review of your notes, be sure that you write out the complete word or phrase for those abbreviations that you cannot immediately read.

Summary Box   *Note-taking Techniques*

What are they?	Why do you use them?
Numeral-letter format: places main ideas (I.) to the left and major details (A., B., C.) to the right.	To give order to your lecture notes and separate main ideas from major details.
Indenting Format: places main ideas to the left and major details to the right; no numerals or letters are used.	To write down significant information from lectures.
Math-science format: accurately lists and describes the steps necessary for solutions to problems and makes marginal comments when a step is not understood.	To help you remember important material for exams.
Abbreviations: shortened words or symbols for words or phrases	To write down more information.
	To save time when taking notes.

Skills Practice

***Exercise 10.1
Condensing
Sentences from
Lectures***

The following ten sentences are taken from a lecture on Charles Darwin. Your job is to read each sentence and then condense it into a phrase in which only the essential information remains. You will find that sentences from lectures tend to be wordy, a style much different from what you normally read. Use the abbreviation *def* and *ex* where appropriate.

70%

(Score = # correct ×
10)
Find answers on p.
315.

---

1. Today I plan to discuss some of the background material on Charles Darwin—the creator, some of you may know, of the theory of evolution.

   _____

2. Much of his research for the theory of evolution came from his many travels to South America in a ship named the *Beagle*.

   _____

3. This ship stopped many times, and it was during these stops that Darwin collected much information that was useful to his theory.

For example, he collected several bits of data on the finches, birds that frequented these areas.

_____

4. Much of Darwin's research was conducted in a very interesting geographical area known as the Galapagos Islands.

_____

5. Darwin discovered many different kinds of plants and animals on these isolated islands.

_____

6. From his data in the Galapagos Islands, Darwin began to develop his ideas regarding the theory of evolution.

_____

7. Darwin's major concern was to organize his many facts around certain general principles.

_____

8. It is important to remember that with each species of animal, Darwin tried as best he could to locate its one common ancestor.

_____

9. Soon he came upon the very interesting and new idea that certain animals were stronger or won out over others in the course of time. This became part of his controversial definition of natural selection.

_____

10. It must be emphasized that Darwin saw that the pace of natural selection was very slow indeed.[1]

_____

Exercise 10.2
More Condensing of
Sentences from
Lectures

Here are ten more sentences, this time from an anthropology lecture on different kinds of societies. Condense these sentences into phrases that pick up the essential information. Where necessary, use the abbreviations *ex, eff,* and *cause.*

_____

[1] Adapted from Cecie Starr and Ralph Taggart, *Biology: The Unity and Diversity of Life,* 4th ed. (Belmont, Calif.: Wadsworth, 1987), pp. 26–30. Used by permission.

1. Today I want to discuss the two kinds of societies we still find in the world today.

   _____

2. I want to spend some time talking about hunting-and-gathering societies as well as horticultural societies.

   _____

3. Hunting-and-gathering societies, as their name implies, hunt for food and gather necessary materials. An example of such a society is the pygmy society of Africa.

   _____

4. It must be made clear that hunting-and-gathering societies tend to be on the move constantly.

   _____

5. Because of their constant need to move, hunting-and-gathering societies are quite small—no more than twenty-five per community.

   _____

6. The cause for hunting-and-gathering societies becoming horticultural societies was their raising of wheat and their need to store it.

   _____

7. The effect of storing food was that communities could settle and did not need to move regularly.

   _____

8. In horticultural societies, permanent sites such as homes and larger buildings were soon constructed.

   _____

9. Also, it is clear that once horticultural societies developed, different levels of society developed—I mean, that of the rich and the poor.

   _____

10. It seems certain that the rich in each horticultural society had more stored food as well as bigger and more expensive buildings,

whereas the poor had less food and smaller buildings, or less space, to live in.[2]

Exercise 10.3
Using Note-taking
Techniques on Short
Lecture Passages

A. Read the following lecture excerpts. Then, after you have condensed the information into main ideas and major details, complete the outlines that follow. Because you are reading lecture material, you will find some of it repetitious.

70%

(Score: Give yourself 4 bonus points. Then multiply the number of correct answers by 2. Add this total to the 4 bonus points.)
Find answers on pp. 315–317.

1. Before we begin our examination of American politics, we must consider the essential characteristics of politics. What is politics? It has four characteristics, I think. First, at its basest level, politics is power. Second, the power is used to effect change. Third, change comes about when political groups with the most power win out. I know this definition makes politics inhumane, but we will see in later lectures how these qualities explain much of the legislation and executive actions that we will study.

    I.

        A.

        B.

        C.

        D.

2. This will be the first of two lectures on the history of the American city. Here are some facts that I think are revealing. About 200 years ago, about 95 percent of Americans lived on farms. Then, there were only twenty-four urban areas, all of which were under 100,000 people. By the 1960s things had changed dramatically. Consider these facts. In 1960, 70 percent of the American public lived in urban areas. From 5 percent to 70 percent! In 1960 there were over 6,000 cities or urban areas. Why has life in America changed so drastically? We will soon find out.

    I.

        A.

        B.

---

[2] Adapted from Serena Nanda, *Cultural Anthropology*, 3rd ed. (New York: Van Nostrand, 1987), pp. 153–158. Used by permission.

C.

D.

3. Today we will continue our discussion of the Middle Ages by first considering the Black Death, which struck Europe in the 1300s. First, let me give you some information about this dreaded plague. In England, for example, between 1348 and 1349, one-third of the population was taken by this plague. What was the Black Death? It was a disease that was caused by fleas that were found in black rats. And it is for this reason that the disease is called the Black Death. This disease, I want to emphasize, did not die out in the 1300s but attacked Europeans off and on for the next 300 years. A frightening disease indeed!

I.

A.

B.

C.

D.

4. Today we are going to discuss amphibians. Amphibians are animals that live in water at one stage in their lives and on land at another stage. Three animals that I want you to remember as being amphibians are frogs, toads, and salamanders. One more thing to remember: Amphibians are cold-blooded animals. Their body temperature changes as the weather temperature changes.

I.

A.

B.

C.

5. Last class we discussed the westerly winds. Today we are going to investigate winds called monsoons. The first characteristic that you need to remember is that they are seasonal. Second, these winds are found only in Asia. There are two basic kinds of monsoons—summer winds and winter winds. The winter winds blow from the land to the ocean, and the summer winds blow from the ocean to the land. Now we'll talk about why monsoons exist.

I.

    A.

    B.

    C.

    D.

B. Now use the indenting technique to complete outlines for the following lecture excerpts. This time you'll be given no outline format.

6. Let's talk about blood pressure. This pressure is the result of the heart pumping blood in the veins. You need to remember two terms when considering blood pressure. The first term is systolic. This is the process of the heart's contracting, or getting smaller. The second term I want you to remember is diastolic. This is the measurement we take after the heart has contracted, or when it relaxes.

7. Today I want to discuss the various parts of the human heart. First, please remember that it is made up of four chambers. The outside of the heart is made up of a strong protective covering, called pericardium. The middle of the heart is made up of a very thick layer of muscle. This muscle is called myocardium, and it provides the power to force the blood through the heart. Now let's look at a slide of the heart and identify these two parts.

8. Last week we finished our discussion of longitude. This week I want to introduce the important latitudes of the world. Remember that latitudes are defined as imaginary lines north and south of the equator. The Tropic of Cancer is the famous latitude north of the equator, while its double, south of the equator, is the Tropic of Capricorn. The area between the Tropic of Cancer and the Tropic of Capricorn is very hot and makes up the area of the Earth having a tropical climate. Now let's discuss this tropical climate for just a bit.

9. Last week we talked about ferns. This week I want to begin a discussion of conifers. First, I want you to remember that conifers are trees bearing cones, and they have leaves that look and feel like nails. What is amazing about these leaves is that they can stay on the tree for several years, unlike most leaves, which fall each season. Examples of conifers that you should remember are: pine, spruce, and fir—and I'm naming only a few.[3]

10. I want to spend a part of this lecture discussing what the computer is capable of doing. Let me first emphasize that it can only

---

[3] Adapted from Cecie Starr and Ralph Taggart, *Biology: The Unity and Diversity of Life,* 4th ed. (Belmont, Calif.: Wadsworth, 1987), p. 602. Used by permission.

do what the human being can do. The computer's edge over us is that it can perform an amazing number of calculations in a much shorter period of time. It is also infinitely patient. The computer can perform the same operation over and over again without getting bored or anxious. No human being is as patient as this. And finally, the computer frees us from repetitive work and allows us to be creative. But I want to repeat that the computer does not do work that we are incapable of doing.

Exercise 10.4
Using Note-taking
Techniques on More
Short Lecture
Passages

80%

Ask instructor for answers.

A. For the following five lecture excerpts, your job is to read each and then use the numeral-letter format for passages 1–3 and the indenting technique for passages 4–5. An outline format is provided for passages 1–3. As in the previous exercise, condense the information.

1. I will begin my lecture this afternoon by introducing one of my favorite writers. His name is Henry David Thoreau. He did not have a very long life. He was 45 when he died of tuberculosis in 1862. But he left his mark on American literature. He made nature come alive for so many readers. Thoreau believed that to experience nature was to experience a heightened spiritual appreciation. In short, nature for Thoreau was a blessing.

Perhaps Thoreau's most famous work was *Walden.* In this first-person narrative, Thoreau traces his solitary experiences on Walden Pond in Concord, Massachusetts. A major statement that Thoreau makes is one that we can relate to today. He asks us to strip life of its nonessentials. If we do, we will have a greater love of the world around us. Another thought that will stay with you is this: You will learn to understand yourself much better if you understand the workings of nature. Let's now talk further about what these two statements suggest.

I.

    A.

    B.

    C.

II.

    A.

    B.

    C.

2. Last week we finished our discussion of the executive branch of our government. Today let's begin a discussion of the judicial branch—specifically the Supreme Court. What makes up the Supreme Court, and what are some of its powers? The Supreme Court consists of nine justices appointed by the President with the approval of Congress. These justices, I must add, serve a life term.

    Let's talk about three of the court's major duties. First, the Court listens only to cases brought before them—it cannot act on its own in bringing cases to hear. The Supreme Court can listen only to certain kinds of cases. The Constitution spells this out. The Court can hear only cases dealing with ambassadors, statesmen, and problems that occur sometimes between states. Finally—and this is very important—once the Supreme Court has acted, the decision must stand. It becomes the law of the land. Only an amendment to the Constitution can change it. Here, I think, lies much of the Court's respect and power.

I.

    A.

    B.

II.

    A.

    B.

    C.

3. The bulk of today's lecture will concern the territory an animal claims. Let's first define the term. A territory for an animal is a geographical area that the animal chooses to have dominance over. The key word here is dominance. Birds and land animals alike seem to exert control over their territory. Interestingly, animals are more aggressive in defending the center, or core, of their territory and less aggressive in the outer limits of their territory.

What happens to an animal whose territory is disturbed? And do the answers to these questions say anything about human beings? Many psychological studies reveal that animals show greater stress if they are put too close to one another. What does this have to do with us? Aren't people put too close together in cities? And don't city dwellers exhibit more crime and anxiety than rural dwellers? The theory that the human being has a territory is a speculative one and still needs much more careful research.

    I.

        A. def:

        B.

        C.

    II.

        A.

        B.

        C.

    B. Now use the indenting technique on the following two passages. Of course, no skeletal outlines will be provided.

4. Today we are going to begin our discussion of chemical formulas. A chemical formula is defined as a combination of symbols that represents the number of elements in a specific compound. If more than one atom is present in the compound, whole numbers

are written to the bottom right of the symbol, which show the number of atoms of that element. We will be using these formulas for the rest of the semester, so we will spend a lot of time learning how to use them.

Now let's look at some examples. In the formula for water (H_2O), there are two atoms of hydrogen to one atom of oxygen. Note how the 2 comes directly after and below the H, and since oxygen has only one atom, there is no number below it. Now let's look at the formula for sulphuric acid: H_2SO_4. There are two atoms of hydrogen, to one atom of sulphur, to four atoms of oxygen.

5. Today I want to discuss the remarkable ability of certain animals and plants to hide themselves. This process you would know as camouflage. What is camouflage? In camouflage, an animal or plant uses form, color, or action in order to blend in with the environment. It should be emphasized that this blending in allows the plant or animal to escape detection from other animals or plants.

Let's look at the slide of Lithops, a desert plant that looks like a small rock. Only when it rains and the vegetation around Lithops is varied does it bring forth flowers of bright colors. At other times, Lithops takes on a brown appearance and a pattern that looks almost like the rocks that surround it. In this slide it may be difficult to identify the Lithops from the rocks.[4]

---

[4] Adapted from Cecie Starr and Ralph Taggart, *Biology: The Unity and Diversity of Life,* 4th ed. (Belmont, Calif.: Wadsworth, 1987), p. 681. Used by permission.

**Exercise 10.5
Writing
Abbreviations from
Memory**

Go back to the section in the introduction called "Using Abbreviations" (p. 175) to learn all of the abbreviations that are listed. Then, without referring to those pages, complete the following questions. Place all answers in the answer box.

Write the abbreviations for:

1. equals
2. greater than
3. and
4. imply
5. regarding
6. necessary
7. positive
8. increase
9. large
10. maximum

Write the correct word or words for the following abbreviations.

11. w/o
12. cf
13. vs
14. inc
15. imp't
16. prin
17. cont'd
18. #
19. ∴
20. → ←

1. _____
2. _____
3. _____
4. _____
5. _____
6. _____
7. _____
8. _____
9. _____
10. _____
11. _____
12. _____
13. _____
14. _____
15. _____
16. _____
17. _____
18. _____
19. _____
20. _____

80%

(Score = # correct × 5)

Find answers on p. 317.

Exercise 10.6
Making Your Own
Abbreviations

For the following twenty words and phrases, write your own abbreviations, using the rules given in the introduction. Your answers may vary from those devised by other students. Discuss your answers with your instructor and classmates. Place all answers in the answer box.

1. republic
2. existentialism
3. *The Scarlet Letter* (used several times)
4. arguments for God's existence (used several times)
5. art
6. phenomenology
7. competitive
8. urbanize
9. climate
10. philosophy
11. *Moby Dick* (used several times)
12. grammatical
13. shipments
14. irrigation
15. pollution
16. pesticide
17. first law of thermodynamics (used several times)
18. theory of relativity
19. atmosphere
20. background

1. _____
2. _____
3. _____
4. _____
5. _____
6. _____
7. _____
8. _____
9. _____
10. _____
11. _____
12. _____
13. _____
14. _____
15. _____
16. _____
17. _____
18. _____
19. _____
20. _____

(Score: answers will vary.)
Ask instructor for suggested answers.

Exercise 10.7
Reading and
Writing
Abbreviations in
Sentences

80%
(Score = # correct ×
10 for 1–10. Answers
will vary for 11–20.)
Find answers on pp.
317–318.

A. Assume that the following abbreviated sentences on Pablo Picasso are from your art history lecture notes. Your job is to rewrite each sentence, changing the abbreviations to words.

1. Picasso is an imp't fig w maj of critics.

   _____

2. Helped develop the sig theory of Cubism.

   _____

3. C makes objs look diff.

   _____

4. Viewers see an obj from sev prspctvs.

   _____

5. C can be cf to Impressionism.

   _____

6. Pic influ by prim African art as well.

   _____

7. Viewers need to view P w a diff set of rules.

   _____

8. P's art ≠ read wrld.

   _____

9. P's art work = P's interp of the wrld.

   _____

10. ∴ it is nec to understnd some of P's ideas re the wrld.

    _____

B. Now write your own abbreviated sentences from the sentences on Cubism that follow. Be sure to condense and to make up your own abbreviations where necessary.

11. Georges Braque began to work with Picasso in the first half of the twentieth century.

    _____

12. It is often difficult to tell the work of these significant artists apart.

_____

13. Both began to make old scraps of materials part of their paintings.

_____

14. Their artistic creations implied a significant change in how the viewer saw their works.

_____

15. These old materials were both part of the work of art and separate objects as well.

_____

16. Picasso and Braque were making a significant statement.

_____

17. Pieces of trash could become important subjects in art.

_____

18. Their technique was usually called collage.

_____

19. Picasso's and Braque's Cubism also caused changes in the style of sculpture and architecture.

_____

20. Therefore, we can conclude by saying that Picasso had a tremendous influence on several aspects of modern art.

_____

Exercise 10.8
Outlining Lecture
Excerpts and Using
Abbreviations

A. Following you will find five lecture excerpts. Use all of your note-taking skills (condensing, abbreviating, and the numeral-letter format) to outline the first three passages.

1. Today I want to give you a little background on the use of personal computers in the United States. In 1977 there were 20,000 general-purpose computers in the United States. What is the personal computer? It is usually a microcomputer with a tape-cassette player or a disk drive that uses floppy or hard

(Score: answers will
vary.)
Ask instructor for
sample answers.

disks. The personal computers generally employ one of three
languages: machine, assembly, or BASIC.[5]

2. I want to give you a very short biography of Herman Melville,
the great American novelist whom we will be discussing this
week. Born to a wealthy merchant family in 1819, Melville
learned the Bible from his mother when he was a very young
child. At the age of fifteen, Melville stopped going to school.
At this time his principal teachers became his experiences and
his own reading. He spent the main part of his early years as a
seaman. From these experiences came many books, the most
important being *Moby Dick,* in 1851.

3. Let's talk a bit today about how television advertising affects its
viewers. Each television commercial suggests a certain set of
values. First, you will find that good-looking people are usually
actors in commercials. Advertisers are suggesting that attrac-
tive people are generally better people. Second, you will find
that soap ads are suggesting that to be physically clean from
their product makes you a better person. Third, beer commercials are suggesting that the definition of happiness for the
American male is drinking with the boys and having a loud,
good time. Somehow fun for men is associated with alcohol.

---

[5] Adapted from Perry Edwards and Bruce Broadwell, *Data Processing* (Belmont, Calif.:
Wadsworth, 1980), p. 357. Used by permission.

Fourth, sex is almost everywhere in ads. This suggests, I think, that sex is the most significant part of life.

B. Now use the indenting format to outline the following excerpts. Be sure to condense information and use abbreviations where it seems appropriate.

4. Let's talk a bit about the history of the radio, the first electronic mass medium. It was developed at the end of the nineteenth century. It was Guglielmo Marconi who was the main contributor. And in 1920 the Westinghouse Company became the very first company to set up a radio station. Then between 1921 and 1922, new radio stations were born everywhere—increasing eight times, to 254 stations. For the next twenty years, it is safe to say that the radio became a significant part of the American family's educational and social life.[6]

5. Let's talk a little about converting temperature from one scale to another. There are two major temperature scales I want you to know: Fahrenheit and Celsius. On the Celsius scale, zero degrees is the freezing point of water, and 100 degrees is the boiling point of water. On the Fahrenheit scale, 32 degrees is the freezing point of water, and 212 degrees is the boiling point of water. If you want to convert Celsius to Fahrenheit

[6] Adapted from Earl R. Babbie, *Sociology: An Introduction* (Belmont, Calif.: Wadsworth, 1980), pp. 431–432.

and vice versa, you should use the following equations: temperature Celsius = 5/9 × (temperature Fahrenheit − 32) and temperature Fahrenheit = (9/5 × temperature Celsius) + 32. You will be using these formulas often for the rest of the semester.

6. Let's look at the effects of the Industrial Revolution on energy and society. The first principal effect was that more work could be done in less time. And this is an important effect. Steam and coal became the major energy sources to power the very big machines that were being built. Today we find that oil and nuclear fission are even more powerful energy sources. The introduction of technology also caused a change in people's socializing—at least the way people socialized while they worked. Workers in large factories or companies no longer boasted about knowing how to do all the tasks that went into making a product. They were assigned to do only one small task. It is this sociological and psychological aspect to technology that I want to discuss next time.

Exercise 10.9
Taking Notes on a
Long Lecture
Passage and Using
Abbreviations

The following is a longer anthropology lecture excerpt on language. Your job is to take notes on this passage. Use the indenting format, condense information where necessary, and abbreviate where appropriate. After you have taken your notes, give the lecture an appropriate title.

(Score: answers will vary.)
Find sample answers on p. 318.

Title: _____

(1) We are going to begin a discussion of language. And I think it is best to consider what are its possible origins. We first need to look at our human ancestors to see what it was that made it necessary for them to develop language. I must emphasize that language's development was a gradual process indeed.

(2) One theorist suggests in an interesting way that language began to be needed once these ancestors moved from the protection of the forest to the more open grasslands. First, on grass, you must understand, our ancestors had to learn to walk efficiently on two feet. Walking on two feet caused better vision, better use of the hands, and a brain that became more complex. Our ancestors needed these skills for two reasons: to protect themselves against predators and to find food more easily.

(3) What did language sound like at this time? It was likely at first no different from the howl of chimps. New sounds may have emerged as our ancestors found themselves in play. It is important to note here that any language that they had was tied to the present, not to the past or future. Language, in other words, was not related to human memory.

(4) Then something very important occurred. Our ancestors needed to tie language to memory. Some language experts believe that hunting was the major cause of this; I tend to agree. Hunters had to communicate both to those who were hunting with them and to those who were close behind. These hunters would need to say things such as "I killed an animal," or "The animal got away," or "I need another spear."

(5) Once our ancestors began to settle in larger social groups, their need to organize became even more complex. Language theorists and anthropologists speculate that a more advanced social organization led to more advanced speech. This last idea is quite an interesting one for me.

(6) I must emphasize that these comments are only theories. Language is still a mysterious mechanism. Its histories and its origins are just as unclear as the language mechanism itself.

(7) Tomorrow we will begin to talk about how people acquire language, now that you know a bit about its origins.[7]

Outline the passages here:

---

[7] Adapted from Serena Nanda, *Cultural Anthropology*, 3rd ed. (New York: Van Nostrand, 1987), pp. 39–42. Used by permission.

Exercise 10.10
Writing a
Paragraph from
Your Lecture Notes

Now use only your lecture notes to answer the following essay question. Begin with a main-idea sentence and support it with relevant details.

Essay Question: In a paragraph, discuss the various theories regarding the origins of human language. In your discussion, be sure to include the relevance to language of our human ancestors moving from forests to grasslands as well as the importance of hunting and socialization on language development.

80%

Ask instructor for answers.

11

Alternate Note-taking Techniques; Mapping, Laddering, and the Cornell Note-taking System

Explanation of Skills

Now that you have studied three traditional note-taking techniques, you will find the alternate techniques of mapping, laddering, and the Cornell note-taking system helpful. Both mapping and laddering are visual note-taking systems. You can best use these two techniques when you are editing your notes. Mapping and laddering are especially helpful for those who are artistic or have strong visual abilities. The Cornell system is an effective recall system that uses traditional note-taking techniques as well as a systematic strategy for remembering.

What Is Mapping?

Mapping is a note-taking technique that uses geometric shapes and pictures to show the relationship of main ideas to their details. Mapping is individual; you choose your own design to show the relationship between general and specific. The most commonly used shapes are circles, squares, rectangles, and radiating lines. Because maps are individual, they help you to retain the material more easily. Maps, often called study maps or advanced organizers, reduce large amounts of information to the essentials; thus they are ideal when you study for exams.

Maps may be large or small. If they are large, they need to be put on a separate sheet of paper. If you place additional information on this page, you take away from the study map and distort the visual picture of main ideas tied to details.

Let's say you are studying your notes in British literature and you come across the following statement: "Alexander Pope and Samuel Johnson are the most famous writers in eighteenth-century English

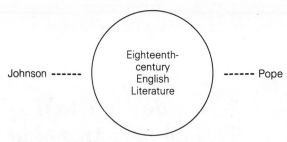

Figure 11-1   *Map of a statement.*

literature." You can map this statement as shown in Figure 11-1. In this map, you see eighteenth-century English literature as the general category, with Pope and Johnson as examples.

Let's say you want to show how the two characters Huckleberry Finn and Tom Sawyer in Mark Twain's *Huckleberry Finn* share the traits of playfulness and love of adventure. You can map these similarities by using intersecting circles. Using intersecting circles is an effective way of mapping similarities (see Figure 11-2).

Mapping is also effective in showing sequences. Arrows can join one step to the other. If you came across the following statement in your health notes, how could you map it? "When a patient contracts this year's Type W influenza, the following symptoms occur: (1) soreness in joints, (2) upset stomach, (3) vomiting, (4) fever of at least 102 degrees." (See Figure 11-3.) Do you see how this map shows both the symptoms and their sequence?

A map using arrows is similar to a *flowchart,* a visualization often used by programmers to set up the logic of their computer programs. Flowcharts are now widely used by people outside programming to list the steps in a procedure. Look at Figure 11-4, which shows the career ladder in a computer company. Follow the arrows from bottom to top; each arrow points to a higher-level position. Also note that some arrows are joined with broken lines and point in two directions, suggesting the double-career option that a person at that level has.

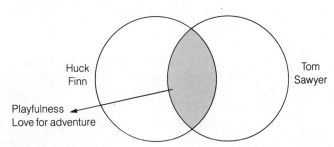

Figure 11-2   *Map of shared traits.*

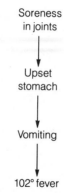

Figure 11-3 *Map showing sequence.*

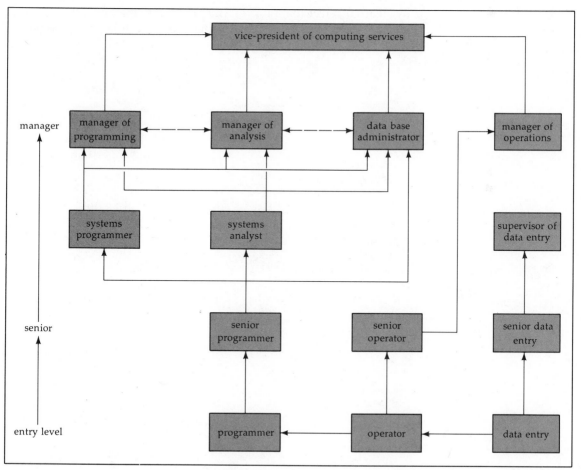

Figure 11-4 *Career ladder. From Perry Edwards and Bruce Broadwell,* Data Processing, *2nd ed. (Belmont, Calif.: Wadsworth, 1982), p. 560. Used by permission.*

All of the aforementioned visual techniques can be combined into larger maps that tie together larger chunks of information—several lectures or an entire textbook chapter. Pretend that you are reviewing your notes in anthropology on the evolution of the human species, and you want to map this information. Your map could look something like the one shown in Figure 11-5. This map reduces several paragraphs into half a page, listing each human ancestor and noting its important characteristics. You also see how Dryopithecine evolved into a species different from the apes.

More complex study maps, also known as advanced organizers, can also show the relationships among topics, main ideas, and supporting details. The topic is usually in the center, the main ideas branch out from the center, and details of support branch out from the main idea lines. See Figure 11-6. These study maps can be used to summarize an entire lecture or a complete textbook chapter.

A second way of presenting much information in a study map is by means of a tree diagram. The main idea is at the top of the tree, the major details branch out from the main idea, and the minor details in

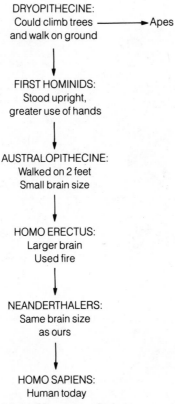

Figure 11-5   *Map of human evolution.*

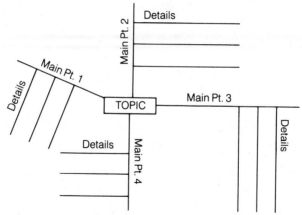

Figure 11-6   *Diagram of a study map.*

turn branch out from the main ideas. Figure 11-7 shows the tree study map.

Many students have found that these larger study maps are effective study aids for midterm and final examinations. With these maps, students are forced to condense material, and they are made to see relationships between general and specific types of material. Further, the visual nature of the study map allows students to "see" the whole and its parts when they take their exams.

Keep in mind that mapping requires few rules and is, for the most part, individual. If you have a visual aptitude, make some study maps as you edit your notes. Even if you don't have strong visual abilities, try to use study maps to help you study for your exams.

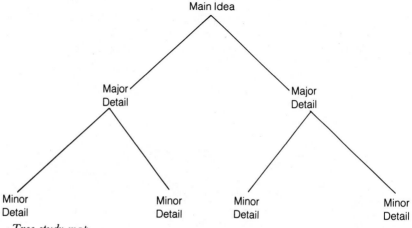

Figure 11-7   *Tree study map.*

```
    ┌─ Family structure
    │       In all societies
    │       Very strong
    │
    │
    │
    └─ Modern family
            Weaker than older family
            More responsibility given to society
```

Figure 11-8   *Laddering of main ideas.*

What Is Laddering?   Laddering is a fairly new note-taking system that also relies on your visual aptitude. Laddering visually ties main ideas to main ideas and relates details to details. Like study maps, laddering can best be used when you are editing your notes and see relationships emerging.

Here is how laddering works. Draw a solid vertical line just to the right of your main ideas. You should use a different colored pencil or pen so the line stands out. Then draw a perpendicular line from this vertical line to each main idea, so that these main ideas are connected. The vertical and horizontal lines then look like part of a ladder. Look at the main ideas in Figure 11-8 to see how laddering brings them out.

You follow this same procedure with the details under each main idea, as shown in Figure 11-9. As it does with main ideas, laddering groups supporting details under each main idea. Place all major-detail ladders along the same plane, so that your eyes see one solid vertical line for main ideas and a broken vertical line for supporting details. See Figure 11-10.

Laddering works best if you use it in conjunction with the indenting format, which does not use numerals and letters. If you added lines to your numerals and letters, you would be cluttering the page. Also, laddering works best if you use it while you are reviewing your notes, not when you are taking your lecture notes.

Like mapping, laddering is another way to bring out the connections between general and specific chunks of information.

Family structure

```
    ┌─ In all societies
    │
    │
    └─ Very strong
```

Figure 11-9   *Laddering of details.*

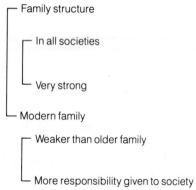

Figure 11-10   *Laddering of main ideas and details.*

What Is the Cornell Note-taking System?

A system developed at Cornell University incorporates several of the strategies that you already know and includes a successful recall strategy. To use this system correctly, follow these ten steps:

1. When taking notes, use three-ring notebook paper and place all of your lecture notes in chronological order in a loose-leaf notebook. By using these two items, you can include material without destroying the sequence of the lectures.

2. Draw a vertical line 2½ inches from the left edge of the page. You will have the remaining 6 inches of paper to write down your lecture notes.

3. During lectures, take notes in any format that you prefer—numeral-letter, indenting, or even short paragraphs.

4. Concentrate on writing only main ideas and significant details during lectures.

5. Skip lines between main ideas, and use only one side of the paper.

6. Read through your notes after class, filling in any incomplete information and rewriting any illegible words.

7. As you review your notes, underline all main ideas or box them.

8. After you have reviewed your notes once, jot down in the 2½-inch margin key phrases that summarize what you have learned.

9. Cover up the 6-inch side of your notes to see whether you can recall the important parts of the lecture with only these key phrases as clues.

10. Continue this procedure until you can easily recall the important parts of the lecture.[1]

Look at the following lecture notes dealing with the family. This student has correctly employed the Cornell system:

2½ inches ←   *6 inches* →

def of family	Nature and Function of the Family 4/12/89
	Definition and strength of the family
	    Def: "Basic unit of kinship or relatedness
	      through blood."

2 chars of fams in all societies	Most fundamental of social structures All societies have families
	Functions of families

3 functs of fams	Essential in caring for and raising children
	    Sexual outlet for spouses
	    Emotional and physical comfort

As you can see, the Cornell note-taking system is sophisticated. Use this technique only after you have mastered the numeral-letter and indenting systems. The Cornell system is basically a refinement of these two systems.

Summary

Mapping and laddering are new note-taking formats. You can use them most effectively when you are editing your notes. Both techniques are visual. Mapping is individualistic, allowing you to create your own shapes to illustrate relationships. Mapping reduces information to its essentials and serves as an excellent review for exams. Laddering works by placing vertical and horizontal lines next to main ideas and supporting details. These two systems work best if you have a visual aptitude, but all students will benefit if they use these techniques as study aids. Like the traditional note-taking systems, mapping and laddering help you see the relationships between main ideas and supporting details.

The Cornell note-taking system helps you remember what you learned in lectures. It breaks up a page into 6 inches of lecture notes next to 2½ inches of summary phrases. The Cornell note-taking system is efficient because it makes you review your notes. In Chapter 12, you will study the SQ3R system, which teaches you a similar recall strategy.

---

[1] Adapted from Walter Pauk, *How to Study in College,* 2nd ed. (Boston: Houghton Mifflin, 1974), pp. 126–132.

Summary Box   *Mapping, Laddering, and the Cornell Note-taking System*

What is it?	*Why use it?*
Mapping: shapes used to relate general and specific information; information reduced to its essentials. Laddering: vertical and horizontal lines are drawn, joining main ideas to main ideas and supporting details to supporting details.	Mapping and Laddering: to show visually how main ideas relate to major details.
Cornell system: the lecture page is divided into 6 inches of notes and 2½ inches of summary; the system insists on recall of important points.	Cornell system: to help ensure recall of material. All three techniques: to remember more information; to prepare better for exams.

Skills Practice

Exercise 11.1
Mapping Statements
from Lectures

The following ten statements are taken from lecture notes. Your job is to create, on a separate sheet of paper, a map for each statement that will show the relationship between main ideas and major details. Remember that mapping is individual, so do not expect your map to be exactly like the one in the key.

70%

(Score = # correct × 10)
Find answers on pp. 318–321.

---

1. Impressionism was a school of painting that emphasized the capturing on canvas of a fleeting moment. The most famous Impressionists were Manet, Monet, and Degas.

2. There are only a few pure substances in nature. Gold, diamonds, and sulfur are found in pure form.

3. British literature to 1800 is usually broken up into the following categories: Medieval, Renaissance, and Restoration-Eighteenth Century.

4. There are many kinds of coal. Lignites are the least pure and most immature. Bituminous coal is a medium-quality coal, while anthracite is the most compact and the purest form of coal.

5. F. Scott Fitzgerald is especially known for two novels: *The Great Gatsby* and *Tender Is the Night.* In *The Great Gatsby,* Fitzgerald develops the character of fated idealist Jay Gatsby, and in *Tender Is the Night,* Fitzgerald traces the mental collapse of psychiatrist Dick Diver.

6. Three of the most important causes of the Great Depression of 1929 were: (1) a decline in industrial production, (2) an increase in the consumer debt, and (3) overpricing of common stocks.

7. Here are three important rules of algebra: (1) the commutative law of addition (a + b = b + a), (2) the associative law of addition [a + (b + c) = (a + b) + c], and (3) the commutative law of multiplication (ab = ba).

8. One of the similarities between whales and chimpanzees is that they both breast-feed their young.

9. Language development usually occurs in four stages. First, one understands a language, then one speaks, then one reads, and finally one writes in this language.

10. There are several causes of inflation. The three most commonly mentioned are: (1) a large federal deficit, (2) high interest rates, and (3) an annual increase in salaries.

Exercise 11.2
Using Laddering on
Short Passages

In the following five lecture excerpts, you will be asked to use the laddering technique to outline each passage. First use the indenting format; then use the laddering technique to highlight the main ideas and major details.

70%

Ask instructor for answers.

---

1. I want to discuss the implications of my statement in the last lecture that the world is divided into two groups—the rich and the poor. Here are some startling facts. One-fourth of the world's population lives in the so-called developed, or industrialized, countries. Three-fourths of the world's population lives in the poorer, developing nations. Examples of developed countries are the United States, Japan, and Germany. Examples of developing countries are Guatemala and Nigeria.

   Yet one-fourth of the population—the developed nations—effectively controls the world. Isn't that amazing! For example, did you know that the developed countries use 80 percent of the resources of the world and that they account for 85 percent of the total expenditures of the world? What, you ask, are the implications of these facts?[2]

---

[2] Adapted from G. Tyler Miller, Jr., *Living in the Environment*, 2nd ed. (Belmont, Calif.: Wadsworth, 1979), p. 118.

2. I want to make a few comments on the unique properties of water, a substance that you and I cannot live without but generally take for granted. For one, of all the liquids we know, water takes the most amount of heat to make it a vapor. This characteristic makes evaporated water a storehouse of energy. Also, water in liquid form can store amazing amounts of heat. Water, therefore, heats and cools more slowly than other liquids. For this reason, you'll be pleased to know that water protects the Earth from sudden temperature changes.

I also want to discuss how water is used in the human body. It dissolves very easily almost all the substances that our body carries. Water can carry vitamins and minerals throughout our body with ease. Water can also be used to clean the body of its wastes. But you must also remember that, because so many things are soluble in it, water in our body can also be easily polluted by poisons and bacteria.

3. It's strange to realize that our Sun, though we think it special to us on Earth, is really quite an ordinary star in the universe. It is as hot and as large as many other stars in the universe. To us, the Sun is very impressive, because it is only 93 million miles away. The star that is next closest to the Sun is 300,000 times farther away than the Sun.

Let's talk a bit about the Sun's composition. It is a ball of extremely hot gases. Do you know that it equals 1 million Earths in size? At its surface, its temperature is extremely hot—10,000 degrees Fahrenheit. Scientists think that at the Sun's core its temperature is unbelievably hot—25 million degrees Fahrenheit or greater.

4. Last lecture I talked about forests. Today, I want to concentrate on grasslands. Where are they? Grasslands used to cover 40 percent of the land on Earth. Much of this land has since been cleared for agricultural use. The great grasslands today are to be found in South Africa, South America, North America, and the Union of Soviet Socialist Republics.

What are some of the characteristics of grasslands? First, the land is flat or rolling. Second, remember that grasslands have dry soil. The rainfall on grasslands is approximately ten to thirty inches a year. This rainfall allows grasslands to have a soil composition that is midway between that of deserts and forests. Finally, animals that graze and burrow are often found on grasslands.

5. We are going to spend the next two lectures discussing density. You will need to understand this concept in many of the laboratory problems you will be assigned. Let's first define density as the mass of a substance in relation to its volume. The formula I want you to remember is this one: Density $= \dfrac{\text{mass of a body}}{\text{volume of a body}}$. As you can see from studying this formula for awhile, a dense body has much mass in a small amount of area.

How is density measured? There are several ways of measuring density. The density of solids and liquids is often measured in grams per cubic centimeter. The gram refers to the mass of an object, and the cubic centimeter measures the volume. The chemical abbreviation I want you to remember is this: gm/cm^3. Sometimes you will see density measured in the English system. This system uses pounds per cubic feet. The chemical abbreviation is lb/ft^3. The density of gases is measured differently.

Exercise 11.3
Mapping a Longer
Lecture Passage

Your job is to read the following lecture excerpt on nuclear energy. As you read, take notes, condensing information and using the indenting format. Then, on a separate sheet of paper, create a study map that includes the important points made in your notes. Remember that mapping is individual, so your map may not look like the sample one in the answer key. Complete your notes in the space provided.

Today my subject is nuclear energy—both its uses and its dangers. First, here are some facts that I want you to know. Current statistics suggest that nuclear energy produces about 8 percent of all electricity in the United States. Scientists predict that by 1990 nuclear power will be only slightly more expensive than power from coal.

Are nuclear power plants safe? The facts suggest that the amount of radiation escaping from a nuclear power plant is in fact less than that from a coal-burning plant of equal size. A second point to be made is that nuclear power plants do not let out carbon dioxide as do coal-burning plants.

The important question, I think, is: What happens if a nuclear accident does occur? There is a chance for a meltdown or a nuclear accident. The process of meltdown is complex. Meltdowns occur when the nuclear fuel overheats. This overheating can cause the water used to cool the material to turn to steam. This steam can cause pressure that could make the entire plant explode if the steam is not checked. When the plant explodes, then the major problems occur: radioactive material is sent throughout the environment.

The last consideration I want to talk about today is that of nuclear waste. What happens to the radioactive material that is used, even if it does not explode into the environment? Where can we store it? Radioactive waste, remember, is dangerous and must be removed to central locations. Radioactive materials decay so slowly that they need to be hidden for thousands of years. No nuclear waste has yet been permanently sealed. Yet, plans are to put these wastes in steel cylinders in areas that are not prone to earthquakes and to water exposure. There are no guarantees that these cylinders will still not contaminate the environment.[3]

Place lecture notes here, but put study map on a separate sheet of paper.

Title: _____

80%

(Score: Give yourself 15 bonus points. Then multiply the number correct by 5 and add this total to the 15 bonus points.) Find answers on pp. 321–322.

Exercise 11.4 Writing a Paragraph from a Study Map

Your job is to write a paragraph from the information that you gathered in the previous lecture on nuclear energy. Use only the information from your study map to answer the following question.

Essay Question: In a well-organized paragraph, present the two sides of the nuclear energy argument: (1) Show that nuclear reactors are relatively safe, and (2) present evidence suggesting that nuclear reactors are unsafe, especially if one considers the possibility of melt-

---

[3] Adapted from Cecie Starr and Ralph Taggart, *Biology: The Unity and Diversity of Life,* 4th ed. (Belmont, Calif.: Wadsworth, 1987), pp. 746–747.

down and the problem of storing nuclear waste. Be sure your evidence is accurate.

70%

Ask instructor for answer.

Study Skills Systems and Strategies

Having mastered reading and note-taking skills, you are now ready to read textbook selections and learn examination strategies. In this part, you will learn about the SQ3R study system, which is an efficient way to read and remember textbook material. You will also learn how to take objective, essay, and math or science tests. Examinations are important indicators that tell instructors how well you are doing.

12

The SQ3R Study System

Explanation of Skills

Now that you have had practice in locating main ideas and major details and have used several note-taking techniques, you are ready to combine these skills when you study your textbook. A successful study system is the SQ3R system, which gives you both reading and note-taking strategies as you read your textbook.

The letters in SQ3R stand for *survey, question, read, recite,* and *review.* Let's look at each of these steps.

Survey

In the survey step, you preview what you intend to read. Surveying is not word-for-word reading; rather, it is selective. Surveying is a central step in study reading; research has repeatedly shown that if you survey material before you read it, your comprehension significantly improves. In surveying, you should (1) determine the length of the chapter, (2) estimate the time it will take you to read the chapter, (3) determine what sections you are already familiar with, and (4) predict whether the material will be difficult or easy for you to understand. In answering these questions, you establish a reading focus.

Surveying an Entire Textbook. When you first get your textbook, you should briefly survey all of the chapters. Consider the following suggestions for doing this:

1. Read the preface—the introductory material written to the student. In the preface, the author gives reasons for writing the book, the topics covered, and suggestions for using the text.

2. Look carefully at the table of contents, which comes after the preface. See how the book is organized. Is the organization simple or complicated? Are there a few divisions or several? If there are exercises, do the explanations come before the exercises, or are all the exercises at the end of the book? Since you will be using this text all semester, you need to know the answers to these questions.

3. See whether there is an index, the alphabetical listing of topics found at the end of the textbook. Indexes are helpful when you want to find information fast. If your textbook has an index, familiarize yourself with it, so that you can use it as a study aid.

4. See whether there is a glossary before the index. A glossary defines important terms that are used in the textbook. Instead of referring to a dictionary, you can use the glossary. Often, students do not even realize that their textbook has a glossary.

5. In some math and science textbooks, students will find an appendix, which comes before the index. The appendix contains charts, graphs, and tables that you need to use in solving problems found in the textbook.

6. In your survey of the entire textbook, you may also discover an answer key. You will often find answer keys at the end of the book. Occasionally, you will find answer keys at the end of an exercise or at the end of a chapter. Some keys provide all of the answers, others just some. This book, for example, gives answers only to odd-numbered exercises. In some math texts, the author will provide answers to the even- or odd-numbered problems within an exercise.

7. Now you are ready to get a sense of the entire textbook. Read through parts of the beginning, middle, and end of the textbook. In this way, you can determine the author's style. Is it formal or conversational? It is helpful to have some sense of the author's style before you begin reading a specific chapter.

Surveying a Chapter of Text.   Consider the following suggestions in surveying a specific chapter:

1. Study the title of the chapter. Having read the title, do you think you know anything about the subject? Has your instructor covered this topic in lecture? Or is this an entirely new topic for you? By answering these questions, you will give focus to your reading.

2. At the beginning of many textbook chapters, you will find an outline or list of objectives that the author intends to address. Since this is the significant information in the chapter, read it over carefully.

3. Most textbook writers divide their chapters up into divisions and subdivisions. These headings are usually in boldface print or italics. Thumb through the chapter divisions. If there are no divisions, read through the first paragraph, the first sentence of the following paragraphs, and the last paragraph of the chapter. By doing this, you determine the outline of the chapter.

4. If there are illustrations, graphs, or charts in the chapter, study them. See how this material relates to the chapter's divisions and subdivisions.

5. See whether discussion or study questions come at the end of the chapter. By reading these questions beforehand, you will know what topics are most important for the author. Also, check to see whether a bibliography is included at the end. A bibliography lists additional books that you may wish to consult after you have study read the chapter.

This chapter survey should take you no more than 3 or 4 minutes, but it is time well spent. Having surveyed, you now have a better idea of what to look for in the chapter.

Question

Before reading for main ideas and supporting details, you need to make up a series of questions that you want the chapter to answer. If the author has already provided study questions, use these, since they are the questions the author thinks are most important for you to answer. As you study read, keep these questions in mind, answering them as you go along.

In many cases, the author does not provide study questions. Then, it is up to you to make up your own questions. This will be difficult at first. You need to study boldface print, italics, and the first sentences of paragraphs, and from this material, make questions of your own. For example, if your economics chapter has **Deficit Spending** in boldface, you could write: "What is deficit spending?" Or if your consumer behavior chapter begins its first paragraph with, "Husbands and wives influence each other's buying preferences," you could turn this statement into a question: "How do husbands and wives influence each other's buying preferences?"

By the time you are ready to study read a textbook chapter, you should have written ten or fifteen questions that you plan to answer while you are reading.

Read

Only after surveying and questioning are you ready to study read— an active skill using all of the critical reading skills you have learned.

Along with your questions, you should have a pen or felt-tip marker. Whenever you come upon a main idea in a paragraph or a detail that supports this main idea, mark this information either by underlining or highlighting the words. Remember, *do not underline too much.* In most cases, all you need to mark is the part of the sentence where you read the important, or core, information. If you overmark a page of text, you will become confused when you review for an exam, not knowing what to review, and finally often reading the entire page over.

Here are ten tips for marking your textbooks:

1. Mark main ideas with a <u>double line</u> or a <u>curved line</u>, or use a marker to shade the <u>main idea</u>. Mark only one main idea per paragraph, and mark only the key parts of this main idea. If the main ideas in a group of paragraphs are related, number them 1, 2, 3, and so on.

2. Mark major details with a <u>single line,</u> or use your felt marker. Try not to underline more than two details per paragraph, and mark only the key parts of these detail sentences. If you find that the details follow a pattern, number these details 1, 2, 3, and so on.

3. For very important statements, place an asterisk (*) in the margins next to these statements. This asterisk will become your signal to study this important piece of information.

4. Important details may be examples, causes, effects, steps, or characteristics. In some cases, you may want to mark both the detail and its type. If you do, use the following abbreviations in the margins: *ex, cause, eff, step,* or *char.*

5. Circle the key parts of a definition if the author has not already highlighted it in boldface or italics. Remember the importance of definitions in learning a subject. You should place the abbreviation *def* in the margin to direct you to the definition when you review your markings. You may also want to write the term on one side of a 3 × 5 card and its definition on the opposite side, so that at the end of the semester, you have collected all of the important definitions for your course on these cards.

6. If a sentence is particularly difficult to understand even after rereading it, place a question mark in the margin next to this sentence. When you review, you will be alerted to what you did not understand.

7. Do not include too many written comments in the margins. If you do write marginal comments, include them anywhere in the margins—top, bottom, left, or right. You should reserve these comments for short summaries of important points, paraphrases of difficult sentences, and inferences that you make. For example, if you note that one main idea or supporting detail is more important than the others, you might want to state in the margin: "Most important main idea" or "Most important supporting detail."

8. Do not begin marking your chapter right away, because once you have marked something, you will have a hard time erasing it. Read through several paragraphs first. Then go back to underline main ideas and supporting details. Often in rereading, you can more easily pick out the important parts of a paragraph.

9. Be consistent with your markings. Use the system just suggested, or make up your own. Just be sure that you use the same underlining symbols and abbreviations throughout the textbook. Otherwise, when you review, you will not be able quickly to separate main ideas from supporting details.

10. See textbook marking as active reading. These markings should be your signals that you understand the form and content of the chapter. If you passively mark, you will not retain the important points made in the chapter.

Figure 12-1 shows an example of a successfully marked textbook page.

These ten steps show how complex study reading really is. Sometimes, even after marking your chapter, you will not completely understand what you have read. Almost everyone has to reread all or part of a textbook chapter sometime during the semester. If a chapter is difficult, you may want to put it aside after you have read it once, and reread it in a day or two. Often if you reread difficult material after it has "settled" for awhile, you will find the material more accessible.

Recite

Having study read and marked the important parts of your chapter, you are now ready to write what you have learned. In the recite step of the SQ3R system, you summarize what you have read. This step is critical because it shows you how much material you have understood and remembered.

When you begin to recite, read for a short period of time—approximately ten minutes. During this time, mark the passage and make marginal comments. Then, close your textbook, and in the section of your notebook designated for study reading notes, take notes on what you read, using any note-taking format that you are comfortable with. Title and date each study reading entry, as in the following example:

Culture and the Consumer   *pp. 24–25*   *3/12/88*

In the beginning, your reciting notes may not be very good. With the first few sets of notes, you may have to review your textbook to see whether your notes are both accurate and thorough. As the semester progresses, extend your study reading sessions from ten to fifteen minutes, then from fifteen to twenty minutes. By the end of the semester, you should be able to study read for fifty minutes and

AFL = American
Federation
of Labor

Ex. of
splitting
of power

CIO = Congress of
Industrial
Organizations

1955 – imp't
date for AFL-CIO
merger

Only 2 big
unions do not
belong

AFL-CIO really
a political grp

By far the largest organization of unions is the *AFL-CIO*. Until the 1930s, the *AFL*, the *American Federation of Labor*, consisted of craft unions of workers such as carpenters, electricians, plumbers, and others involved with specific trades. Oftentimes workers in a given factory were fragmented into many of these craft unions, and there were times when they could not agree with one another during negotiations with the employer. For instance, in 1919 the unions tried to coordinate a steel strike with a committee representing more than 20 crafts. Even today the carpenters and machinists are still unable to settle some of their differences as a result of this experience.

① To overcome this splitting of union power, in 1935 John L. Lewis of the United Mine Workers and Sidney Hillman of the Amalgamated Clothing Workers formed the *Congress of Industrial Organizations (CIO)*. The CIO aimed at unionizing entire factories with one union and became so successful that the AFL felt obliged to copy it with some industrial organizations of its own.

After considerable fighting among themselves involving *jurisdictional strikes*—strikes to force workers to join one union or another ②—the two giant organizations merged into one federation in 1955. In 1972, 16.5 million workers belonged to the AFL-CIO, out of a total of 19.4 million Americans in all unions. There are still two large unions that do not belong to the federation, however—the Teamsters Union (1.9 million members) and the United Automobile Workers (1.4 million).[1]

The AFL-CIO, with its offices in Washington, D.C., exists mainly to exert political influence on the President and the Congress. However, the real power of the union is with the locals, organizations of workers in specific towns and factories. The locals collect the dues and conduct negotiations with employers. The locals belong to national organizations and sometimes international ones (Canadian locals belong, too), both of which belong to the AFL-CIO.

Figure 12-1 *A carefully marked page of text. From Philip C. Starr,* Economics: Principles in Action, *2nd ed. (Belmont, Calif.: Wadsworth, 1978), p. 138. Used by permission.*

accurately recite what you have read. Even for the best students, one hour of concentrated reading of textbook material is all they can effectively do at one sitting.

With particularly difficult chapters, you may want to break up your reading into shorter sessions. If you do this, you may even want to write out some short, specific goals to complete. Look at the following goals for reading a chemistry chapter:

1. Read for ten minutes, or complete two pages of the chapter on temperature conversions.
2. Summarize these pages.
3. Break for five minutes.
4. Read for ten more minutes, recite, and take another five-minute break.
5. Complete at least fifty minutes of study reading in this chapter before you do something else.

Once you have finished your recitation notes for an entire chapter, you may want to read them carefully to see whether you can make a study map out of them. A carefully designed study map is a helpful study aid.

Review

Review is the final step in the SQ3R system. You will study this step thoroughly in Chapters 14 and 15 on test-taking procedures. For now, just remember that to review is your insurance that you will remember what you worked hard to learn. When you review, you (1) study your lecture notes, (2) reread your text markings, (3) review your study reading notes, and (4) study your study maps or design study maps for what you have read. You should not review the night before the exam. You need to review throughout the semester. You will retain more of the reading material if you edit and review your notes after every study reading session. Review all your markings and your study reading notes one week before a major exam. Cramming may help you pass the test, but it will not help you retain the material.

Summary

The SQ3R system is a study system for you to use when you read your textbooks. The S stands for survey—taking a general look at your reading task. Q stands for questioning—writing key questions whose answers will help you understand the reading. The first R, read, is the step where you mark up key points and make accurate inferences. In the second R—recite—you summarize what you have read; this step is critical because it tells you what you have learned. The last R stands for review; here, you go over your markings and notes to retain what you have learned.

The SQ3R system is a sensible study reading system. By using the SQ3R, you approach your study reading in an orderly fashion of surveying, questioning, reading, reciting, and reviewing.

Summary Box   *SQ3R*

What is it?	Why do you use it?
A systematic approach to reading textbook material. S = survey Q = question R = read R = recite R = review	To understand textbook material. To recall the material for exams. To retain textbook material.

Skills Practice

Exercise 12.1
Underlining from
Textbook Excerpts

(Score: answers will vary.)
Find sample underlinings on pp. 322–324.

The following three excerpts are from textbooks in various fields. Your job is to read each excerpt. Then, in each paragraph, underline the main idea twice and one or two major details once. Be sure to mark only the important parts of the main ideas and major details.

1. Catching More Fish and Fish Farming

Fish are the major source of animal protein for more than one-half of the world's people, especially in Asia and Africa. Fish supply about 55 percent of the animal protein in Southeast Asia, 35 percent in Asia as a whole, 19 percent in Africa, about 25 percent worldwide—twice as much as eggs and three times as much as poultry—and 6 percent of all human protein consumption. Two-thirds of the annual fish catch is consumed by humans and one-third is processed into fish meal to be fed to livestock.

Between 1950 and 1970, the marine fish catch more than tripled—an increase greater than that occurring in any other human food source during the same period. To achieve large catches, modern fishing fleets use sonar, helicopters, aerial photography, and temperature measurement to locate schools of fish and lights and electrodes to attract them. Large, floating factory ships follow the fleets to process the catch.

Despite this technological sophistication, the steady rise in the marine fish catch halted abruptly in 1971. Between 1971 and 1976 the annual catch leveled off and rose only slightly between 1976 and 1983. A major factor in this leveling off was the sharp decline of the Peruvian anchovy catch, which once made up 20 percent of the global ocean harvest. A combination of overfishing and a shift in the cool, nutrient-rich currents off the coast of Peru were apparently the major factors causing this decline, which also threw tens of thousands of Peruvians out of work. Meanwhile, world population continued to grow, so between 1970 and 1983 the average fish catch per person declined and is projected to decline even further back to the 1960 level by the year 2000.[1]

2. Traditional Jazz

Two types of Afro-American folk music existed before and during the early years of jazz and later merged with it. One of these was **ragtime**. It featured the piano, occasionally in combination with other instruments. The music sounds like a polished, syncopated march with a decorated right-hand part. Early musicians associated with ragtime are Scott Joplin in Sedalia, Missouri, and Ben Harvey, who published his *Ragtime Instructor* in 1897. In 1974 the film *The Sting* caused a renewed interest in Joplin's rags.

The other type of music involved with early jazz was the folk **blues**. Its musical characteristics will be discussed shortly. Some of the most famous names associated with blues are Leadbelly, whose real name was Huddie Ledbetter; W. C. Handy, who was known for his "Memphis Blues" and "St. Louis Blues"; and Ferdinand "Jelly Roll" Morton, whose first published blues appeared in 1905—the "Jelly Roll Blues."

Like folk music, jazz was created by generally untutored musicians who could not have written down what they played or sang, even if they had wanted to. Jazz is different from most folk music in two respects. It has sprung from the cities rather than the fields and forests; it is an urban form of music. And for most people, it is a spectator experience. Usually only a few people perform, although listeners may contribute a little hand clapping and foot stomping.[2]

3. Matter: Types, States, Properties, and Changes

A lump of coal, an ice cube, a puddle of water, air—all are samples of matter. Matter is anything that occupies space and has mass. **Mass** is the quantity of matter in substance.

A substance or pure substance is one of millions of different types of matter found in the world. Any substance can be classified as either an element or a compound. An element is one of the 108 basic building blocks of all matter. Examples include iron, sodium, carbon, oxygen, and chlorine. Scientists have discovered 90 naturally occurring elements on Earth and have made small quantities of 18 others in the laboratory.

A compound is a form of matter in which two or more elements are held together in a fixed ratio by chemical bonds. Water, for example, is a combination of the elements hydrogen and oxygen, and sodium chloride (the major ingredient in table salt) is a combination of the elements sodium and chlorine. About 5 million compounds of the 108 known elements have been identified, and about 6000 new

---

[1] G. Tyler Miller, Jr., *Living in the Environment,* 4th ed. (Belmont, Calif.: Wadsworth, 1985), p. 153. Used by permission.

[2] Charles R. Hoffer, *The Understanding of Music,* 5th ed. (Belmont, Calif.: Wadsworth, 1985), pp. 492–493. Used by permission.

compounds are added to the list each week. With proper guidance, you could make a new compound yourself. At least 63,000 compounds are combined in the food we eat, the air we breathe, the water we drink, and the countless products we use.[3]

Exercise 12.2
More Underlining
from Textbook
Excerpts

The following are three more excerpts from textbooks in different fields. Again, underline main ideas twice and major details once, and mark only the important parts.

1. Early Primate Evolution

(Score: answers will vary.)
Ask instructor for sample underlinings.

The evolutionary history of the primates is not clear-cut, with one form gradually replacing another. Fossils have not yet been recovered for a few critical time periods. Moreover, there are periods in which closely related forms coexisted for some time, with some destined to leave descendant populations and others to become evolutionary dead-ends. What we will be describing, then, are some of the known branches on a very "bushy" evolutionary tree.

The oldest known primate fossils date from the Paleocene (65 million to 54 million years ago). Again, they were morphologically similar to existing tree shrews, with a relatively small brain and a long snout. Although many of those forms died out, some left descendants that evolved into the true prosimian forms of the Eocene (54 to 38 million years ago).

The Eocene climate was somewhat warmer than the Paleocene, and tropical rain forests flourished—as did the early prosimians. These primates were characterized by an increased brain size, an increased emphasis on vision over smell, and more refined grasping abilities. This was the time of divergences that led, eventually, to the modern-day lemurs, lorises, and tarsiers. It was also the time of divergences that led to the first anthropoids.[4]

2. Humans in Nature: Hunter-Gatherers

Early humans survived without claws, fangs, or great speed. That they did so, and multiplied, is due to three major cultural adaptations—all the product of intelligence: (1) the use of *tools* for hunting, collecting, and preparing food and making protective clothing, (2) learning to live in an often hostile environment through effective *social organization* and *cooperation* with other human beings, and (3) the use of *language* to increase the efficiency of cooperation and to pass on knowledge of previous survival experiences.

Our early hunter-gatherer ancestors cooperated by living in small bands or tribes, clusters of several families typically consisting of no more than 50 persons. The size of each band was limited by the availability of food. If a group got too large it split up. Sometimes

---

[3] G. Tyler Miller, Jr., *Chemistry: A Basic Introduction*, 4th ed. (Belmont, Calif.: Wadsworth, 1987), p. 2. Used by permission.
[4] Cecie Starr and Ralph Taggart, *Biology: The Unity and Diversity of Life*, 4th ed. (Belmont, Calif.: Wadsworth, 1987), pp. 644–645. Used by permission.

these widely scattered bands had no permanent base, traveling around their territory to find the plants and animals they needed to exist. Hunter-gatherers' material possessions consisted mostly of simple tools such as sharpened sticks, scrapers, and crude hunting weapons. Much of their knowledge could be described as ecological—how to find water in a barren desert, and how to locate plant and animal species useful as food. Studies of Bushmen, Pygmies, and other hunter-gatherer cultures that exist today have shown the uncertainty of success in hunting wild game; thus often most of the food of primitive people was provided by women who collected plants, fruits, eggs, mollusks, reptiles, and insects.

Many people tend to believe that hunter-gatherers spent most of their time in a "tooth and claw" struggle to stay alive. But research among hunter-gatherer societies in remote parts of the world casts doubt on this idea. These "primitive" people may hunt for a week and then spend a month on vacation. They have no bosses, suffer from less stress and anxiety than most "modern" people, and have a diet richer and more diverse than that of almost everyone else in the world today, rich and poor alike.[5]

3. Cultural Continuity and Discontinuity

Ruth Benedict (1938) characterized American culture as containing major discontinuities between what is expected of children and what is expected of adults. Children in our culture are not expected to be responsible; they are supposed to play, not work. Few children in America have the opportunity to contribute in any meaningful way to the basic tasks of society. Children take on responsibility only when they become adults. A second major discontinuity is that children are required to be submissive, but adults are expected to be dominant. This is especially true for males. Sons must obey their fathers, but as fathers they must dominate their sons. A third major discontinuity has to do with sex. As children, Americans are not allowed to engage in sexual behavior, and for many people, just the thought of childhood sexuality is repellent. As adults, however, especially as men and women marry, sex is considered to be a normal, even valued, activity.

In great contrast to the discontinuities experienced by the individual learning to participate in American culture is the continuity of socialization among many native American societies. The Cheyenne, a Plains Indian tribe, exhibit a great degree of continuity in their culture. Cheyenne children are not treated as a different order of people from adults. They are regarded as smaller and not yet fully competent adults, although by American standards the competence of Cheyenne children is quite astounding. The play of small children centers on imitation of, and real participation in, adult tasks. Both boys and girls learn to ride horses almost as soon as they can walk. This skill is related to the importance of the horse in traditional Cheyenne culture, in which buffalo were hunted on horseback. By

---

[5] G. Tyler Miller, Jr., *Living in the Environment*, 4th ed. (Belmont, Calif.: Wadsworth, 1985), p. E2. Used by permission.

the time they are six, little boys are riding bareback and using the lasso. By eight, boys are helping to herd the horses in the camp. As soon as they can use them, boys get small but good-quality bows and arrows. Little girls who are just toddlers help their mothers carry wood and water. Boys and girls learn these activities in play, in which the routine of family life is imitated. Girls play "mother" to the smallest children; boys imitate the male roles of hunter and warrior and even the rituals of self-torture that are part of Cheyenne religious ceremonies.

Control of aggression is an important value among the Cheyenne, and aggression rarely occurs within the group of adults. A chief rules not by force and dominance but by intelligence, justice, and consideration for others. The needs of the group are more important than the needs of the individual. The Cheyenne learn this lesson at an early age. Infants who cry are not physically punished, but they will be removed from the camp and their baskets hung in the bushes until they stop. This is an early lesson in learning that one cannot force one's will on others by self-display. Aggression and lack of control of one's emotions do not bring rewards for either children or adults; rather, they result in social isolation.[6]

Exercise 12.3 Using the SQ3R System on a Textbook Excerpt

In this exercise, you will be reading a longer text excerpt, titled "The Less-developed Countries." You will be asked to survey, make up questions, read, recite, and review. When you have completed these five steps, you will be asked to answer some questions that will demonstrate your comprehension of the excerpt.

A. Survey

Give yourself one minute to survey the following excerpt, noting (1) the title and subtitles, (2) words in italics and boldface print, and (3) any graphs or charts. If you have extra time, begin reading the first paragraph or two. When your time is up, answer the questions that follow without looking back at the excerpt.

---

[6] Serena Nanda, *Cultural Anthropology*, 3rd ed. (Belmont, Calif.: Wadsworth, 1987), pp. 131, 134. Used by permission.

Chapter 21
The Less-developed Countries
Challenge for the Future

Philip C. Starr

This last chapter is about poverty among nations. Poverty is, of course, a relative matter. Whenever there is any inequality in the distribution of income, some people will always be poor *relative* to others. But much of the world is so abjectly poor that some observers speak of *absolute* poverty—"a condition of life so degraded by disease, illiteracy, malnutrition, and squalor as to deny its victims basic human necessities."[1]

One billion people—one-quarter of the world's population—are in this category. One-quarter of a million people in Calcutta are homeless. They eat, live, and die in the streets. Three million people in Bolivia out of a total population of 5 million have a life expectancy of 30 years of age. The average Bolivian eats less than one-half of one ounce of meat per year, which in effect means that the peasant population is too poor to eat any meat at all.[2]

These problems are hard for Americans to appreciate. The problem is not like that of an American black male who cannot get a college education or like that of a female of any color who cannot get admitted to medical school. The problem is that two-thirds of the world's population have not made it in terms of income to first grade, while the other one-third has relatively easy access to wealth and income. The problem is not the typical American one of reducing the number of high school dropouts: The problem is how to give more than 2 billion people the means and the opportunity to make some investment in their own human capital. Our point is that only when *individuals* begin to have some perception of their own impact (positive or negative) on our planet can

Starr, Economics, *pp. 350–352. Used by permission.*

we begin to appreciate our *collective* responsibility to help one another.

Note that the chapter title refers to *less-developed countries* (abbreviated LDCs). Several terms are used to describe countries that are poorer than others: Underdeveloped countries, developing countries, Third World countries. We prefer the term "less developed."*

Economists have no specific dividing lines or explicit definitions of such terms. A nation's position on the ladder is usually determined by dividing its GNP by population (*per capita GNP*) so that there is a spectrum of nations from rich to poor—from $6,300 per person per year in Sweden to $70 per person per year in Burundi (both in 1973). (There are probably poorer countries than Burundi, but in those cases GNP and/or population is usually unknown.)

This chapter reviews the plight of the less-developed countries from the point of view of economic analysis. The chapter is divided into four parts: (1) Why should we bother? (2) Problems that must be solved. (3) What can be done to help. (4) Conclusions.

Why Should We Bother?

There are five basic arguments.

1. Our Need for Strategic Materials

An industrial society like the U.S. cannot function without certain raw materials. One esti-

---

* All countries, rich or poor, are to some extent "developing." The difference is relative; so, by "less developed," we simply mean that such countries are less developed than others. The term "third world" is a conversational term implying poverty, but occasionally one will hear of "fourth" and "fifth" world countries, depending on how far down the economic ladder they are.

mate[3] is that there are 13 such materials essential to the U.S. Some examples are asbestos, bauxite (aluminum ore), chrome, cobalt, copper, lead, manganese, nickel, petroleum, platinum, silver, tin, and titanium—not to mention bananas, coffee, tea, and Scotch. Many of these essentials come from the less-developed countries, and our dependence on other countries is growing. In 1950 we relied on other countries to provide us with more than half of only 4 of the 13 materials. By 1985 we will want more than half of 9 of the 13 from other countries.

2. *Closer Social and Economic Ties*

We are more closely bound than ever to all countries. Americans worry about the international traffic in drugs, some of which comes from the LDCs. We worry about inflation that comes from higher coffee, tea, and oil prices.

Many of the less-developed countries are following the lead of *OPEC,* the *Organization of Petroleum Exporting Countries,* and forming cartels. Cartels have formed among the countries that export bauxite, tin, coffee, bananas, tea, rubber, and pepper, to name a few. The intent of these cartels is to control supply and raise the price. The United States will have to learn to deal with and be on good relations with the countries that belong to these cartels.

3. *The Need for Political Stability*

It is sometimes said that "only the rich can afford democracy." Consider a nation of starving, bewildered, uneducated people. It is easy for them to turn to a dictator who persuades them that he or she can solve their problems. If the dictator becomes the source of international tension, or even war, as in some of the African or Latin American states, the peace of the world may be threatened. No one (rich) nation like the United States can afford to permit a people's suffering to threaten the orderly progress of economic development throughout the world. We mean to be cautious here. We do not suggest military intervention to remove the dictator but rather sufficient help for such a people to make the dictator unnecessary.

4. *The Moral Question*

We are often viewed as the rich kid who pays no attention to the kids in the slums. Americans consume 40 percent of the world's resources with 6 percent of the world's population. Many people believe we are indifferent to the problems of the poor countries. The United States has a reputation for being miserly with its foreign aid. In terms of economic assistance as a percentage of GNP, we rank 14 among 16 developed nations.[4] For our own peace of mind, we cannot afford to be viewed

---

CONCEPTS TO REMEMBER

Less-developed countries (LDCs)	Social overhead capital
Per capita GNP	Zero population growth (ZPG)
Organization of Petroleum Exporting Countries (OPEC)	Physical Quality of Life Index (PQLI)
	Group of 77
Revolution of rising expectations	Official government aid (OGA)
Nonrenewable resource	Intermediate technology
Capital-output ratio	Green Revolution
Infrastructure	Triage

as a "global parasite"[5] that consumes the world's resources while millions starve.

5. Time Is Running Out

In a world of growing populations and declining food reserves, the time left to solve the world's poverty problems is getting short. The world's population is increasing at the rate of 64 million* per year now, rising to 100 million per year by the year 2000.[6] Roughly 87 percent of these new mouths to feed will be in the LDCs.

Running Out of Food To feed this present yearly addition of 64 million people will require nearly 20 million tons of grain each year, which is more than the total Canadian wheat crop. (The population problem will be discussed in more detail in a later section.)

The Malthusian moment of truth has arrived. Although all countries are currently using only about 44 percent of an estimated 7.9 billion acres of arable land for food production, *all* of that land will be in use by the year 2080 if present population trends continue— *even if the yield per acre is quadrupled.*

The world's grain reserves are dropping as they are used up to meet increasing demand. Table 21-1 shows how the world's grain reserves have declined to a point where we had only a 35-day supply in 1975.

---

* We obtained this by multiplying 3.92 billion people by 1.64 percent, the growth rate in 1975.

Table 21-1
Declining Grain Reserves

Year	Reserves (days of consumption)
1961	105
1965	91
1970	89
1975	35

Source: Lester R. Brown, "The World Food Prospect," *Science,* 12 December 1975.

Notes

1. Robert S. McNamara, "The Moral Case for Helping the World's Poor," *Los Angeles Times,* 28 September 1973, pt. II, p. 7.

2. Harvey Morris, "Life of Bolivian Indians Remains Harsh," *Los Angeles Times,* 31 March 1977, pt. I-A, p. 1.

3. Charles W. Maynes, Jr., "Are the World's Poor Undeserving?" *Los Angeles Times,* 8 December 1974, pt. VI, p. 1.

4. McNamara, "The Moral Case for Helping the World's Poor."

5. Maynes, "Are the World's Poor Undeserving?"

6. See Nathan Keyfitz, "World Resources and the Middle Class," *Scientific American,* July 1976; "Running Out of Food," *Newsweek,* 11 November 1974; Lester R. Brown, "The World Food Prospect," *Science,* 12 December 1975; Thomas Y. Canby, "Can the World Feed Its People?" *National Geographic,* July 1975; and Douglas N. Ross, *Food and Population: The Next Crisis,* The University Library, 1975.

1. _____

2. _____

3. _____

4. _____

5. _____

(Score = # correct ×
20)
Find answers on p.
324.

1. The chapter excerpt lists concepts to remember.

    a. true
    b. false

2. The excerpt does not use italics for emphasis.

    a. true
    b. false

3. The excerpt makes use of boldface print.

    a. true
    b. false

4. The table that appears in the excerpt shows:

    a. grain reserves
    b. the industrialized countries of the world
    c. the poorer countries of the world
    d. overpopulation

5. The title suggests that this chapter will mainly concern itself with:

    a. the wealthy countries of the world
    b. the industrialized countries of the world
    c. the poorer countries of the world
    d. overpopulation

B. Question

Now go back to the excerpt and from the title, subtitles, and italics write six questions that this excerpt raises.

1.

2.

3.

4.

5.

6.

(Score: answers will
vary.)
Find sample answers
on p. 324.

C. Read and Recite

Begin study reading, underlining main ideas and major details. Read from the beginning of the excerpt to the end of "2. Closer Social and Economic Ties." Then close the book and recite, using the indenting format.

(Score: answers will vary.)
Find sample outline on p. 324.

Now study read the rest of the excerpt from "3. The Need for Political Stability" to the end. When you finish, write down the most important points using the numeral-letter format. Remember, don't look back.

(Score: answers will vary.)
Find sample outline on p. 325.

Now look back at your two outlines. From them, make up a study map that ties all of the information together.

D. Review

Now study your underlinings, outline, and study map. When you think that you have learned the most important points of the excerpt, answer the following questions without looking back.

Examination: The Less-developed Countries   Directions: Choose the letter that correctly answers the following ten questions. Place all of your answers in the answer box.

1. How many people in the world are in absolute poverty?

   a. 5 million
   b. 1 billion
   c. 2 billion
   d. 3 billion

2. The country with the highest gross national product (GNP) is:

   a. Burundi
   b. United States
   c. Sweden
   d. France

3. The excerpt says that the less-developed countries are rich in:

   a. raw materials
   b. educated people
   c. foodstuffs
   d. both a and c

4. The United States's reliance on raw materials from other countries is:

   a. decreasing
   b. increasing
   c. staying the same
   d. none of these

1. _____

2. _____

3. _____

4. _____

5. _____

6. _____

7. _____

8. _____

9. _____

10. _____

_____
80%

(Score = # correct ×
10)
Find answers on p.
325.

5. From the excerpt you can tell that a cartel is a group of countries:

    a. controlling the price of a product or products
    b. controlling the supply of a product or products
    c. with similar political beliefs
    d. both a and b

6. The excerpt suggests that less-developed countries:

    a. tend to be democratic
    b. tend to live under dictatorships
    c. believe in elections
    d. have access to the atomic bomb

7. The excerpt states that the United States:

    a. is concerned with the poor in other nations
    b. gives more aid to developing nations than most other developed nations give
    c. gives less, percentage-wise, than most other developed countries give
    d. has a reputation in the world for being generous

8. In the excerpt it it suggested that the rising world population is not an alarming problem.

    a. true
    b. false

9. The grain reserves in the world are:

    a. rising
    b. dropping
    c. staying the same
    d. none of these

10. In the excerpt it is suggested that the problems of the developing nations will be:

    a. a major problem in the future
    b. a minor problem in the future
    c. resolved by the year 2000
    d. resolved by developed nations

Exercise 12.4
Writing a
Paragraph Using
SQ3R

Once again review your text markings, study notes, and study map for the previous textbook excerpt. When you can remember the important points in this excerpt, close your book and notes and answer the following essay question.

Essay Question: In an organized paragraph, discuss three reasons the author gives for wanting the United States to help the less-developed countries. Begin with a topic sentence.

Use the following outline to jot down the important points you want to make in your paragraph.

I. _____

80%

Ask instructor for answers.

A. _____

B. _____

C. _____

13

Mnemonic Strategies

Explanation of Skills

A good memory, of course, is a key to learning. Knowing how memory is stored in the brain will give you a better understanding of how to become a more successful student. Also, in understanding how memory works, you can see how memory aids, called **mnemonic strategies**, help you learn.

How Does Memory Work?

The study of the brain and learning, called cognitive psychology, is new. All that students in this field have to work with at this time are theories, at best.

Cognitive psychologists are now suggesting that there are two kinds of memory: short-term and long-term. Everything you learn begins in short-term memory; you read or listen to something, and it enters short-term memory. Almost everything that goes into short-term memory is quickly forgotten, because forgetting is much easier for the brain than remembering. When something stays with you, it has entered long-term memory.

The best way to put information into long-term memory is through **rehearsal**. Rehearsal involves practice; with study material, that would involve rereading, discussing, summarizing, or paraphrasing. When you rehearse information, the brain records it, something like how a computer records bits of information on tape or chips. When you learn, the brain records the information with a physical mark on the cerebrum (the learning part of the brain). These marks are called *neural traces*, or memory grooves. Well-rehearsed information creates well-defined neural traces. If you learn something improperly, the neural trace will not be well defined, and it will likely return to short-term memory and be forgotten. Study Figure 13-1 on how the brain remembers.

How do you keep information in long-term memory? To remember, you should (1) study for short periods, (2) take short rest periods between study periods, (3) review what you have learned, and (4) study different subjects in succession.

Studying for short (twenty-five to fifty minute) intervals has several advantages. First, realize that the brain forgets more than it remembers; so if you take in less information, you have a better chance of remembering it. Remember, though, that these study periods must be concentrated. You need to reread and recite what you have read. This concentrated reading is what you have learned to do in the SQ3R system.

Another characteristic of the brain is that it tends to rehearse what you have learned even after you have stopped studying. You are unaware of this rehearsal. When you read for a certain length of time, you need to take a relaxing break. Even if the break has nothing to do with what you have studied, your brain will still be rehearsing this new material. Like food being digested, new information needs to sit in the brain awhile before it can enter long-term memory. Remember, though, that you need to schedule carefully your study breaks. Reading for twenty minutes and then taking a three-hour break will not train your brain to remember. If you plan to study in three intervals at night, for example, your breaks should be no more than twenty minutes long.

A third fact to know about the brain is that it tends to forget more during the first twenty-four hours than at any other time. Since you tend to forget more at first, make a point of reviewing what you have learned soon after you have read your textbook or listened to a lecture. What you review today will have a better chance of staying in long-term memory.

A final characteristic of memory is that the brain tends to forget if it is processing similar bits of information. This mental process is known as **interference**. The brain seems to take in more if two chunks

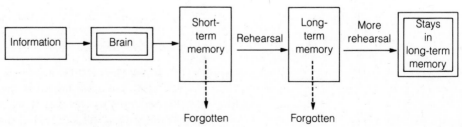

Figure 13-1   *How the brain remembers.*

of information are different. So it is wiser to study for two dissimilar courses than two similar courses in succession. For example, you will remember more of your psychology chapter if you do some chemistry problems afterward than if you were to follow your psychology reading with reading a chapter of sociology.

Memory Tips

From this very general introduction to learning theory, you can design certain successful learning strategies. Consider the following learning hints:

1. Something learned well the first time is not easily forgotten. Study new information slowly and carefully, asking questions as you go along.

2. Relate new information to several contexts. Putting information into proper context is called **association**. The more contexts that you place information in, the more likely you are to remember this new material. If you are learning the meaning of *ostentatious,* for example, it is best for you to learn both its dictionary meaning as well as its synonyms; its history, or etymology; and words related to it, such as *ostensibly, ostentation,* and *ostentatiousness.* With each new context that you place the word in, you are creating more memory grooves, all of which are associated with *ostentatious.*

   Similarly, the more you read in several fields, the more contexts you make, and the easier it will be for you to attach new information to them. Many composition theorists and language experts are now saying that students learn to speak and write better if they read widely. Creating several contexts seems to be central to successful learning.

3. Organize any information that you read or study into patterns, often into main ideas and major details. Organizing information into recognizable patterns is known as **categorization**. When students categorize information, they have a better chance of keeping it in long-term memory. Even if information seems disorganized, try to find an order; most information is built upon patterns.

4. Reviewing is another important way to remember. Psychological studies have shown that if you have once learned something and have forgotten it, you will have an easier time relearning it. Spaced review helps keep information in long-term memory. Don't leave your reviewing of notes and textbook markings until the night before an exam.

5. On a few occasions, you will be asked to learn a particular sequence or list that has no pattern, such as the colors in the light spectrum or the planets in the solar system. When this happens, use one of the following four mnemonic strategies: (1) a mnemonic sentence,

(2) an acronym, (3) an abbreviation, (4) a visualization, or (5) a gimmick.

A Mnemonic Sentence. Your biology instructor may want you to remember the order of classifications in the animal kingdom. There is no logic to this nomenclature, so you might want to create a mnemonic sentence that will help you recall each term. Your job is to remember the following divisions in the animal kingdom and their proper sequence: kingdom, phylum, class, order, family, genus, and species. You note that the beginning letters for the classifications are: K, P, C, O, F, G, S. Thus, to remember each term, think of a seven-word sentence whose words begin with the seven letters in the biology classifications. You might think of something like: "King Paul called out for Gus and Sam." This sentence will likely stay with you during an exam, when you need to recall this classification sequence.

Acronyms. You use an acronym to abbreviate a phrase. **Acronyms** are made up of the first letter of each word of the phrase; these letters make a word or a new word. NATO, for example, stands for North Atlantic Treaty Organization, and its initial letters can be pronounced as a word. You can make up your own acronyms when you cannot use categorization to remember a particular chunk of information. For example, if you cannot remember the parts of an atom, you can create the acronym PEN to stand for *proton, electron,* and *neutron.*

Abbreviations. You can use abbreviations in a similar fashion. **Abbreviations** are made up of the first letter of each word in a phrase. Unlike acronyms, these abbreviations do not spell out a word. MVM could be your abbreviation for remembering the three planets besides the Earth that are closest to the Sun: Mercury, Venus, and Mars.

Visualizations. Another successful memory aid is called a **visualization**. In a visualization, you attach what you need to learn to something visual. You have already learned something about visualizing when you studied the spatial geographic pattern (pp. 80–81). Here, you learned that in biology and geography courses, it is helpful to see how one part of an organism or location relates to another.

Visualizing can also prove helpful in learning unrelated pieces of information; you create a picture that incorporates the information into it. For example, if you cannot remember that *lapis lazuli* is a semiprecious stone, you may want to invent a scene in which a queen has a beautiful stone in her lap. Note the pun on the word *lap.* This scene with the jewel on the queen's lap should help you recall the first part of the word (*lap*) and the fact that this stone is precious, worn by queens. You should use such an elaborate visual strategy, though, only when association and categorization have failed to make the proper learning connections for you.

Gimmicks.   Gimmicks can also be used to trigger your memory when the conventional learning strategies have failed. **Gimmicks** are simply word games or tricks to help you remember; they are often used in learning to spell difficult words. If you have difficulty spelling *conscience,* for example, you might remember its spelling if you learned the slogan "There is a *science* to spelling the word *conscience.*" Similarly, if you cannot remember that the noun *principal* refers to a person, you could think of your principal as your *pal.* By remembering *pal,* in this slogan, you will no longer confuse *principal,* the person, with *principle,* the rule or belief. Instructors will often teach you these spelling gimmicks, but you may be imaginative enough to make up your own.

Summary

The brain has two storage capacities—short-term and long-term memory. As a student, it is your goal to transfer as much information as possible to long-term memory. You can place more information into long-term memory by studying in short, concentrated periods, by taking spaced study breaks, and by regularly reviewing what you have studied. You will also remember more if you relate what you have learned to several contexts. By studying the same material in lecture, in your textbook, and in your study notes, you begin to see this information from several perspectives. Along with association, categorization is another key learning principle; whenever possible, try to divide up information into general and specific categories.

When information has no particular pattern, you may want to use verbal and visual gimmicks to learn the material. Generally, though, the most effective way to learn new material is to learn it right the first time—by putting it into logical categories and associating it to what you already know about this material.

Summary Box   *Memory Aids*

What are they?	*Why do you use them?*
Study techniques that help place information into long-term memory. The three basic learning principles are: (1) rehearsal, (2) association, and (3) categorization. Some of the more successful learning gimmicks are: (1) mnemonic sentences, (2) acronyms, (3) abbreviations, (4) visualizations, and (5) spelling gimmicks.	To help you retain information and easily recall it on examinations.

Skills Practice

Exercise 13.1
Applying Memory
Aids to Study
Material

(Score: answers will vary.)
Find sample answers on p. 329.

For the following ten pieces of information, your job is to use a memory aid to learn them. Your answers, of course, will vary.

1. Think of a gimmick to help you remember the difference in spelling and meaning between *stationery* (writing paper) and *stationary* (not moving).

2. Think of a gimmick that will help you remember the difference in spelling and meaning between *allusion* (reference) and *illusion* (unreal image).

3. Think of a gimmick that will help you remember the difference in meaning between *among* (used in comparing three or more) and *between* (used in comparing no more than two).

4. Think of a gimmick that will help you remember the difference in spelling and meaning between *capital* (meaning chief, or principal) and *capitol* (meaning a building that is the seat of government).

5. Think of a visualization that will help you remember that Nimrod was a mighty hunter referred to in the Bible. Describe the scene in a sentence or two.

6. Think of an acronym that will help you remember the colors of the light spectrum: red, orange, yellow, green, blue, indigo, and violet. Remember that an acronym is a word that is made up of the first letter of each word in the series you want to learn.

7. Think of a mnemonic sentence that will help you remember the first five presidents of the United States: Washington, Adams, Jefferson, Madison, and Monroe.

8. Think of an abbreviation that will help you recall the three most populous cities in the world: Mexico City, Tokyo, and Moscow.

9. You need to remember for your anthropology class the three different kinds of societies: egalitarian, rank, and stratified. Think of an abbreviation to help you recall these three types of societies.

10. Assume that you have to learn the meaning of *zealous* (eager or passionate). Use the learning theory of association to help you recall the meaning and uses of *zealous*. Add prefixes and suffixes to this word.

Exercise 13.2
Self-Evaluation:
Applying Memory
Tips and Theory to
Your Studies

The following nine questions will test the learning theories that you learned in the introduction. Answer these questions as they pertain to your studies. It would be helpful to share your answers with other students and your instructor. There are no right or wrong answers.

(Score: answers will vary.)

1. To test the theory of interference, study back to back for courses that are similar in content. What problems did you find?

2. To test the theory of interference, study back to back for courses that are different in content? What happened? Did you learn more easily?

3. To test the theory of rehearsal, read for thirty to fifty minutes, but do nothing else. Do not take notes, do not discuss the material, and do not review. Then take a ten-minute break. After the break, recite what you remember. Was your summary complete? What information did you miss?

4. To again test the theory of rehearsal, read for thirty to fifty minutes, but this time take notes, discuss, and review. Then take a ten-minute break. Finally, recite what you remember. Was your summary complete? Was it better than the summary in 3?

5. To test your rehearsing skills, go over the study notes, lecture notes, text markings, and study maps for one of your classes. See which rehearsal techniques you find most helpful. In a sentence or two discuss how the following rehearsal techniques helped you remember the material:

   a. underlining _____

   _____

   b. making marginal notes _____

   _____

c. summarizing _____

_____

d. paraphrasing _____

_____

e. making study maps _____

_____

f. reviewing your textbook underlinings and notes _____

_____

g. reviewing your study maps _____

_____

h. other techniques: _____

_____

6. Of the courses you are taking, choose one that requires you to memorize. Make up an acronym to help you remember a chunk of information.

7. Of the courses you are taking, choose one that requires you to memorize certain material. Make up an abbreviation or mnemonic sentence to help you learn this material.

8. Choose a course you are taking that has a difficult word you need to learn. Think of a gimmick that will help you remember either its spelling or its meaning.

9. Find another word for the course that you used for question 8. Create a visualization that will help you remember the meaning of that word.

14

Examination Strategies; Objective Tests

Explanation of Skills

So far you have learned to read your textbook critically, take notes from your textbook and from lectures, and use mnemonic strategies when you cannot remember information. You use all of these skills when you prepare for an exam. In most courses, how well you do on exams determines how well you do in the course.

You will be taking two kinds of exams: objective and essay. Each type of exam requires a different strategy. Let's look at the objective test first.

What Are Objective Tests?

On objective tests, you often need to have learned many details and understood the basic concepts. You will have little or no writing to do, because objective exams are often machine scored, usually requiring you to mark the correct response from two to five choices on the answer sheet. Objective tests are often in three formats: multiple-choice, true-false, and matching. You will study each type later in this introduction.

How to Prepare for Objective Tests

If your economics instructor announces that you will be taking a 100-question multiple-choice exam the following week, how should you study for it? Cramming the night before, of course, goes against the principle of learning effectively through spaced intervals. Preparing for a 100-question exam should take you three to five days.

In this period, you should first review your textbook markings. You should be looking for highlighted main ideas and supporting details. Then, read your marginal comments, which often give in-

NET NATIONAL PRODUCT (NNP)		gross national product
		without depreciation
Blank Side		Lined Side

Figure 14-1   *Study card defining* net national product.

sights not stated in the textbook. If you come upon any new insights or want to underline additional information, do so at this time.

Third, review your study reading notes. These notes will likely repeat much of what you studied in your textbook, but reading the same information from a new perspective will provide an additional context for you to remember the material. Fourth, review your lecture notes, underlining key points and making marginal comments as you did in your textbook. Study especially carefully those parts of your notes that are not mentioned in your textbook.

As you study your lecture and study notes, you will come across definitions that you need to remember. Put these terms on 3 × 5 cards, with the term on the blank side of the card and the definition on the lined side. The night before the exam, study these cards carefully. Divide your cards up into two piles as you study—those terms that you know and those that you don't. By the end of the night, you need to have all of your cards in the "I know" pile. Your cards should look like the one shown in Figure 14-1, which defines "net national product."[1] Some students prefer to write these definitions on a sheet of paper, with the term on the left side of the page and the definition to the right, as in the following list of economic terms:

Term	*Explanation*
1. Net National Product (NNP)	gross national product without depreciation
2. Gross National Product (GNP)	sum of government purchases, consumption, investments, and exports
3. National Income (NI)	net national product without indirect business taxes

The only problem with such a study sheet is that you cannot prove that you have learned the term, as you can with the cards. On your sheet, you cannot separate the "I knows" from the "don't knows."

Along with note cards and study sheets, you should also design study maps. Look at how the study map in Figure 14-2 relates the

---

[1] Walter Pauk, *How to Study in College,* 2nd ed. (Boston: Houghton Mifflin, 1974), p. 172.

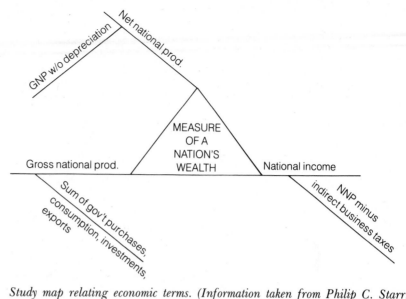

Figure 14-2 *Study map relating economic terms. (Information taken from Philip C. Starr,* Economics: Principles in Action, *2nd ed. [Belmont, Calif.: Wadsworth, 1978], pp. 174–175.)*

same economic terms. The visual nature of study maps may help you remember these terms more easily.

Finally, you should carefully read any instructor handouts. These handouts often present important material, and your instructor may even design questions from them. Also, if your instructor has provided you with a syllabus, you may want to review the titles of each class meeting to see how the topics relate to each other. If the syllabus does not have titles, review the titles that you have given each lecture.

The night before the exam, concentrate on concepts; do not cram for details the night before the exam.

How to Answer Multiple-Choice Questions

Multiple-choice questions are the most commonly used objective questions. In the multiple-choice format, a question or statement is posed; this section is called the **stem**. Three to five choices follow, which either answer the question or complete the statement. It is up to you to eliminate the incorrect choices and find the correct one. Look at the following multiple-choice example on Sigmund Freud:

stem 1. According to Freud, the three parts of human consciousness are:

choices
  a. the ego, the id, and the libido
  b. the id, the alterego, and the ego
  c. the id, the ego, and the superego
  d. the child, the adult, and the parent

If you know something about Freudian psychology, you know what the correct answer is (c). You either write (c) on your answer sheet or darken (c) on your answer grid.

Hints on Taking Multiple-Choice Exams.   Here are some strategies to use when you answer a multiple-choice question:

1. Read the stem and each choice as if it were a separate true-false statement. In the previous example, you would have read: "According to Freud, the three parts of the human consciousness are the ego, the id, and the libido." Then determine whether this statement is true or false.

2. If you determine the statement to be false, draw a line through it (if your instructor allows you to mark on the exam), as in the following:

    1. According to Freud, the three parts of the human consciousness are:

        a. ~~the ego, the id, and the libido~~

    By crossing out, you eliminate choices. You also save yourself time by preventing your eyes from returning to incorrect choices.

3. Continue to eliminate incorrect choices until you find the correct answer. In some difficult questions, two choices may appear correct to you. If this happens, reread the stem to the question to pick up any shades of meaning in the words; then reconsider the two choices. Look at the following question on short-term memory, from which two choices have already been eliminated:

    2. The best example of the use of short-term memory is:

        a. reciting key points in reading material
        b. repeating a phone number just told to you
        c. ~~understanding what categorization means and using this information on an essay exam~~
        d. ~~remembering the name of a friend whom you have not seen for eight years~~

    You can eliminate (c) and (d) because both are examples of information that has been in long-term memory for a long time. Both (a) and (b), however, refer to recently learned information. In rereading the stem, you note that the question is asking for the *best* example of short-term memory. You remember that reciting helps put information into long-term memory, so (b) is the best answer. You need to use your best skills in logic and critical reading when you come upon two choices that both seem correct.

4. Question choices that include absolute terms of qualification such as *always, never,* and *only*. Choices using these terms are frequently incorrect because they need to be true in every case; and few statements are always true. Look at the following question on categorization:

> 3. Which statement best describes categorization?
>> a. Categorization and association are never both used to learn new information.
>> b. Categorization is always used to learn disorganized information.
>> c. Categorization is an unsuccessful learning technique.
>> d. Categorization is an effective learning technique used by students in several disciplines to learn new material.

You would be correct in omitting both (a) and (b) as correct answers because the qualifiers *never* and *always* insist that these statements be true in every case. If you can think of one exception for each choice, you can eliminate that choice. You are then left with (c) and (d). Knowing that categorization is a basic learning principle, you would choose (d) as the correct answer.

5. Look for choices that give complete information. Although incomplete answers may not be false, they do not qualify as acceptable choices. Study this question on rehearsal:

> 4. Which statement gives the best definition of rehearsal?
>> a. Rehearsal is a learning process involving rereading.
>> b. Rehearsal is a learning process involving rewriting.
>> c. Rehearsal is a learning process that helps put information into long-term memory.
>> d. Rehearsal is a learning process that may use all of the senses to place information into long-term memory.

Though choices (a), (b), and (c) are all partially correct, choice (d) is like the main idea for the three preceding choices, so it is the best choice.

6. Read carefully for the terms *not, except,* and *but* in the stem. These words change completely the meaning of the question. If you skip over these terms, you may know the answer yet still choose incorrectly. Consider the following question on rehearsal:

> 5. As a learning process, rehearsal includes all of the following activities except:
>> a. rereading
>> b. reciting

c. discussion
d. reading

Note how the word *except* reverses the question, asking you to choose the activity that does not involve rehearsal. Choice (d) is that activity. If you had overlooked *except,* you could have chosen (a), (b), or (c)—all acceptable rehearsal activities.

7. Be careful to read all of the choices, especially those that say "all of these," "both (a) and (b)," or "none of these." Instructors who carefully design multiple-choice questions often make "all of these" or "both (a) and (b)" correct choices. "None of these" frequently serves as a filler choice, when the test maker has run out of interesting choices. Look at the following question on neural traces and see how the option "both (a) and (b)" is thoughtfully designed as the correct choice:

6. A neural trace is:

    a. a mark on the cerebrum
    b. also called a memory groove
    c. only induced by drugs
    d. both (a) and (b)

Had you not read all of the choices, you could have marked (a) as the correct choice.

8. With multiple-choice questions, make educated guesses. If you can eliminate two of the four choices, you have a 50 percent chance of choosing the correct answer. Be sure that your instructor or the test does not penalize you for guessing. Some standardized tests do. Even if there is a guessing penalty, if you have narrowed your choices down to two, make an educated guess. If you cannot eliminate two or more of the choices, don't spend too much time on that particular question. If there is no guessing penalty, make your choice quickly, and move on to the next question. If there is a guessing penalty and you cannot narrow your choices down to two, leave that answer blank.

Many instructors criticize multiple-choice exams, saying that the best indicator of what a student knows is an essay exam. Although this is a valid objection, multiple-choice questions are the most frequently used type of objective question on standardized tests. You will be taking such tests in your college career, so you need to design an efficient strategy for taking them.

How to Answer True-False Questions

True-false questions are also popular on objective exams. Unlike multiple-choice questions, which may have up to five choices, true-false questions have only two. Your chance of being correct is always 50 percent. Instructors emphasize details when they design true-false questions; so when you study for a true-false test, you need to look carefully at the details.

Hints on Taking True-False Exams.   Here are some strategies to follow when taking a true-false test:

1. For a statement to be true, each part must be true. One detail in the statement can make the entire statement false. When you read a true-false statement, look for the following: the "who," the "what," the "why," the "when," the "where," and the "how much." The answer to each of these questions must be correct for you to mark the entire statement true. Look at the following true-false question on Jean Piaget, and see if it correctly answers the "who," the "what," and the "when":

   Jean Piaget made some revolutionary discoveries about child behavior during the nineteenth century.

   The "who" (Jean Piaget) and the "what" (child behavior) are correct, but the "when" is not. Piaget did his research during the twentieth century.
   Study the key parts of this statement on the Los Angeles School District:

   With 48 percent of its 490,000 students Latin speakers, the Los Angeles School District continued to search for competent bilingual teachers in 1987.

   With this question, the "who," the "what," and the "when" are correct. The Los Angeles School District was concerned with hiring more bilingual teachers in 1987. But the "how many" is incorrect; the correct enrollment for this school district in 1987 was 590,000. Because this one bit of information is incorrect, you must mark the entire question incorrect.

2. Like multiple-choice questions, true-false questions also may use qualifiers such as *never, always,* and *only.* These qualifiers frequently make the statements false. On the other hand, less definite qualifiers such as *often, may, many, most, frequently,* and *usually* tend to make the statement true. Read the following true-false statement on association:

   The memory technique of association is always used when you learn a new word.

   Although association is successfully used in vocabulary learning, it is not always used. The word *always* makes this statement false. If you can think of one case in which the statement is untrue, then the statement is false. But see how a less inclusive qualifier can make the same statement true:

The memory principle of association is often used when a student learns new words.

The word *often* allows for the statement to have some exceptions. Because of the flexibility that *often* gives this statement, you can mark this statement true.

3. In designing true-false questions, instructors frequently match terms with inappropriate definitions. So in preparing for a true-false test, be sure that you know your definitions and your people. Read this example on categorization:

Categorization involves placing a word in several contexts in order to remember it. Association, not categorization, is the process of placing a word in several contexts. The test maker consciously exchanged *association* with *categorization*. If you did not know the meaning of both words, you may not have chosen the correct answer.

How to Answer Matching Questions

Of the three kinds of examination questions, matching questions are the hardest to answer correctly by guessing. In answering matching questions, you need to know the information very well. In the matching format, you are given a list of words in one column and a list of explanations of these words in a second column, often to the right of the first list. It is your job to match correctly the word with the explanation.

Hints on Taking Matching Exams.   Consider the following strategies for taking a matching test:

1. Look at both columns before you begin answering. Are there terms in one column and definitions in another? People in one column and descriptions of them in another? People in the left column and quotations in the right column? What pattern do you detect in the following example from learning theory?

1. neural trace	a. a process of placing information into several contexts to ensure retention
2. rehearsal	b. a process of transferring information from short-term memory to long-term memory
3. association	c. a physiological mark on the cerebrum storing a bit of information

In this set, terms are on the left, definitions on the right.

2. With each correct match, cross out the term and the explanation of it (if your instructor does not plan to reuse the test). In this way, you save time by not rereading material that you have already treated. Look at how crossing out is used for the following matching questions.

___c___ 1. ~~neural trace~~	a. a process of placing information into several contexts to ensure retention
_____ 2. rehearsal	b. a process of transferring information from short-term memory to long-term memory
_____ 3. association	c. ~~a physiological mark on the cerebrum storing a bit of information~~

3. In the information in the right-hand column is lengthy, begin reading in this column first. Read the explanation; then match it with the appropriate term. In this way, you save time by not rereading the lengthy explanations.[2]

How to Take Objective Tests

Here are some strategies to use when you are taking an objective test.

1. Read over all of the directions carefully. Know what you need to do.

2. Plan your time. If your test has three parts—true-false, multiple-choice, and matching—divide your exam hour into equal time allotments. Check your watch so that you do not stay on any one section of the exam for too long.

3. Read through the questions quickly to determine the difficulty level of the exam.

4. Answer the easiest sections first. Since you have a better chance of getting the easier questions right, do not wait until the end of the hour to answer them.

5. Do not spend too much time on any one question. If you are unsure about an answer, make an educated guess. Then place a mark to the left of the question so that if you have time, you can go back to it.

6. Check your numbering so that the number on your answer sheet corresponds to the number on your exam booklet. Students often place a correct answer on the wrong number of their answer grid and get the question wrong.

---

[2] James Shepherd, *RSVP: The Houghton Mifflin Reading, Study, and Vocabulary Program* (Boston: Houghton Mifflin, 1981), p. 321.

7. If possible, leave five to ten minutes at the end of the exam to review your answers. Check for carelessness. Change only those answers you are reasonably sure are incorrect. Do not change a guess; more often the guess is correct and the correction is not.

Summary

There are three major types of objective tests: multiple-choice, true-false, and matching. Each type of question requires a different strategy. The multiple-choice question is the most commonly used objective question. With multiple-choice and true-false questions, you can make educated guesses; matching questions, on the other hand, leave little room for guesswork. With matching questions, you need to know names and definitions well.

Multiple-choice questions are frequently used on entrance and professional exams. So it is important to develop a successful strategy in answering them.

Summary Box   *Objective Tests*

What are they?	How do you take them?
Examinations, frequently machine scored, that test the breadth of your knowledge on a subject. The three most common types are multiple-choice, true-false, and matching.	Multiple-choice: learn to eliminate incorrect answers; cross them out, and consider other choices. True-False: look for statements that are absolute; they are frequently false. Matching: see how the columns are organized; with each match that you make, cross out the statement in one column and the name or term in the other.

Skills Practice

Exercise 14.1
Answering
Multiple-Choice
Questions

Read the following textbook excerpt about the incest taboos. Underline important points and make marginal comments. After reading, recite either by taking notes or by making a study map. When you think you know the material, answer the five multiple-choice questions that follow. Before you answer these questions, you may want to refer to pp. 249–252 in the introduction, which deal with strategies to use when answering multiple-choice questions.

Marriage Rules: Incest Taboos

Every society has rules about mating. In all societies, there are some prohibitions on mating between persons in certain relationships or from certain social groups. The most universal prohibition is that on mating among certain kinds of kin: mother-son, father-daughter, and sister-brother. The taboos on mating between kin always extend beyond this immediate family group, however. In our own society, the taboo extends to the children of our parents' siblings (in our kinship terminology called first cousins); in other societies, individuals are not permitted to mate with others who may be related up to the fifth generation. These prohibitions on mating (that is, sexual relations) between relatives or people classified as relatives are called **incest taboos**.

Because sexual access is one of the most important rights conferred by marriage, incest taboos effectively prohibit marriage as well as mating among certain kin. The outstanding exception to the almost universal taboo on mating and marriage among members of the nuclear family are those cases of brother-sister marriage among royalty in ancient Egypt, in traditional Hawaiian society, and among Inca royalty in Peru. Incest taboos have always been of interest to anthropologists, who have attempted to explain their origin and persistence in human society, particularly as they apply to primary (or nuclear) family relationships. Many theories have been advanced, and we will look here at four major ones.

Inbreeding Avoidance   The inbreeding avoidance theory holds that mating between close kin produces deficient, weak children and is genetically harmful to the species. The incest taboo is therefore adaptive because it limits inbreeding. This theory, proposed in the late nineteenth century, was later rejected for a number of decades on the ground that inbreeding could produce advantages as well as disadvantages for the group, by bringing out recessive genes of both a superior and an inferior character. Recent work in population genetics has given more weight to the older view that inbreeding *is* usually harmful to a human population. The proportion of negative recessive traits to adaptive recessive ones is very high, and in the human animal, inbreeding has definite disadvantages. Furthermore, these disadvantages are far more likely to appear as a result of the mating of primary relatives (mother-son, father-daughter, sister-brother) than of other relatives, even first cousins. It would seem, then, that the biological adaptiveness of the incest taboo as it applies to the nuclear family must be considered in explaining both its origins and its persistence.

The question raised here, of course, is how prescientific peoples could understand the connection between close inbreeding and the biological disadvantages that result. But the adaptive results of the incest taboo need not have been consciously recognized in order to persist; rather, groups that had such a taboo would have had more surviving children than groups without the taboo. This reproductive advantage would eventually account for its universality as groups without the taboo died out.[3]

Directions: Choose the correct letter to answer the following questions. Place all answers in the answer box.

1. Which of the following is not an example of the incest taboo?

   a. mother mating with son
   b. brother mating with sister
   c. close friends mating with each other
   d. father mating with daughter

2. Exceptions to the incest taboo have sometimes been allowed with:

   a. the lower class
   b. royal families
   c. the middle class
   d. all of these

3. The inbreeding avoidance theory suggests that incest leads to:

   a. miscarriages
   b. marital problems
   c. genetically weak children
   d. none of these

4. Recent research in genetics has:

   a. rejected the inbreeding avoidance theory
   b. supported the inbreeding avoidance theory
   c. neither supported nor rejected the inbreeding avoidance theory
   d. questioned the need for the incest taboo

5. Anthropologists believe that the incest taboo evolved in prescientific cultures because:

   a. of their strong religious beliefs
   b. of their rigid family structure
   c. ancient cultures passed on all of their traditions from one generation to the next
   d. those who ignored it died out

1. _____

2. _____

3. _____

4. _____

5. _____

80%

(Score = # correct × 20)
Find answers on p. 329.

Exercise 14.2
Answering
True-False
Questions

Read the following textbook excerpt on the sun. Underline the important points and make marginal comments. After reading, recite either by outlining or by making a study map. When you think that you have learned the information, answer the five true-false questions

[3] Serena Nanda, *Cultural Anthropology*, 3rd ed. (Belmont, Calif.: Wadsworth, 1987), pp. 205–206. Used by permission.

that follow. You may want to refer to pp. 252–254 of the introduction, which present strategies to use in answering true-false questions. Remember that true-false questions often test your knowledge of details.

The Sun: Source of Energy for Life on Earth

Just as an economy runs on money, the ecosphere runs on energy. *The source of the radiant energy that sustains all life on Earth is the sun.* It warms the Earth and provides energy for the photosynthesis in green plants. These plants, in turn, synthesize the carbon compounds that keep them alive and that serve as food for almost all other organisms. Solar energy also powers the water cycle, which purifies and removes salt from ocean water to provide the fresh water upon which land life depends.

The sun is a medium-sized star composed mostly of hydrogen. At its center, the sun is so hot that a pinhead of its material could kill a person over 161 kilometers (100 miles) away. Under the conditions of extremely high temperatures and pressures found in the interior of the sun, light nuclei of hydrogen atoms are fused together to form slightly heavier nuclei of helium atoms. In this process of *nuclear fusion* some of the mass of the hydrogen nuclei is converted into energy.

Thus, the sun is a giant *nuclear-fusion reactor* 150 million kilometers (93 million miles) away from the Earth. Every second, the sun converts about 3.7 billion kilograms (4.1 billion tons) of its total mass into energy. Nevertheless, we need not worry about the sun running out of energy. It has probably been in existence for 6 billion years and estimates are that it has enough hydrogen left to keep going for at least another 8 billion years.[4]

Directions: Read the following statements. Write A for true and B for false. Place all answers in the answer box.

1. The major element that makes up the sun is nitrogen.
2. In the sun's middle, the heat transforms lighter helium to heavier hydrogen.
3. The sun is 140 kilometers (92 million miles) away from the earth.
4. The sun has been called a giant nuclear-fission reactor.
5. The sun was created 8 billion years ago and will not die for another 6 billion years.

1. _____
2. _____
3. _____
4. _____
5. _____

____

80%

Ask instructor for answers.

____

[4] G. Tyler Miller, Jr., *Living in the Environment,* 4th ed. (Belmont, Calif.: Wadsworth, 1985), p. 32. Used by permission.

Exercise 14.3
Answering Matching
Questions

Read the following excerpt, which defines musical terms. Underline important points and make marginal comments. After reading, recite either by outlining or by making a study map. When you think that you know the material, answer the five matching questions that follow. You may want to refer to pp. 254–255 of the introduction, which present strategies to use in answering matching questions.

Musical Terminology

Certain musical terms are basic to an understanding of music literature. The first term to learn is *music,* which is defined as a combination of sounds that are organized and meaningful, occurring in a prescribed span of time and usually having pitch. In the definition of music is another term, *pitch,* which is defined as the degree of highness or lowness of a sound. Related to pitch is *interval.* Interval is defined as the distance between two pitches. The most fundamental interval is an *octave.* Finally, *melody* is defined as pitches sounded one after another, presented in a logical series that forms a satisfying musical unit.[5]

Directions: Match the letter of column B with the appropriate number in column A. Place all answers in the answer box.

Column A	Column B
1. octave	a. a combination of pitches forming a pleasing unit
2. pitch	b. a combination of organized sounds that happen in time and usually have pitch
3. melody	c. the distance between two pitches
4. interval	d. the highness or lowness of a sound
5. music	e. the most fundamental interval

1. _____

2. _____

3. _____

4. _____

5. _____

_____
80%

(Score = # correct ×
20)
Find answers on p.
329.

---

[5] Adapted from Charles Hoffer, *The Understanding of Music,* 5th ed. (Belmont, Calif.: Wadsworth, 1985), pp. 22–24. Used by permission.

15

Examination Strategies: Essay Tests and Math or Science Tests

Explanation of Skills

Essay exams are different in many ways from objective tests. Unlike objective tests, which ask you to remember many details, essay exams make you choose main ideas and major details from a large body of material and then form an organized response. When you are writing an essay exam, you need to recall main ideas and major details quickly. Problem-solving questions in math and the sciences are similar to essay questions. The major difference is that instead of using words, you are using numbers and symbols. In both an essay exam and a math or science problem, you need to use skills in logic and organization. Unlike objective exams, the best essay and math or science exams ask you to generate important information yourself.

How to Prepare for an Essay Exam

When preparing for an essay exam, you again need to review your textbook underlinings, textbook comments, study reading notes, lecture notes, and study maps. (See the section in Chapter 14 titled "How to Prepare for Objective Tests.") Instead of trying to remember many details as you would in preparing for an objective test, on an essay exam, you need to concentrate on significant main ideas and details of support. Your job is to reduce much information into its significant points. This may not be easy for you at first.

If your instructor has provided you with several possible essay topics, find information in your study material to answer them. If your instructor does not provide you with questions, check to see whether there are discussion questions at the end of your textbook chapters. Find the ones that you think are most important, then locate information that would best treat each question. As you study, you

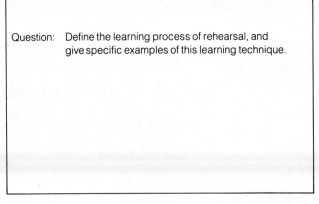

Front Side

Figure 15-1   *Front of study card with essay question.*

should formulate your own essay questions from topics that you think are important. You can often design your own essay questions from the divisions and subdivisions of your textbook chapters or from the lecture titles in your syllabus or lecture notes.

After you have reviewed your notes and underlinings, write the three or four most likely essay topics on a separate sheet of paper or on the blank side of 5 × 8 notecards. These sheets and cards are similar to those mentioned in Chapter 14 on preparing for an objective exam. On the back side of the paper or the lined side of the card, answer the question, giving pertinent main ideas and major details. Use a numeral-letter or indenting format. Don't write this information in paragraph form at this time. Save your more thorough sentence writing for the essay exam itself. The cards or sheets of paper should look something like what is shown in Figures 15-1 and 15-2.

```
Rehearsal

    Def:   the active use of the senses to place information
              into long-term memory

    Specific expls:

            rereading—of sig info in your text (seeing)
            writing—making study sheets or maps in the forms of
                     summaries (touching)
            discussion—verbal exchange w yourself or in a disc
                       grp to put info into your own wds (hearing)
```

Back Side

Figure 15-2   *Back of study card, answering the question.*

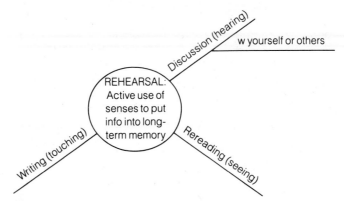

Figure 15-3   *Study map showing answer to essay question.*

Once you have completed the study sheets or cards, turn each over to the question side to see if you can orally respond to the question. See if you can quickly remember the main idea and the necessary supporting details. If it is hard for you to remember the supporting details, use a memory aid. RWD is an abbreviation that you could design to remember rereading, writing, and discussion—the details for the essay question in Figure 15-3. Review these cards or sheets until your response to each question is fast. A key to doing well on an essay exam is your being able to recall main ideas and accurate details with ease.

Study maps are also good tools to use when you study for essay tests. Figure 15-3 shows how the information on rehearsal can be neatly arranged into a study map.

How to Read an Essay Question

Having studied well for your essay test, you are now ready for the questions. Understanding the intent of the question is as important as being prepared for the exam. Study the following key terms, which are commonly used in essay questions, and learn how they are used.

Words That Ask for Retelling of Material

summarize, survey, list, outline

If these words appear in your question, you are being asked to give only the important points. You should not concentrate on many details or on analyzing any one point in depth.

Example Question: List the major stages in the development of the human fetus.

To answer this question well, you should list each step in the fetal development of the child. You should then briefly comment on each stage, but you do not need to discuss the relationship of one stage to another or the importance of any of these stages.

Words That Ask You to Make Inferences

discuss, explain

These are two of the most frequently used words in essay questions. They ask you to give the "why" of an argument. You must carefully choose those details that clarify your main idea.

Example Question: Discuss four reasons for the entry of the United States into World War II.

In this question, you need to choose those examples that account for the United States's entry into World War II. These reasons are often your own, so be sure to include terms of qualification when you are presenting opinions—words such as *may, might, likely, it is suggested,* and so on. See p. 78 for a more thorough list of qualifiers.

A Word That Asks You to Define

define

Define usually asks you for a short answer. You are not asked to analyze, just to give the term's major characteristics. Just as a dictionary definition is concise, so should your response be concise.

Example Question: Define prejudice as used in sociology.

Here you are being asked to explain prejudice from a sociological perspective. You are not being asked to list its various meanings or to explain its history. Your focus should be on how prejudice relates to sociology.

Words Showing Similarities and Differences

compare, contrast

Compare means to show both similarities and differences. To avoid confusion, some instructors use the phrase "compare and contrast." *Contrast* used singly means to show differences. With contrast questions, you are treating opposite sets of information, so use transitions of contrast: *similarly, oppositely, conversely,* and so on. With strict comparison questions, you are treating similar sets of information; here, use transitions of similarity such as *likewise, similarly,* and so on. See pp. 82–83 for a more thorough list of transitions of comparison and contrast.

Example Question: Compare and contrast the attitudes of Presidents Reagan and Carter regarding social welfare programs.

In this question, you need to cite programs and legislation from both administrations that show similarities and differences.

Words That Ask You to Critique

analyze, examine, evaluate

Questions using these words are asking you to express a point of view. When you evaluate, you must even judge the merit of your topic. The details you choose are important because they present the bulk of your argument. Critique words are often used in essay questions in the humanities—literature, art, music, film—where you are asked to judge the value of a poem, a painting, or a film. These questions can be difficult because you are being asked to do more than summarize.

Example Question: Analyze the major characters in Dickens's *Great Expectations.* Are these characters successful?

This question is asking you to choose characters in the novel whose actions and traits make them believable. Ultimately, you are judging the success of Dickens's characters. So you need to choose carefully those details that demonstrate Dickens's success or failure in rendering character.

A Word That Asks You to Take a Stand

defend

Defend is often used in speech topics or in essay questions in political science or history. With defend questions, you take a definite stand, only presenting evidence that supports this position. In this sense, defend questions ask you to ignore evidence that goes against your position.

Example Question: Defend the premise that nuclear arms will one day lead to nuclear holocaust.

In answering this question, you should discuss only how nuclear arms are a threat to peace. If you suggested that nuclear arms are a deterrent to war, you would weaken your argument.

A Word That Shows Connections

trace

Trace is mainly used in history essay questions where you are asked to discuss a series of events and show their relationship to one other. Again, you need to be selective in choosing details that support the connections you see.

Example Question: Trace the development of labor unions in the United States from 1900 to the present.

In this question, you need to choose the important figures and events that led to the formation of unions in the United States; you also need to show how events or individuals influenced other events or individuals.

Words That Ask for Important Information

significant, critical, key, important, major

In most subjects, instructors use these words to guide you in presenting only meaningful evidence. These terms subtly ask you to distinguish the significant from the insignificant. An instructor using these words will often criticize your essay if you fail to choose the important evidence.

Example Question: Discuss three key factors that led to the Great Depression in the United States.

Your instructor may have discussed ten factors, but you are asked to discuss only three. Here, you need to review the ten factors to determine which three have priority. This is difficult to do because you are both summarizing and evaluating information.

Kinds of Essay Questions

There are three basic types of essay questions used on exams: those that ask for the short answer, the short essay, or the extended essay. Each type asks you to use a different strategy.

The Short-Answer Question. In the short-answer question, you are asked to respond to a question in a phrase, a sentence, or several sentences. In a one-hour exam, you can expect to answer up to twenty short-answer questions. The key to doing well on these questions is to be as concise and specific as you can. In biology and geology courses using short-answer questions, instructors are often looking for the breadth and accuracy of your knowledge, not your writing style. Ask your instructor whether you need to answer the short-answer question in sentences. If the answer is no, answer in phrases; you will be able to write more during the hour. In contrast, in an English course, your instructor will likely want you to answer the short-answer questions in complete sentences that are correctly punctuated.

Look at the following short-answer question and study the response that received full credit.

Question: Name and identify the three branches of the federal government.
Answer:

1. legislative: makes laws; made up of House and Senate
2. executive: sees that laws are carried out; president
3. judicial: sees that laws are enforced; Supreme Court and other federal courts

This student has presented accurate information in an organized way. Beside each government branch, the student describes the activity, then names the person or agency responsible.

Now see how this same question is answered poorly.

Question: Name and identify the three branches of the government.
Answer:

1. legislative: works on laws; made up of two houses
2. executive: the president
3. judicial: courts

This student has not presented the information in an organized way or with enough detail. Although the student names the legislative branch, "works on laws" is vague. With the executive branch, the student names the president but does not describe the function. With the judicial branch, the Supreme Court is not specifically named, nor does the student mention the Court's function.

The Short-Essay Question. The short-essay question asks you to write an organized paragraph of several sentences. In an hour, you should be able to answer up to five such questions. Your strategy when writing the short-answer question is to present your main idea or thesis right away, then present accurate details of support. These details must follow logically from your main idea. If you have completed the writing assignments in this book, you are familiar with how a convincing paragraph is put together.

Read the following short-essay question and the response that received full credit.

Question: Discuss the three major characteristics of human language.
Answer:

> Human language has three qualities that distinguish it from animal communication. First, human language uses a limited number of sounds that produce thousands of utterances. Second, human speech is not imitative. The human being can generate a sentence never heard before. Finally, human language can discuss what is not there. Human beings can discuss the past and future as well as the present.

Do you see how the student directly addresses the question? The main-idea sentence comes first, stating that there are three characteristics of human language. Then the sentences of support discuss these characteristics. The student has used the transitions "first, second, and finally" to direct the reader to these three characteristics.

Now consider this second response, which is both poorly organized and less detailed.

Question: Discuss the three major characteristics of human language.
Answer:

> Human language has three qualities. Human language uses few sounds. Also, human language uses sentences. Humans can also discuss what is not there. Philosophers have spent centuries discussing what language is all about.

Note how the main-idea sentence is too general, so the student makes no attempt to distinguish human language from animal language. Note how the second detail sentence, "Also, human language uses sentences," does not discuss how the human being can generate sentences that have never before been uttered. So this supporting detail does not directly address the uniqueness of human language. Note how the last sentence, "Philosophers have spent centuries discussing what language is all about," introduces an entirely new topic, so the paragraph loses its focus.

The Extended Essay Question.   You will often be asked to write on only one topic during a one-hour exam. Obviously, your instructor is expecting you to write more than one paragraph during this hour. In an hour, you should be able to write several organized paragraphs. This type of essay response is known as the extended essay.

In structure, the extended essay resembles the short essay. The main idea of the paragraph becomes the first paragraph, or introduction, of the extended essay. The detail sentences of the paragraph then each become separate paragraphs. Together, these paragraphs are referred to as the body. Unlike the short essay, the extended essay has a concluding paragraph, called the conclusion, which often summarizes the key points of the essay. Look at Figure 15-4, which shows the structure of the extended essay and states the purpose of its three parts.

The extended essay is difficult to write well at first because you must successfully use several organizational skills. Start by committing the information in Figure 15-4 to memory, so that each essay you write has a recognizable introduction, body, and conclusion. Also, begin using transitions to join sentences and to hook one paragraph to another. By using such transitions as "for example" or "to conclude," you will give additional order to your essay. In Chapter 5 on organizational patterns, there are lists of several transitions that you may want to review and use in your extended essays. Read the following extended essay question and response. See if you can locate the introduction, the body, and the conclusion, and note how transitions are used.

Question: Discuss the three major functions of religion.
Answer:

(1) Every society has a religion of some sort. Although the beliefs and expressions of religion vary from one culture to another, three basic functions of religion emerge when you study all religions. For one, religion helps clarify the unexplained. Second, religion helps reduce anxiety among its followers. Third, religion helps give order to society.

(2) Every culture has tried through religion to answer such questions as where the universe came from and where we go after death.

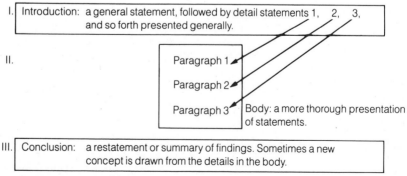

Figure 15-4   *Diagram of an extended essay.*

Western religions explain their origin in the Book of Genesis. In this book, we learn that one God created parts of the universe and the world on separate days. Eastern religions see many gods as creating the universe. Western religions believe that human souls live after death, whereas Eastern religions such as Hinduism believe that human beings are reincarnated into other beings after death.

(3) Prayer seems to be part of all religions. In each culture, prayer seems to relieve anxiety. In many African cultures, tribesmen perform rituals to help crops grow or to cure the sick. Prayer in Western cultures works similarly. Western priests often ask their parishioners to pray for the health of their sick loved ones. In each case, prayer becomes an outlet to relieve anxiety.

(4) Finally, religion has an important ordering effect on society. Religious services almost always accompany births, baptisms, marriages, and deaths. And the faithful are invited to witness these events. Such group activities give to the members of the religion a sense of community. Just think of how many wars have been fought over religious beliefs, and you will realize how closely tied religion is to social structure.

(5) In conclusion, it is clear that religion still plays an important role in human life. Religion has through the ages helped explain the mysteries of the universe, comforted people in their grief, and given to each culture a set of social rules.

Note how paragraph 1 presents the three issues that the essay intends to discuss. Paragraphs 2, 3, and 4 give the necessary support for the main idea that religion is found in every society. Each paragraph in the body centers its discussion on a separate function of religion. Nowhere in these paragraphs does the discussion lose its focus.

Note also the transitions that signal different sections of the essay: "for one," "second," and "third" in paragraph 1, and "in conclusion" in paragraph 5. Finally, note that the conclusion summarizes the major points made in the essay.

If you want to study other acceptable models of the extended essay, read some of the longer passages that come at the end of most exercises in various chapters in this book. These longer passages are often modeled after the extended essay.

Now consider how this same question is answered in a disorganized way. Look at this essay to see what is lacking in the introduction, the body, and the conclusion.

Question: Discuss the three major functions of religion.
Answer:

(1) Religion has been used to explain the unexplainable. Each culture has certain creation myths and beliefs about an afterlife. There are many similar creation myths in Western and Eastern religions.

(2) All cultures seem to pray. Prayers help people's problems. People pray in various ways throughout the world. The end is always the same.

(3) Religion has a purpose in society. Many social functions are somehow related to religion. People get together and feel a bond. That is another important function of religion.

Did you note that this essay has no introduction? If you did not have the question before you, you would not know what question this essay was trying to answer. Further, the evidence is vague. In the body, creation myths are mentioned, but no specific creation myths of East and West are discussed. Similarly, the relationship between social functions and religion is presented, but no rituals such as marriage and funerals are introduced. An instructor evaluating this essay would mark it down for its lack of direction and relevant details.

In the next section of this chapter, you will analyze math and science problems and tests. In studying this section, you will see parallels to what you have just learned about essay tests.

How to Prepare for a Math or Science Test

As in preparing for exams in other courses, for a math or science test you will be studying lecture notes, textbook underlinings and comments, and study notes. The study notes are usually solutions to problems. Before you begin studying for your math or science test, see if your instructor has provided you with some sample problems. Also, be sure you know whether or not the test will be open book or notes.

You should spend a week reviewing all important material. Because the last class session before an exam in math and science courses is usually a review, it would be helpful if you had done most of your studying before this session. In this review session, you will have the opportunity to ask questions that may have come up during your studying.

When you study, spend most of your time reviewing the problems and solutions shown in your textbook, completed in lecture and study notes, and done as homework. Trace the logic used to solve each problem. While you are reviewing, use note cards to write down important theorems, laws, formulas, and equations. Know these cards well because you will probably need to recall this information quickly on the exam.

Look at the sample study card in Figure 15-5 from a chemistry study review. Note that the name of the formula is listed on the blank side, and the formula itself and a sample solution using the formula is on the lined side. Using the blank side of the card, you can test yourself to see whether you can recall the variables of the formula.

When it is possible to design a study map of math and science information, do so. Since math and science courses build from one lecture to another, seeing connections among units is most helpful; study maps often help you see these connections more easily. Figure

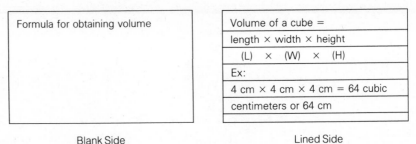

Volume of a cube =
length × width × height
(L)   ×   (W)   ×   (H)
Ex:
4 cm × 4 cm × 4 cm = 64 cubic
centimeters or 64 cm

Formula for obtaining volume

Blank Side   Lined Side

Figure 15-5   *Study card from a chemistry study review.*

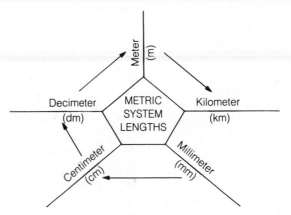

Figure 15-6   *Study map of the metric system.*

15-6 shows how the metric system is presented via a study map. In this map, the units of measure become progressively larger as your eyes move clockwise.

Once you have made these study cards and study maps, choose three to five problems that you have never done and that will likely be on your test. Complete each problem, and time yourself. If you have difficulty moving from one step to another, try to figure out your confusion. Go back to your notes and textbook.

If your instructor allows crib notes, or notes that list certain formulas and rules, write these out neatly. But do not use these notes as a crutch. Crib notes should be used when you need to use a formula or theorem that is hard to remember.

The night before the exam, do not cram. Just go over your study cards and maps.

The Math or Science Test

Instructors in math or science generally score an exam by looking at the steps that you used to arrive at a solution. They are often more interested in the way you solved the problem than in the correct answer.

Before you start solving a problem on your test, be sure you know what is being asked of you. The two most commonly used words on math and science tests are *solve* and *prove*. Both words ask you to present the logic of your solution, not just give an answer. Look at the following question on the metric system and its solution.

Question: How many kilograms are there in 2543 grams?

Solution	*Vague Solution*

1. 1 kg = 1000 grams

$$\frac{2543}{1000} = 2.543$$

2. $kg = \dfrac{g}{1000}$

3. $kg = \dfrac{2543}{1000}$

4. kg = 2.543

5. 2.543 kg

Do you see how you can easily follow the pattern of thought in the first solution? Step 1 shows the conversion, step 2 the formula, and steps 3 and 4 the procedures used to solve the equation. The second answer does not present any of these steps and so does not explain why 1000 is to be divided into 2543.

Hints to Use in Solving Math or Science Problems

Use these steps to solve math or science problems on homework or on exams.

1. Read the question carefully. Determine the unknown. If you have to, write out the unknown in the margin. In the previous solution, kg is the unknown.

2. Reread the question to determine the known quantities. In the previous solution, 2543 grams is the known. You may want to write out the known in the margin as well.

3. Then ask what the problem is asking you to do.

4. Write out the formulas or equations you need to solve the problem. In the example, the needed formula is 1000 g = 1 kg. Then, plug your knowns into the formula, and solve for the unknown.

5. When you get an answer, check it by rereading the question. Is it reasonable? In the example, 254,430 kg would be illogical because you know that kilograms are heavier than grams. You can often spot a simple computational error, such as multiplying when you should have divided, by rereading the question with your answer in mind.

6. If you cannot solve the problem, list the formulas that you know can be used to solve it. Most instructors give partial credit.

Hints in Taking Math, Science, or Essay Tests

Here are some tips in taking all the kinds of examinations discussed in this chapter.

1. Read the directions carefully. Know how many questions you have to answer and the point value assigned to each question.

2. Read through each question, underlining key words such as *analyze, solve,* or *major.*

3. Answer the easiest questions first.

4. Jot down a brief outline of what you intend to say for each question or a list of equations you need to use in solving each problem. With these phrases and formulas, you will be able to structure your answers. They will also help you if during the exam you draw a momentary blank.

5. Plan your time wisely. If you are to answer two essay questions or two problems during the hour, be sure to start the second question or problem halfway through the hour.

6. When writing the essay or solving the problem, use only one side of the paper and leave margins, so if you want to add information, you can put it either in the margins or on the back side of the paper.

7. If you are pressed for time, list the equations that you intended to use or an outline of the rest of your answer. You will likely get partial credit by including these abbreviated responses.

8. Save at least five minutes at the end of the exam time to review for errors in computation or in spelling, punctuation, and diction.

9. With essay exams, do not expect to write the perfect essay. Your goal is to present accurate information in an organized way.

Summary

Different from objective tests, essay tests ask you to present the important points of what you have studied in an organized way. Unlike objective exams, which ask you to remember many details, essay tests ask you to reduce what you have learned to its essentials. This process of evaluating all that you have studied to find the significant points may be difficult at first. The three most commonly used essay exams are: the short-answer exam, the short-essay exam, and the extended essay exam.

Math and science questions are like essay questions; for both, you must present information in a logical way. In place of words, math and science tests use numbers and symbols. Instructors are often looking not just for the correct answer but for how you arrived at your answer.

Developing effective writing skills and knowing how to solve math and science problems are skills that employers are coming to value more and more. Two of your more important goals in college should therefore be to develop efficient writing and problem-solving skills.

Summary Box   *Essay Exams and Math or Science Exams*

What are they?	*How do you do well on them?*
Essay: exams that ask for orga- nized responses on material that you have studied. They can be short answer, short essay, or extended essay.	By reducing information to its essentials. By presenting accurate informa- tion in an organized way.
Math or science: exams that ask you to use numbers and sym- bols to solve a problem in a logical way.	By determining known and un- known quantities. By choosing correct formulas. By showing the steps that you used to arrive at you answer.

Skills Practice

Exercise 15.1
Answering Short-
Essay Questions

Read the following excerpt on China. Underline the important points, and make marginal comments. After reading, recite what you have learned either by taking notes or by creating a study map. When you think that you know the information well, answer the essay question that follows. You may want to reread pp. 267–268 in the introduction on the short essay.

The People's Republic of China

On October 1, 1949, **Mao Tse-tung*** (1884–1976) announced to the Chinese people that Chiang Kai-shek's armies were defeated. The Chinese people call this day a day of liberation, and today when they talk of history they speak of "before liberation" and "after liberation." They have good reason.

---

* The spelling of Mao Tse-tung is from the Wade-Giles system. At the start of 1979, the Chinese officially adopted a new system called the "Pinyin" (phonetic) system which more closely approximates Chinese pronunciation. Under the Pinyin system, Mao Tse-tung becomes Mao Zedong; Peking becomes Beijing; Teng Hsaio-ping becomes Deng Xiaoping, and so forth. We'll stick with the older, Wade-Giles system on the theory that it is still more familiar to most readers.

Before and After Liberation

Before liberation, people died in the streets on cold nights. An American newspaper in Shanghai ran an article in early 1949 stating that eighty corpses had been found in the morning after a cold wind the night before. Young girls were forced to become prostitutes. Drug addiction from opium was widespread. Rich peasants charged 100 percent interest every six months on loans to tenant farmers. Taxes were repeatedly collected by warlords until the people were paying taxes a year in advance. Large cities like Canton, Nanking, Peking, and Shanghai were divided up into walled "concessions" owned by foreign companies or governments. In one such concession in Shanghai there was a park with a sign that read NO CHINESE OR DOGS ALLOWED.

People were often treated like beasts of burden, forced to work in the factories and fields from the age of seven. Work was long, averaging twelve hours a day, and wages were barely sufficient to maintain life. Workers and peasants were so poor they could not maintain their families and often sold their babies into slavery for a few pennies. No wonder the Chinese were ready to overthrow their economic system.

Today, the Chinese economy is growing rapidly. Despite the fact that there are tremendous masses of people—more than four times the number in the United States in a country only 2.5 percent larger geographically—all receive, at minimum, a subsistence diet; all have a place to live, adequate clothing, medical care, and free education. Illiteracy, starvation, prostitution, sexually transmitted disease, and drug addiction have, with some exceptions, been reduced or eliminated. Cities are clean. Flies, mosquitoes, and other common pests have almost disappeared. A near-miracle seems to have occurred. How has this come about?[1]

Essay Question: The author asserts that China today is a much better place than it was in 1949 under Chiang Kai-shek. To support this point of view, describe China "before liberation" and China "after liberation." Cite at least three details portraying China before liberation and at least three details of China after liberation.

80%

(Score = number correct × 10)
Find answers on pp. 329–330.

---

[1] Philip C. Starr, *Economics: Principles in Action*, 4th ed. (Belmont, Calif.: Wadsworth, 1984), p. 48. Used by permission.

Exercise 15.2
Answering
Problem-Solving
Questions

Read the following excerpt on the metric system. Underline the important points, and make marginal comments. After reading, recite what you have learned either by taking notes or by creating a study map. When you think that you know the information well, solve the following problem. You may want to refer to pp. 273–274 in the introduction, which discuss strategies to use in solving math or science problems.

Metric (SI) Prefixes

Values of measurements can be expressed in the fundamental metric or SI units such as meters, kilograms, and seconds. They can also be expressed in larger or smaller units by multiplying the fundamental unit by 10 or some multiple of 10, such as 1000 (or 10^3) or 0.001 (10^{-3}) (see Table 2-2). Note that any multiple of 10 can be expressed as a positive power of 10 such as 10^3 and 10^6 or a negative power of 10 such as 10^{-3} and 10^{-6}. The power to which 10 is raised is called an **exponent** and numbers such as 10^3, 10^{-6}, and 8.2×10^4 are called **exponential numbers.**

In the metric or SI system, prefixes are used to indicate how many times the base unit is to be multiplied or divided by 10 to form larger or smaller units. The SI prefixes most commonly used in introductory chemistry are given in Table 2-2.

In the metric or SI system, units are based on 10, and prefixes are used to indicate how many times a base unit is to be multiplied or divided by 10 to form larger or smaller units.

Table 2-2 *Commonly Used Prefixes and Multiplier Factors for the Metric System*

Prefix	Abbreviation	Multiply Base Unit By
kilo	k	10^3 or 1,000
deci	d	10^{-1} or 0.1
centi	c	10^{-2} or 0.01
milli	m	10^{-3} or 0.001
micro	μ	10^{-6} or 0.000001

Table 2-3 *Metric Prefixes and Units for Length and Mass*

Length	Mass
1 km (kilometer) = 1,000 m (meters)	1 kg (kilogram) = 1,000 g (grams)
1 dm (decimeter) = 0.1 m (meter)	1 dg (decigram) = 0.1 g (gram)
1 cm (centimeter) = 0.01 m (meter)	1 cg (centigram) = 0.01 g (gram)
1 mm (millimeter) = 0.001 m (meter)	1 mg (milligram) = 0.001 g (gram)
1 μm (micrometer) = 0.000001 m (meter)	1 μg (microgram) = 0.000001 g (gram)

Table 2-3 summarizes the use of these prefixes for units of length and mass. The values in metric units for some common objects are

width of home movie film = 8 mm

average ski length = 1.60 m to 1.80 m, or 160 cm to 180 cm

mass of a new nickel = 5 g

mass of a 150-lb human = 68.2 kg[2]

Problem: How many millimeters are there in 27.5 kilometers? In arriving at a solution, show all of your work. List the known quantity, the unknown quantity, and the conversion formulas.

75%

Ask instructor for answer.

---

[2] Miller, *Chemistry*, pp. 35–36. Used by permission.

Applying SQ3R to Text Excerpts

The following three reading selections are all excerpts from college textbooks. In each selection, you will be applying all of the skills that you have studied in previous parts. If you do well on the examinations to these three selections, you should be adequately prepared to do well in most college courses.

Study Reading 1

Global Patterns of Climate

Vocabulary (Words Not Defined in This Excerpt)

topography: the surface features of a region including hills, valleys, lakes, rivers, canals, bridges, roads, etc.

This excerpt from an environmental science text discusses weather and those variables in nature that influence it. This excerpt relies on three basic organizational patterns: definition, cause-effect, and spatial geographic. Read over the following strategies; they should help you learn this information more easily.

1. Read over the definitions carefully. Mark the key words and phrases that explain these terms. Since there are many definitions in this excerpt and since they are critical to understanding the physical laws related to weather and climate, concentrate on learning these words and on seeing how the various terms relate to each other.

2. Study the cause-effect statements carefully. Many of them relate to the effect of warm and cold winds or fronts on the weather. Be sure you can identify both cause and effect. If you do not remember the characteristics of the cause-effect pattern, refer to pp. 77–78.

3. Much of what is said in this excerpt can be visualized. Study the two illustrations carefully; also, when wind and precipitation movements are described, use your spatial geographic abilities to

visualize these processes. If you do not remember the spatial geographic pattern, refer to pages 80–81.

4. Because of this excerpt's reliance on the cause-effect and spatial geographic structures, you can best remember much of this information by designing study maps that illustrate various natural processes of weather and climate. When you are reviewing the material, you may want to design a few study maps.

5. Before you take the quiz on this excerpt, you should not only know the meanings of the key terms but also be able to explain the important cause-effect patterns that underlie the physical processes involved in weather and climate.

A. Survey

Take three minutes to survey this chapter excerpt. Read the title of the excerpt, the titles of the various sections, and any terms that are highlighted. Also, study the two illustrations to see how they relate to the excerpt. Finally, if time permits, read through the first and last paragraph of the excerpt to get a sense of its style and level of difficulty.

When you have finished with your survey, answer the following questions without looking back at the excerpt. Place all of your answers in the answer box.

Global Patterns of Climate

G. Tyler Miller, Jr.

Weather and Climate

(1) **Weather** is the day-to-day variation in atmospheric conditions, such as temperature, moisture (including precipitation and humidity), sunshine (solar electromagnetic radiation), and wind. When the atmosphere thins to nothing, as on the moon or in space, there is no weather. **Climate** is the generalized weather at a given place on Earth over a fairly long period of time such as a season, 1 year, or 30 years. Climate involves seasonal and annual averages, totals, and occasional extremes of the day-to-day weather pattern for an area. Climate is the

weather you expect to occur at a particular time of the year in your hometown, whereas weather is the actual atmospheric conditions in your hometown on a particular day.

Global Air Circulation Patterns

(2) Heat from the sun and evaporated moisture are distributed over the Earth as a result of global circulation patterns of atmospheric air masses. Three major factors affecting the pattern of this global air circulation are **(1)** the uneven heating of the equatorial and polar regions of the Earth, which creates the driving force for atmospheric circulation; **(2)** the rotation of the Earth around its axis, which causes deflection of air masses moving from the equator to the poles and from the poles back to the

G. Tyler Miller, Jr., Living in the Environment, 4th ed. (Belmont, Calif.: Wadsworth, 1985), pp. 41–43. *Used by permission.*

equator; and **(3)** unequal distribution of land masses, oceans, ocean currents, mountains, and other geological features over the Earth's surface.

(3) An *air mass* is a vast body of air in which the conditions of temperature and moisture are much the same at all points in a horizontal direction. A warm air mass tends to rise, and a cold air mass tends to sink. Air in the Earth's atmosphere is heated more at the equator, where the sun is almost directly overhead, than at the poles, where the sun is lower in the sky and strikes the Earth at an angle. Because of this unequal heating, warm equatorial air tends to rise and spread northward and southward toward the Earth's poles as more hot air rises underneath, carrying heat from the equator toward the poles. At the poles the warm air cools, sinks downward, and moves back toward the equator. In addition, because of the Earth's annual rotation around the sun, the sun is higher in the sky in summer (July for the northern hemisphere and January for the

southern hemisphere) than in winter (January for the northern hemisphere and July for the southern hemisphere). Such annual variations in the duration and intensity of sunlight lead to seasonal variations in the different hemispheres and at the poles (Figure 3-8).

(4) The Earth's daily rotation on its axis (Figure 3-8) not only results in night and day; it also produces the major wind belts of the Earth. The general tendency for large air masses to move from the equator to the poles and back is modified by the twisting force associated with the Earth's rotation on its axis. This force deflects air flow in the northern hemisphere to the right and in the southern hemisphere to the left (Figure 3-9). This distortion of the Earth's general air circulation causes the single air movement pattern that would exist in each hemisphere on a nonrotating Earth to break up into three separate belts of moving air or *prevailing ground winds:* the polar easterlies, the westerlies, and the tradewinds (Figure 3-9). The equatorial calm is known as the dol-

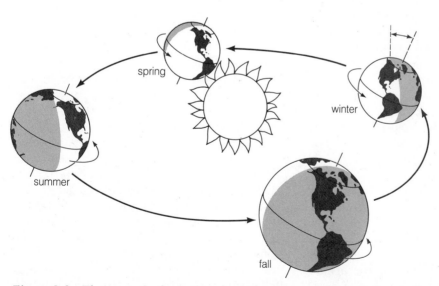

Figure 3-8   *The seasons in the northern hemisphere are caused by variations in the amount of incoming solar radiation as the Earth makes its annual rotation around the sun. Note that the northern end of the Earth's axis tilts toward the sun in summer, making the northern hemisphere warmer, and away from it in winter, making the northern hemisphere cooler.*

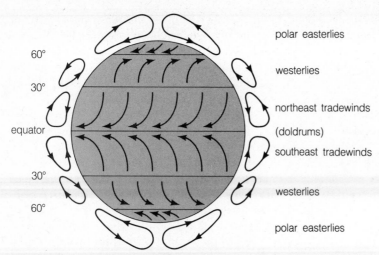

polar easterlies

westerlies

northeast tradewinds

(doldrums)

southeast tradewinds

westerlies

polar easterlies

60°

30°

equator

30°

60°

Figure 3-9 *The Earth's daily rotation on its axis deflects the general movement of warm air from the equator to the poles and back to the right in the northern hemisphere and to the left in the southern hemisphere. This twisting motion causes the air flow in each hemisphere to break up into three separate belts of prevailing winds.*

drums (Figure 3-9). These three major belts of prevailing winds in each hemisphere contribute to the distribution of heat and moisture around the planet that leads to differences in climate in different parts of the world.

(5) A *front* is the boundary between two colliding air masses. When a warm air mass and a cold air mass collide, the warm air flows up the front slope of the cold air as if it were a mountain slope, and the cold air forms a wedge near the ground. If prevailing winds cause the cold air mass to push the warm air mass back, we have an advancing *cold front*. If the reverse happens, we have an advancing *warm front*, and when no motion of the air masses takes place, we have a *stationary front*. An advancing cold or warm front usually brings bad weather because of the rain, snow, and strong winds that are found in the vicinity of its moving air masses.

(6) The boundary where the warm tropical air masses pushed from the south by the prevailing westerlies collide with the cold polar air masses pushed from the north by the polar

easterlies (Figure 3-9) is known as the *polar front*. This front is of major importance in determining the weather and climate of the North American continent. Depending on the relative strength of the polar easterlies and the westerlies, the polar front swings northward and southward in a rather unpredictable way. In general, it moves toward the equator during the winter and recedes to the poles during the summer.

(7) The general global circulation pattern of air masses (Figure 3-9) also influences the distribution of precipitation over the Earth's surface. A great deal of the sun's heat goes not just into warming the Earth's surface but also into evaporating water from the oceans and other bodies of water that cover about three-fourths of the Earth's surface. Evaporation of water from the land and transpiration of moisture from the leaves of plants also contribute water vapor to the atmosphere. A single apple tree, for example, may transpire 6,790 liters (1,800 gallons) of water vapor into the atmosphere during its six-month growing season.

The amount of water vapor in the air is called its *humidity*. The amount of water vapor the air is holding at a particular temperature expressed as a percentage of the amount it could hold at that temperature is known as its *relative humidity*. When air with a given amount of water vapor cools, its relative humidity rises; when this same air is warmed, its relative humidity drops. Thus, warm air can hold more water vapor than cold air, explaining why the humidity tends to rise in warmer summer months.

(8) When an air mass rises it cools, which causes its relative humidity to increase. Once the relative humidity of the rising air mass reaches 100 percent, any further decrease in temperature causes tiny water droplets or ice crystals to condense on particles of dust in the atmosphere to form *clouds*. As these droplets and ice crystals in clouds are moved about in turbulent air, they collide and coalesce to form larger droplets and crystals. Eventually they can become big enough to be pulled downward by gravitational attraction toward the Earth's surface in the form of *precipitation* such as rain, sleet, snow, or hail. Thus, almost all clouds and forms of precipitation are caused by the cooling of an air mass as it rises. Conversely, when an air mass sinks, its temperature rises and its relative humidity can decrease to the point where it can't release its moisture as rain or snow.

(9) Air rising in the tropics is both hot and moist. As this air rises and cools, some of its water vapor is converted to water droplets, giving up some heat in the process. These droplets form the clouds from which tropical rains fall, helping explain why the tropics are wet and thus covered with lush vegetation. Conversely, areas north and south of the equator where the airflow is mainly downward—such as the deserts of the U.S. Southwest and the Sahara—tend to be dry because sinking air can hold more moisture.

(10) An air mass tends to take on the temperature and moisture characteristics of the surface over which it moves. Thus, the climate and weather of a particular area are also affected by the distribution of land and water over the Earth's surface because these surfaces react differently to the incoming rays of the sun. In general, land surfaces are heated rapidly by the sun. Because this heat does not penetrate deeply, land surfaces also cool rapidly. This means that interior land areas not near a large body of water usually have great differences between daily high and low temperatures. Water, however, warms up slowly, holds a much larger quantity of heat than the same volume of land surface, and cools slowly. As a result, the surface layer of air over the oceans is cooler in summer and warmer in winter than that over the continents. Because warm air rises, a net inflow of cool ocean air moves onto the continents in summer, and in winter there is a net outflow of cool air from the continents onto the oceans. Land and sea breezes result from the land being colder than the water at night and early morning but warmer later in the day.

(11) The Earth's rotation, prevailing winds, and variations in water temperature give rise to ocean currents such as the Gulf Stream, which carries warm waters from the Florida Straits northward along the Atlantic Coast and on to the British Isles. Such currents affect the climate of coastal areas near their flow. For example, air moving across the warm Gulf Stream acquires heat and moisture and influences the climate and weather along the East Coast. The climate of the East Coast is also affected by the cold Labrador Current, which flows southward as far as Norfolk, Virginia. The cool Japan Current has a major effect on the climate and weather of the West Coast of the United States.

Effects of Topography on Local Climate and Weather

(12) Topographical factors can often make local climatic conditions different from the general climate of a region. Such local climatic patterns are called *microclimates*. For example, forests have lower wind speeds and higher rel-

ative humidity than open land. Buildings in cities also disrupt wind-flow patterns and heat-absorption patterns and cause cities to have different microclimates than surrounding nonurban areas.

(13) Climate is also modified locally by the presence of mountains. An increase in altitude results in a decrease in the density (mass per unit of volume) of the atmosphere, which in turn leads to a decrease in the temperature of the atmosphere. Thus, because of their higher altitudes, mountains tend to be cooler and windier than adjacent valleys. They also act as barriers to interrupt the flow of prevailing winds and the movement of storms. For example, because most U.S. mountain ranges run north and south, they disrupt the flow of the prevailing westerlies.

(14) Mountain ranges also affect precipitation patterns. When prevailing winds reach a mountain range, the air rises and may decrease in temperature to the condensation level (100 percent humidity). When this occurs, precipitation may occur on the windward side of the range as the air flows upward. After flowing over the mountain crests, the air flows down the lee side of the range. As this happens, it becomes warmer and its relative humidity can decrease to the point where it can't release its moisture as air or snow. Thus, slopes on the lee side of the mountain range and the land beyond these slopes generally lack abundant precipitation. This *rain shadow effect* is the main reason that arid and semiarid deserts lie to the east of the Coast Ranges and the Cascade and Sierra Nevada ranges of California.

---

1. _____

2. _____

3. _____

4. _____

5. _____

_____
80%

Ask instructor for answers.

---

1. This chapter excerpt makes use of:

    a. boldface print
    b. italics
    c. underlining
    d. both a and b

2. The two illustrations relate weather to the Earth's:

    a. annual rotation
    b. daily rotation
    c. annual and daily rotation
    d. mountain ranges

3. A topic that will not be covered in this excerpt is:

    a. air circulation
    b. weather and climate
    c. topography and weather
    d. the greenhouse effect

4. This excerpt makes no use of mathematical equations.

    a. true
    b. false

5. The title of this excerpt suggests that climate will be analyzed in relation to:

    a. all the continents of the Earth
    b. North America

c. the North and South Poles

d. the mountainous areas of the Earth

B. Question

Having surveyed this excerpt, make up five questions that you will answer as you study read. Use the chapter title, subdivision titles, and italicized terms to help you to make up these questions. Write your questions in the space provided.

> Ask instructor for
> sample questions.

1.

2.

3.

4.

5.

C. Read and Recite

1. Having written these five questions, you can begin study reading. Underline important points and make marginal comments. Remember, do not underline too much. Read paragraphs 1–7. Afterward, on a separate sheet of paper, recite what you have read. When you have finished, go back to these seven paragraphs to see if your summary is complete and accurate.

2. Now read paragraphs 8–14. Follow the same procedures as you did for paragraphs 1–7: (1) recite on a separate sheet of paper, (2) then return to these paragraphs to see if your summary is complete and accurate. Make any necessary additions to your summary.

D. Review

Now you are ready to review all of your material. Read over text underlinings, marginal comments, and your two summaries. You may also want to make study maps from some of this material. Finally, go back to your original five questions to see if you can answer them without any help.

Examination: Global Patterns of Climate.   Directions: Give yourself fifty minutes to complete the following questions. Be sure to budget your time to answer all three parts: matching, multiple choice, and short essay.

I. Matching: Match up the following terms with the appropriate definitions. Each term should be matched up to only one definition. Place the letter of the correct definition in the answer box next to the appropriate number. (24 points)

1. _____

2. _____

3. _____

4. _____

5. _____

6. _____

7. _____

8. _____

9. _____

10. _____

11. _____

12. _____

13. _____

14. _____

15. _____

16. _____

17. _____

1. microclimate
2. climate
3. weather
4. front
5. air mass
6. precipitation
7. humidity
8. relative humidity

a. amount of water vapor in the air at a specific temperature in comparison to what it could be at that temperature
b. rain, sleet, snow, or hail
c. the boundary between two colliding air masses
d. general weather at a specific place on Earth over a long period of time
e. local patterns of climate
f. day-to-day change in atmospheric conditions
g. a body of air with similar temperature and moisture
h. amount of water vapor in the air

II. *Multiple Choice:* Choose the letter that correctly completes each question or statement. Place all answers in the answer box. (36 points)

9. Warm air masses are:

  a. below cold air masses
  b. above cold air masses
  c. mixed in with cold air masses
  d. only found at the equator

10. The Earth's wind belts are caused by:

  a. the Earth's annual rotation
  b. the Earth's daily rotation
  c. ocean currents
  d. land masses

11. The belt of moving air at the equator is known as the:

  a. westerlies
  b. easterlies
  c. tradewinds
  d. doldrums

12. Bad weather is usually caused by the movement of a:

  a. cold front
  b. warm front
  c. stationary front
  d. both a and b

13. An important force determining weather conditions in North America is the:

  a. polar front
  b. westerlies

    c. doldrums

    d. tradewinds

14. Humidity in the air increases when:

    a. an air mass heats up

    b. an air mass cools

    c. a cold front meets a stationary front

    d. it is midday

15. Land tends to be heated:

    a. rapidly by the sun

    b. slowly by the sun

    c. as fast as water

    d. as slow as water

16. An important factor affecting the weather of the British Isles is the:

    a. Arctic snow

    b. doldrums

    c. westerlies

    d. Gulf Stream

17. Weather and climate seem to be influenced by:

    a. unknown variables

    b. few variables

    c. several variables

    d. the Earth's rotation only

III. Short Essay: In a paragraph, discuss how mountains affect weather patterns. In your paragraph, mention: (1) mountain altitude and air density, (2) how U.S. mountains affect the westerly winds, and (3) precipitation differences between windward and leeward sides of mountains. (40 points)

70%

Ask instructor for answers.

Study Reading 2

From Classicism, Classical Music, and Sonata Form

This excerpt on Classicism and Mozart is from a music history textbook. It is essentially divided into two parts. The first describes the characteristics of the Rococo style and Classicism, and the second section gives a quick biography of Mozart, the great classical composer. The excerpt is structured around two organizational patterns: description and sequence of events.

Use the following strategies to master the important material in this excerpt:

1. Determine the significant characteristics of the Rococo style and Classicism. You may want to write these characteristics down in the margins as you read. You will be reading many details about the Rococo style and Classicism; concentrate only on the important characteristics of each style. If you do not remember what kinds of details characteristics are, reread p. 56.

2. When you begin reading about Mozart's life, you need to put the information about him into its proper sequence. In this section, you will read several details about his life, and sequencing the material should help you remember more of the facts. Refer to pp. 79–80 on sequence of events to determine the important aspects of this organizational pattern.

3. One part of the test will include true-false questions on Mozart. So commit to memory many of the details of his life.

A. Survey   Take two minutes to survey this excerpt. Read the chapter title, the section titles, and any terms that are highlighted. If time permits, read the first few and last few paragraphs to get a sense of the style and difficulty level of the excerpt.

When you have finished surveying, answer the questions that follow without looking back at the excerpt. Place all of your answers in the answer box.

Classicism, Classical Music, and Sonata Form

Charles R. Hoffer

(1) By the time of Bach's death in 1750, the Baroque style had faded in popularity. In fact, Bach's own sons thought of their father as something of an out-of-date old man, a not unknown attitude of sons toward their fathers. But the world *was* changing. Passing was the intensity of religious feeling. Gone was the love of the dramatic and grandiose. A new age had arrived, one that would see significant changes in the style of art and music.

Rococo Style

(2) Like all stylistic periods in music, the Classical period did not have a clearly marked beginning. An early instance of the gradual transition from the heavy, complex Baroque style was the **Rococo**, or *galant,* style, which began early in the eighteenth century in the courts of Europe, especially France. It was the art of the aristocracy, of the people at the lavish courts of Versailles and similar places. Like the aristocracy, Rococo music and art were light, elegant, and frivolous. In painting, the Rococo was represented by Fragonard, Watteau, and Boucher. Their subject matter was often fanciful love, and their pictures were laced with figures

Charles R. Hoffer, The Understanding of Music, *5th ed. (Belmont, Calif.: Wadsworth, 1985), pp. 200–205. Used by permission.*

of cupids and thinly clad nymphs. Rococo furniture and clothing were highly decorated. The lace cuff and the powdered wig were in vogue, and elegant manners were cultivated.

(3) François Couperin (1668–1733) is probably most representative of Rococo composers. He wrote a large amount of music, mostly suites, for the clavecin, the French version of the harpsichord. Couperin's music was highly embellished, with many ornaments added to the happy, short melodies.

(4) Although music and art in the Rococo style were not profound, they were pleasant diversions for the aristocracy during much of the eighteenth century. More important, the Rococo represented a break from the complex counterpoint of the Baroque, and it ushered in a new type of music.

Patronage

(5) The patronage system existed for several centuries. However, it is especially associated with the eighteenth century because of the experiences of Haydn and Mozart under it. The system was one in which a composer accepted exclusive employment under the auspices of a patron. Patrons were either the wealthy (and sometimes decadent) aristocracy or the Church. When a composer found a good patron, as Haydn did, a secure position and an

audience for his compositions were assured. The writing of new works was expected. At its best, patronage was a good incubator for creative talent.

(6) There were liabilities, as shown by Mozart's experiences with patronage. Most serious among these was the fact that composers had to please their patrons, or else they found themselves helping in the stables or looking for a new patron. The result was much trivial music written according to standard formulas. Too, the patronage system regarded composers not as unique creative artists but as the source of a product for the privileged classes to use and enjoy.

(7) Since the relationship between composers and their work was taken lightly, it was common practice for composers to borrow themes and ideas from one another. In fact, plagiarism was understood to be a form of flattery and commendation. Legal niceties such as copyrights and royalties were unheard of. Not until the advent of the Romantic philosophy of the nineteenth century did composers feel compelled to create in a way that was uniquely individual.

The Classical Attitude

(8) During the Classical period, which scholars consider to stretch roughly from 1750 to 1825, several conditions in society influenced artists and composers. The first of these was a new intellectual outlook of such scope that the period came to be called the Age of Enlightenment or the Age of Reason. The trend was strongly influenced by Descartes, Diderot, Moses Mendelssohn (grandfather of Felix Mendelssohn, an important composer of the Romantic period), Spinoza, and others who revived and added to the idealistic, idea-centered philosophy of ancient Greece. In fact, the word *classical* traditionally refers to the reason and restraint found in the life of the ancient Athenians.

(9) Briefly, the philosophy of eighteenth-century thinkers was this: First, truth can be realized only by the process of reason, so an emphasis must be placed on learning and intellectual pursuits. Second, the universe is a machine governed by inflexible laws that human beings cannot override. Therefore, what is true is true throughout the world; it is universal. Third, emotions as a guide to truth are false, so rational intellect should control human behavior. The intellectuals of the Classical period were not impressed by the unknown, since they believed that in time they would come to know it through thought and knowledge. They rejected the past, especially the Middle Ages, because they felt mysticism had stifled natural human capacities. Reason, not faith, was to be humanity's beacon.

(10) The American Declaration of Independence written in 1776 is a thoroughly Classical document. It is difficult for us, who tend to think of revolutionaries as bomb-throwing zealots, to consider Jefferson, Washington, Adams, and the others as revolutionaries. But revolutionaries they were, even though their demands and statements of purpose were shaped in the language of reason and Classical thought. These individuals were cultured, intelligent, reasonable men, and their Declaration shows it. Although at its conclusion they pledge "our Lives, our Fortunes, and our Sacred Honor," the Declaration is essentially a legal brief, a list of the colonists' grievances against the King of England. Instead of screaming "Death to the tyrant!" Jefferson begins "When in the course of human events, it becomes necessary for one people to dissolve the political bands which have connected them with another. . . ." At a moment that would seem to require a display of emotion—the declaring of national independence and the pledging of one's life to a cause—these intellectual and political leaders were dispassionate, restrained, sensible, logical.

Wolfgang Amadeus Mozart

(11) Wolfgang Amadeus Mozart stands out among composers. His music has about it a clearness, delicacy, and simplicity that seem to defy analysis. His music is so—musical!

(12) Mozart was born in 1756 in Salzburg, Austria. His father, Leopold, was a recognized violinist and composer in the court of the archbishop. The elder Mozart was quick to realize and capitalize on his son's extraordinary talents. Under his father's teaching, young Mozart showed remarkable mastery of the piano and to a lesser extent the violin. By the time he was five he had composed his first pieces, and at six he performed at the court of the Empress Maria Theresa. When he was seven, Mozart and his sister, who was four years his elder, went on a tour that included Paris, London, and Munich. By the age of thirteen he had written concertos, symphonies, and a comic opera; at fourteen he was knighted by the Pope. ˙

(13) The most phenomenal aspect of Mozart's musical talent was his memory for music and his ability to work out whole pieces in his mind. He once wrote, "Though it be long, the work is complete and finished in my mind. I take out of the bag of my memory what has previously been collected into it. For this reason the committing to paper is done quickly enough. For everything is already finished, and it rarely differs on paper from what it was in my imagination."

(14) Mozart never enjoyed the stability of a good appointment as a composer to a patron.

For a while he worked for the prince-archbishop of Salzburg. The archbishop was a difficult man, and the high-spirited Mozart resented the restrictions of the patronage system. (He wrote his father, "The two valets sit at the head of the table. I at least have the honor of sitting above the cooks.") He quarreled with the archbishop and was dismissed. At the age of twenty-five he left Salzburg to pursue his career in Vienna.

(15) Since Mozart did not fare well under the patronage system, he spent some of the last ten years of his life, as he put it, "Hovering between hope and anxiety." Due in part to his impractical and overgenerous nature in financial affairs, he had to eke out an existence by teaching, giving concerts, composing, and borrowing from friends.

(16) In 1791, at the age of thirty-five, Mozart died of uremic poisoning. Because he was so deeply in debt, he was given the cheapest funeral and buried in a pauper's grave.

(17) Despite his short life and its disappointments, Mozart composed over 600 works, many of them sizable compositions such as operas, symphonies, concertos, and string quartets. He never used opus numbers, although some were added later by publishers. His works were catalogued by a Viennese botanist and amateur musician named Köchel.

1. _____

2. _____

3. _____

4. _____

5. _____

_____
80%

Ask instructor for answers.

1. The excerpt makes use of:

    a. boldface print
    b. italics
    c. underlining
    d. both a and b

2. One section *not* covered in this excerpt is:

    a. the Rococo style
    b. patronage
    c. the Classical attitude
    d. the sonata form

3. It seems that the Rococo style came:

    a. before the Classical
    b. after the Classical

    c. before the Baroque
    d. to be only in France

4. It seems that the section on Mozart discusses only his sonatas.

    a. true
    b. false

5. This excerpt presents several dates to situate the various stages in the Classical period.

    a. true
    b. false

B. Question

Having surveyed this excerpt, write five questions that you intend to answer when you study read. Use the chapter title and section titles to help you write these questions. You may also want to read the first sentence of several of the paragraphs to formulate some of your questions. Write your questions in the space provided.

> Ask instructor for sample questions.

1.

2.

3.

4.

5.

C. Read and Recite

Having written your questions, you are now ready to begin study reading paragraphs 1–7, underlining important passages and making marginal comments about the Rococo style and the Classical attitude. When you have finished reciting, go back to these seven paragraphs to be sure that your summary is both accurate and complete.

Now read paragraphs 8–17. Then recite this material on a separate sheet of paper. In this section, include a definition and list of characteristics for the Classical attitude as well as a list of the important events in Mozart's life. Again, go back to these pages to check for the completeness and accuracy of your summary.

D. Review

Now you are ready to review your: (1) underlinings, (2) marginal comments, and (3) two summaries. You may want to design study maps for the Rococo style and Classical attitude as well as the significant events in Mozart's life. Finally, go back to the five questions you made up in B to see if you can now answer them without any help.

Examination: Classicism and Mozart. Directions: Give yourself fifty minutes to complete the following questions. Be sure to budget your time.

I. Multiple Choice: Choose the letter that correctly completes each question. Place all answers in the answer box. (30 points)

1. _____
2. _____
3. _____
4. _____
5. _____
6. _____
7. _____
8. _____
9. _____
10. _____
11. _____
12. _____
13. _____
14. _____
15. _____
16. _____
17. _____
18. _____
19. _____
20. _____

1. How can you best describe the Rococo style?

    a. light
    b. elegant
    c. frivolous
    d. all of these

2. Rococo music is usually:

    a. serious
    b. simple
    c. ornate
    d. all of these

3. A patron is one who:

    a. tutors young musicians
    b. supports young composers
    c. writes biographies of great composers
    d. attends concerts

4. The Classical attitude emphasized:

    a. reason
    b. emotion
    c. a study of the Middle Ages
    d. a study of mysticism

5. Which characteristic does *not* describe the Classical attitude?

    a. emphasis on learning
    b. emphasis on universal truths
    c. fascination with the unknown
    d. saw universe running much like a large machine

6. According to this excerpt, the Declaration of Independence is:

    a. a reasoned document
    b. a revolutionary document
    c. not Classical in attitude
    d. both a and b

7. The Classical period has also been called the:

   a. Age of Enlightenment
   b. Age of Pessimism
   c. New Renaissance
   d. Noble Age

8. What the Classical period admired most in the ancient Greeks was:

   a. their mythology
   b. their intellectual restraint
   c. Homer
   d. their drama, especially their comedies

9. The Classical mind believed that the unknown was:

   a. God's world
   b. unattainable
   c. attainable through faith
   d. attainable through knowledge

10. What do you think was the attitude of the Classical mind toward the human being's potential?

   a. pessimistic
   b. neutral
   c. optimistic
   d. none of these

II. True-False: Write A for true, B for false. Write all answers in the answer box. (30 points)

11. Mozart's music is often described as complicated.
12. Mozart knew how to play only the piano.
13. At the age of five, Mozart was already composing.
14. As a composer, Mozart had an average memory for musical pieces.
15. Mozart seemingly revised his pieces very little.
16. Mozart spent some of his time composing in Vienna.
17. The Prince Archbishop of France was Mozart's patron early in Mozart's career.
18. In his personal life, Mozart was often in debt because his wife was extravagant.
19. Mozart died of uremic poisoning at the age of 36.
20. To Mozart's credit are over 600 musical works.

III. Short Essay In an organized paragraph, discuss the major characteristics of the Rococo style and the Classical attitude. Show how and where these two schools of thought are similar and different. (40 points)

75%

Ask instructor for answers.

Study Reading 3

Measurements and Units

This chapter excerpt, "Heat and Temperature," is from a chapter in a
college chemistry textbook. This chapter is called "Measurement and
Units." The style is straightforward, but this simplicity is deceiving.
You may need to reread many of the sections in order to master them
and to use this knowledge in solving specific problems. Use the following strategies to master the material in this excerpt:

1. Read the definitions carefully, underlining or circling important
   parts. You need to know what each term in this excerpt means, so
   read to understand every part of each definition.

2. Read for cause-effect patterns. You may want to reread the section
   on cause and effect on pp. 77–78. The cause-effect statements in
   this excerpt are direct, so don't look for terms of qualification.

3. Read the example problems and solutions carefully. Follow the
   solution to each problem step by step. Be sure that you understand
   each step before you go on to the next.

4. Memorize the formulas regarding temperature conversion. Learn
   what each abbreviation means and how each term relates to the
   others.

5. After you finish reading the excerpt, complete the exercises. These problems will give you needed practice in converting the temperatures from one scale to another.

6. By the time you have finished the excerpt, you should be able to recall without help the meanings of the terms. You should also be able to write out the conversion formulas and correctly use each one.

A. Survey

Take three minutes to survey the chapter excerpt. Read the title, the titles of each section, the terms and statements that are highlighted, as well as the summary and exercises at the end of the excerpt. If time permits, begin reading the first several paragraphs.

When you have finished, answer the following questions without looking back at the excerpt. Place all of your answers in the answer box.

Chapter 2
Measurement and Units

G. Tyler Miller, Jr.

2.5   Heat and Temperature

(1) *Heat Units and Measurement*   The official SI unit for heat or any other form of energy is the **joule (J)** (pronounced jool). Many chemists, however, still use an older heat unit known as the calorie (cal). Although the calorie unit is gradually being phased out, it is still widely used so that we need to be able to convert between joules and calories. A **calorie (cal)** is defined as the amount of heat energy required to raise the temperature of 1 g of water from 14.5° to 15.5°C. One calorie is equal to 4.184 joules.

$$1 \text{ cal} = 4.184 \text{ J} \quad \text{or} \quad \frac{4.184 \text{ J}}{1 \text{ cal}}$$

(2) Since both the joule and the calorie represent relatively small quantities of heat energy, the larger quantities of heat usually encountered in physical and chemical changes are often expressed in kilojoules (kJ) and kilocalories (kcal or Cal). Respectively, these units are equal to 1,000 J and 1,000 cal. Since 1 cal equals 4.184 J, 1 kcal (kilocalorie) equals 4.184 kJ (kilojoules).

(3) The kilocalories (also abbreviated Cal with a capital C) is the unit used in dietary tables to show the energy content of various types of food. Thus, a piece of pie containing 500 Cal (or 500 kcal) contains 500,000 or 5×10^5 cal. Individual energy requirements for the human body depend on a number of factors, including body weight and the amount of physical activity. A person weighing 68.2 kg (150 lb) and carrying out moderate physical activity typically needs about 8.4×10^3 kJ or 2.0×10^3 kcal of food energy a day.

(4) *Heat and Temperature*   It is important to distinguish between heat and temperature.

G. Tyler Miller, Jr., Chemistry: A Basic Introduction, *2nd ed. (Belmont, Calif.: Wadsworth, 1981), pp. 51–55; p. 59; p. 61. Used by permission.*

Heat or thermal energy can be roughly described as a measure of the total kinetic energy of all the particles in a sample of matter.[1] The relative "hotness" or "coldness" of a sample of matter is described by measuring its temperature. **Temperature** is a measure of the average (not the total) kinetic energy of the particles in a sample of matter.

(5) The heat (total kinetic energy) and temperature (average kinetic energy) of a given sample of matter are quite different quantities, just as the total mass of the members of a chemistry class is quite different from the average mass of the class. The heat in a given sample of matter depends on the amount of matter present in the sample. In contrast, the temperature of an object does not depend on the amount of matter in the sample. A cup of hot coffee contains a larger quantity of heat than a drop of the same coffee, but the temperatures of the liquid in the cup and the drop are the same.

(6) When one object has a higher temperature than another object, we know from experience that some of the energy from the hotter object will flow in the form of heat to the cooler object. You discovered this the first time you touched a hot stove or other hot object. In more formal language, then, temperature determines the direction in which heat energy flows when two samples of matter are brought into contact with one another.

Heat is a measure of the total kinetic energy of all the particles in a sample of matter.

Temperature is a measure of the average kinetic energy of the particles in a sample of matter.

---

[1] Heat or thermal energy also includes the rotational and vibrational energy of the particles along with the potential energy of attractions between particles. Since these energies are normally small (except at high temperatures), heat or thermal energy is primarily a measure of the total energy of motion (kinetic energy) of the particles.

(7) *Temperature Measurement* A **thermometer** is a device used to measure the temperature of a sample of matter. The most commonly used thermometer is the mercury thermometer. To measure and compare temperatures throughout the world, scientists have established several standard temperature scales. The three major temperature scales are the *Fahrenheit (F) scale,* the *Celsius (C) scale* (formerly known as the centigrade scale), and the *Kelvin (K) scale* (Figure 2-7). A unit of temperature on each scale is called a **degree.** A superscript, °, is used before the C abbreviation for Celsius and before the F abbreviation for Fahrenheit to indicate a degree. This superscript is not used for Kelvin temperature, since the Kelvin is defined as a unit of temperature. Thus, 100°C is read *100 degrees Celsius* and 273 K is read *273 Kelvin.* The term °K or *degrees Kelvin,* however, is still a widely used relic of an earlier version of the metric system. Most everyday measurements of temperature in the United States are reported in Fahrenheit temperature, although this scale is being phased out as the United States converts to the metric system. Scientists use both the Celsius and the Kelvin scales. The official SI temperature scale, however, is the Kelvin (K) scale.

(8) As shown in Figure 2-7, the **Fahrenheit temperature scale** is defined by assigning to the normal boiling point of water a temperature of 212°F and to the freezing point of water the temperature of 32°F. Since the difference between 212 and 32 is 180, the glass length between the two reference points is divided into 180 equal segments, each denoting a Fahrenheit degree. For the **Celsius temperature scale** the boiling point of water is assigned a value of 100°C and the freezing point of water is assigned the value of 0°C. This allows the distance between these two reference points to be divided into 100 equal units, each representing a Celsius degree. On the **Kelvin temperature scale**, the normal boiling point of water is 373.15 K (approximately 373 K) and the freezing point of water is 273.15 K (approximately 273 K). The value of 0 K is the absolute

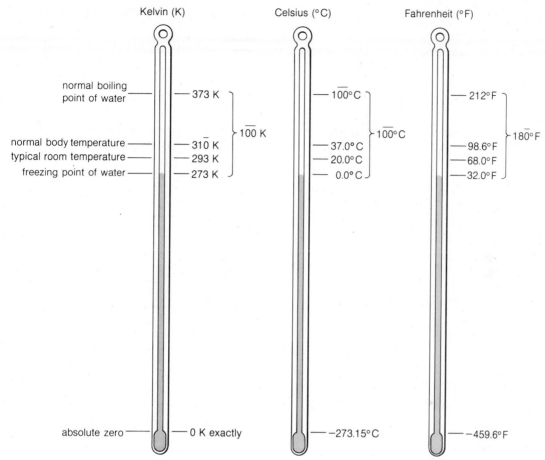

Figure 2-7   *Comparison of the Kelvin (K), Celsius (°C), and Fahrenheit (°F) temperature scales.*

zero of temperature on the Kelvin scale. This value is equal to $-273.15°C$ or $-459.75°F$ (Figure 2-7).

(9) **Temperature   Conversions**   Conversions between Fahrenheit and Celsius temperatures can be made using two simple formulas. Since 100 degrees on the Celsius scale is the same as 180 degrees on the Fahrenheit scale (Figure 2-7), then $1°C = 1.8°F$. Thus, the unit conversion factor between Celsius and Fahrenheit is $1.8°F/1°C$ (or $9°F/5°C$). The zero point on the Fahrenheit scale is $32°F$ compared to $0°C$ for the Celsius scale. Thus, to convert any temperature on the Fahrenheit scale to the Celsius scale, we first subtract $32°F$ from the Fahren-

heit temperature and then multiply by the appropriate conversion factor.

$$°C = \frac{1.0°C}{1.8°F} \times (°F - 32°F)$$

To convert from Celsius to Fahrenheit we multiply the Celsius temperature by the appropriate conversion factor and then add $32°F$ to the result.[2]

---

[2] Another set of formulas relating to Fahrenheit and Celsius scales is

$$°C = \frac{1.0°C}{1.8°F} (°F - 40°F) - 40°C$$

$$°F = \frac{1.8°F}{1.0°C} (°C + 40°C) - 40°F$$

$$°F = \left(°C \times \frac{1.8°F}{1.0°C}\right) + 32°F$$

The following examples illustrate the use of these conversions.

(10) **Example 2.12** To help save energy, Americans have been asked to lower their thermostats to 65°F in cold weather. What is this temperature on the Celsius scale?

Solution

Unknown: °C

Known: 65°F

Plan: $°C = \dfrac{1.0°C}{1.8°F} (°F - 32°F)$

Result: $C = \dfrac{1.0°C}{1.8°F} \times (65°F - 32°F)$

$= \dfrac{1.0°C}{1.8°F} (33°F) = 18°C$

(11) **Example 2.13** On a cold day in Alaska the temperature is −25°C. What is the equivalent Fahrenheit temperature?

Solution

Unknown: °F

Known: −25°C

Plan: $°F = \left(°C \times \dfrac{1.8°F}{1.0°C}\right) + 32°F$

Result: $°F = \left[(-25°C) \times \dfrac{1.8°F}{1.0°C}\right] + 32°F$

$= -45°F + 32°F = \mathbf{-13°F}$

(12) Conversions between the Celsius and Kelvin scales are very easy. From Figure 2.7 we

can see that 0 K = −273°C. Thus, °C = K − 273° and K = °C + 273°. In other words, to convert °C to K we merely add 273 to the Celsius temperature. . . .

(13) ***Accomplishments and Review*** After completing this chapter you should be able to do the following:

2.5 Heat and Temperature

12. Distinguish between heat and temperature and give the units used for heat and temperature measurements.

13. Make conversions between the Fahrenheit (F), Celsius (C), and Kelvin (K) temperature scales.

(14) ***Exercises***

2.5 Heat and Temperature

26. Which of the following is the highest temperature: 250 K, 230°F, 120°C?

27. Make the following temperature conversions:
    a. Room temperature frequently averages 20.0°C. What is this on the Fahrenheit and Kelvin scales?
    b. Milk is pasteurized at 145°F. What is this on the Celsius and Kelvin scales?
    c. What is the normal body temperature of 98.6°F on the Celsius and Kelvin scales?
    d. The normal boiling point of ethyl alcohol is 79.0°C. What is its boiling point on the Kelvin scale?
    e. At normal atmospheric pressure the boiling point of liquid nitrogen is 77 K. What is the boiling point in degrees Celsius? Would nitrogen be a liquid or a gas at −100°C?

1. This excerpt makes use of:

    a. boldface print
    b. italics
    c. illustrations
    d. all of these

2. The boldface statements on heat and temperature:

    a. define both terms
    b. show the difference in the Fahrenheit, Celsius, and Kelvin temperature scales
    c. show the difference between heat and temperature
    d. both a and c

3. The problems that are presented in this excerpt are solved:

    a. step by step
    b. by presenting the formulas
    c. by presenting the known and unknown quantities
    d. all of these

4. It appears that in this excerpt you will learn something about:

    a. the Fahrenheit scale
    b. the Celsius scale
    c. the Kelvin scale
    d. all of these

5. Which topic will not be covered in this excerpt?

    a. heat units
    b. temperature measurement
    c. temperature conversions
    d. specific heat

1. _____
2. _____
3. _____
4. _____
5. _____

_____
80%

Ask instructor for answers.

B. Question

Having surveyed the chapter excerpt, write five questions that you intend to answer when you study read. Use the chapter title, section titles, and boldface print to formulate your questions. Write your questions in the space provided.

1.

2.

3.

4.

5.

Ask instructor for sample questions.

C. Read and Recite

With these questions, you are ready to begin study reading. Use your best underlining and commenting skills, being sparing with what you underline and making marginal notes on important terms and formulas. Read the entire excerpt. Then, on a separate sheet of paper, recite what you have read. When you have completed your summary, go back to the excerpt to be sure that your summary is both accurate and complete. Make any additions to your summary at this time.

D. Review

Now you are ready to review your underlinings, your marginal comments, and your summary. Before you take the exam, you should solve Exercises 26 and 27 on p. 302. There will be a problem-solving section to the exam, and these problems will serve as review.

Examination: Heat and Temperature.   Directions: Give yourself fifty minutes to complete the following questions. Be sure to budget your time.

I. Matching: Match up the following terms with the appropriate definitions. Each term should be matched up to only one definition. Place all answers in the answer box. (18 points)

Answer box	
1. _____	
2. _____	
3. _____	
4. _____	
5. _____	
6. _____	
7. _____	
8. _____	
9. _____	
10. _____	
11. _____	
12. _____	
13. _____	
14. _____	
15. _____	

1. joule
2. calorie
3. heat
4. temperature
5. Celsius temperature scale
6. Kelvin temperature scale

a. amount of heat required to raise the temperature of one gram of water from 14.5°C to 15.5°C
b. measure of the average kinetic energy in a sample of matter
c. official SI unit for heat or any other form of energy
d. boiling point of water about 373°; freezing point of water about 273°
e. boiling point of water 100°; freezing point of water 0°
f. measure of the total kinetic energy of all particles in a sample of matter

II. Multiple Choice: Choose the letter that correctly completes each question or statement. Place all answers in the answer box. (27 points)

7. How many joules are in a calorie?

   a. 4184 J
   b. 418.4 J
   c. 41.84 J
   d. 4.184 J

8. The correct abbreviation for kilocalorie is:

   a. cal
   b. Cal
   c. KC
   d. kc

9. The heat in a given sample of matter depends on the:

   a. average energy of the particles in the sample
   b. amount of matter present in the sample
   c. average kinetic energy of the particles in the sample
   d. none of these

10. Heat tends to flow from a:

    a. cooler object to a warmer object
    b. warmer object to a cooler object
    c. gas to a liquid
    d. liquid to a solid

11. On which temperature scale is the superscript (°) not used?

    a. Fahrenheit
    b. Celsius
    c. Kelvin
    d. metric

12. On the Celsius scale, what is the boiling point of water?

    a. 0°
    b. 212°
    c. 373°
    d. 100°

13. On which scale is the difference between the boiling point of water and the freezing point of water 180?

    a. Fahrenheit
    b. Celsius
    c. Kelvin
    d. metric

14. In which scale is the difference between the boiling point of water and the freezing point of water 100?

    a. Fahrenheit
    b. Celsius
    c. Kelvin
    d. both b and c

15. 0 K is designated as:

    a. absolute zero
    b. the freezing point of water
    c. the boiling point of water
    d. none of these

III. Problem Solving: Complete the following two problems. You will get credit for determining the unknown quantity, the known quantity, the correct formula, and the correct answer. Show all your work.

1. In the desert areas of Southern California the temperature often goes as high as 44°C. What temperature is this on the Fahrenheit scale? (25 points)

    a. unknown: (5 points)

    b. known: (5 points)

    c. formula: (5 points)

    d. work: (5 points)

    e. answer: (5 points)

2. For experimental purposes Dr. Burns placed a virus at 120°F. What is the equivalent Kelvin temperature? (30 points)

    a. unknown: (5 points)

    b. known: (5 points)

    c. formulas: (10 points)

    d. work: (5 points)

    e. answer: (5 points)

> ‾‾‾‾‾ 70%
> Ask instructor for answers.

Answer Key

Answers have been provided for most odd-numbered exercises. You should ask your instructor for the answers to (1) all even-numbered exercises, (2) the essay questions and several short-answer questions, and (3) the study reading selections in Part Five.

Chapter 3
Locating the Main Idea

Exercise 3.1

1. b
2. a
3. c
4. d
5. c

(For 6–10, wording will vary.)

6. types of American literature
7. minorities in the United States
8. stages in a young adult's life
9. symptoms of the flu
10. major divisions of an outline or major divisions in reading, listening, and writing material.

Exercise 3.3

1. b	6. c	11. c	16. a
2. d	7. c	12. c	17. d
3. a	8. b	13. a	18. a
4. c	9. c	14. d	19. d
5. a	10. b	15. d	20. d

Exercise 3.5

1. d
2. c
3. b
4. b
5. a

Chapter 4
Locating Major and
Minor Details

Exercise 4.1

1. c   6. a
2. d   7. c
3. b   8. c
4. b   9. b
5. c   10. a

Exercise 4.3

1. b   6. e
2. c   7. c
3. a   8. a
4. b   9. c
5. d   10. d

Exercise 4.5

1. general   6. general
2. specific   7. specific
3. specific   8. specific
4. general   9. general
5. specific   10. specific

Here are sample revised topic sentences:

1. Cigarette smoking is hazardous to the bronchial tract and lungs.
2. Lake April has been found to have polluted its vegetation and wildlife.
3. The Asian flu has struck our school.
4. Charles Dickens is a great writer because his characters are so carefully drawn.
5. The five-step study method is effective.
6. Abraham Lincoln was a great American president because of his love for his country, his sensitivity to human suffering, and his intelligence.
7. The finances of Haven College have steadily increased over the past five years.
8. The film *The History of Xanadu* is flawed by several historical and technical errors.
9. Crime is a problem in America because our society is becoming more and more alienated.
10. Some ethical questions have been brought up regarding how Senator Washington was elected to the state assembly.

Chapter 5
Identifying
Organizational
Patterns

Exercise 5.1

1. b   6. b   11. a
2. a   7. a   12. d
3. b   8. b   13. a
4. a   9. a   14. d
5. b   10. b   15. d

Exercise 5.3

Answers should be essentially the same as those in the key. Wording may vary. Each definition has two answers, each counting one point.

Term	General Category	Examples
1. depression	severe economic decline	Great Depression of the 1930s
2. mass production	organizing work into special tasks	automobile production
3. monopoly	excessive control of an industry by one company	only one doctor in a town
4. cartel	group producing the same product; agree on production and charge	Civil Aeronautics Board
5. gland	organ or cell secreting a chemical	pituitary or thyroid
6. larva	immature animal form	caterpillar
7. herbivore	animal feeding mainly on plants	cow
8. conglomerate	combination of companies under one management	International Telephone and Telegraph
9. post hoc error	first event the cause of the second	eating potato salad causes stomachache
10. ethics	branch of philosophy dealing with right behavior	biomedical ethics

Exercise 5.5

1. b	**6.** b
2. a	**7.** a
3. d	**8.** b
4. c	**9.** a
5. d	**10.** c

Exercise 5.7

1. d	**6.** d
2. d	**7.** d
3. d	**8.** a
4. c	**9.** b
5. c	**10.** c

Chapter 6
Reading and Listening for Inferences

Exercise 6.1

You may want to go back to the paragraphs marked "B" to see how they could be made more credible.

1. A	**6.** A
2. B	**7.** B
3. A	**8.** A
4. B	**9.** A
5. B	**10.** B

Exercise 6.3

Wording may vary, but the information should be essentially the same. Award one point for each correct answer. You may give yourself partial credit where you think it is appropriate.

1. *Subjugate* means to subdue by force and suggests that the imperialistic nation can be ruthless.
2. *Unquenchable* suggests weakness and vulnerability and implies that the imperialistic nation is always trying to control the weaker nation.
3. *Defenseless* suggests weakness and vulnerability and implies that the imperialistic nation is unjustly combating those countries that cannot defend themselves.
4. *Sacrificed* suggests a ritualistic offering to a god and implies that the imperialistic nation has a barbaric nature.
5. *Greed* has sinful connotations, being mentioned in the Bible as one of the seven deadly sins; it implies that the imperialists are sinners as well.
6. *Influential* has positive connotations of power, suggesting that King changed the course of history for black Americans.
7. *Enlightened* suggests instruction or illumination and is often associated with religious teachings. Applied to King, this word suggests the prophetic and religious side of his character.
8. *Miracle* suggests doing the impossible and is applied to superhuman abilities. These superhuman, godlike associations are applied to King.
9. *Graciously* implies civility and decorum, suggesting the proper, socially poised aspects to King's character.
10. *Senselessly* implies randomness and illogic, and suggests that King's murder was the act of a crazed individual.

Chapter 7
Reading Graphs and
Tables

Exercise 7.1

1. d		6. b	
2. c		7. c	
3. b		8. b	
4. b		9. b	
5. d		10. c	

Chapter 8
Summarizing and
Paraphrasing

From Explanation of Skills

Law of Conservation of Matter: Everything Must Go Somewhere

(1) We always talk about consuming or using up matter resources, but actually we don't consume any matter. We only borrow some of the Earth's resources for a while—taking them from the Earth, carrying them to another part of the globe, processing them, using them, and then discarding, reusing, or recycling them. In the process of using matter, we may change it to another form, such as burning complex gasoline molecules and breaking them down into simpler molecules of water and carbon dioxide. But in every case we neither create nor destroy any measurable amount of matter. This results from the **law of conservation of matter:** In any ordinary physical or chemical change, matter is neither created nor destroyed but merely changed from one form to another.

(2) This law tells us that we can never really throw any matter away. In other words, there is no such thing as either a consumer or a "throwaway" society. *Everything we think we have thrown away is still here with us in some form or another.* Everything must go somewhere and all we can do is to recycle some of the matter we think we have thrown away.

(3) We can collect dust and soot from the smokestacks of industrial plants, but these solid wastes must then go somewhere. Cleaning up smoke is a misleading practice, because the invisible gaseous and very tiny particle pollutants left are often more damaging than the large solid particles that are removed. We can collect garbage and remove solid wastes from sewage, but they must either be burned (air pollution), dumped into rivers, lakes, and oceans (water pollution), or deposited on the land (soil pollution and water pollution if they wash away).

(4) We can reduce air pollution from the internal combustion engines in cars by using electric cars. But since electric car batteries must be recharged every day, we will have to build more electric power plants. If these are coal-fired plants, their smokestacks will add additional and even more dangerous air pollutants to the air; more land will be scarred from strip mining, and more water will be polluted from the acids that tend to leak out of coal mines. We could use nuclear power plants to produce the extra electricity needed. But then we risk greater heat or thermal pollution of rivers and other bodies of water used to cool such plants; further, we also risk releasing dangerous radioactive substances into the environment through plant or shipping accidents, highjacking of nuclear fuel to make atomic weapons, and leakage from permanent burial sites for radioactive wastes.

(5) Although we can certainly make the environment cleaner, talk of "cleaning up the environment" and "pollution free" cars, products, or industries is a scientific absurdity. The law of conservation of matter tells us that we will always be faced with pollution of some sort. Thus, we are also faced with the problem of *trade-offs*. In turn, these frequently involve subjective and controversial scientific, political, economic, and ethical judgments about what is a dangerous pollutant level, to what degree a pollutant must be controlled, and what amount of money we are willing to pay to reduce a pollutant to a harmless level.[1]

I. Law of conservation of matter

   A. Definition: in a physical or chemical change, matter neither created nor destroyed, merely changed from one form to another

   B. Everything that we dispose still with us

---

[1] Miller, *Living in the Environment*, p. 32. Used by permission.

C. Garbage must be burned, thrown in river or ocean, or put in land—each creates pollution (or any other example from paragraph 3)
D. Electric car reduces pollution—but electric power plants must be created (or any other example from paragraph 4)
E. Cleaning up environment an absurdity
F. Pollution problem—involves political, economic, and ethical judgments

Exercise 8.1

Score the five questions, not the underlinings, which will likely vary from this sample underlining. Just check to see that you have underlined main ideas correctly.

First Law of Energy: You Can't Get Something for Nothing

(1) *Types of Energy*   You encounter energy in many forms: mechanical, chemical, electrical, nuclear, heat, and radiant (or light) energy. Doing work involves changing energy from one form to another. In lifting this book, the chemical energy stored in chemicals obtained from your digested food is converted into the mechanical energy that is used to move your arm and the book upwards and some heat energy that is given off by your body.

(2) In an automobile engine the chemical energy stored in gasoline is converted into mechanical energy used to propel the car plus heat energy. A battery converts chemical energy into electrical energy plus heat energy. In an electric power plant, chemical energy from fossil fuels (coal, oil, or natural gas) or nuclear energy from nuclear fuels is converted into mechanical energy that is used to spin a turbine plus heat energy. The turbine then converts the mechanical energy into electrical energy and more heat. When this electrical energy passes through the filament wires in an ordinary light bulb, it is converted into light and still more heat. In all of the energy transformations discussed in this section, we see that some energy always ends up as heat energy that flows into the surrounding environment.

(3) Scientists have found that all forms of energy can be classified either as potential energy or kinetic energy. **Kinetic energy** is the energy that matter has because of its motion. Heat energy is a measure of the total kinetic energy of the molecules in a sample of matter. The amount of kinetic energy that a sample of matter has depends both on its mass and its velocity (speed). Because of its higher kinetic energy, a bullet fired at a high velocity from a rifle will do you more damage than the same bullet thrown by hand. Similarly, an artillery shell (with a larger mass) fired at the same velocity as the bullet will do you considerably more harm than the bullet.

(4) Stored energy that an object possesses by virtue of its position, condition, or composition is known as **potential energy.** A rock held in your hand has stored or potential energy that can be released and converted to kinetic energy (in the form of mechanical energy and heat) if the rock is dropped. Coal, oil, natural gas, wood, and

other fuels have a form of stored or <u>potential energy</u> known as <u>chem-ical energy</u>. When the fuel is burned, this chemical potential energy is converted into a mixture of heat, light, and the kinetic energy of motion of the molecules in the air and other nearby materials.

(5) With this background on the types of energy, we are now prepared to look at the two scientific laws that govern what happens when energy is converted from one form to another.[2]

1. c
2. b
3. a
4. b
5. b

Exercise 8.3

Here is one way to underline this exerpt correctly.

Second Law of Energy: You Can't Break Even

Second Energy Law and Energy Quality   Energy varies in its *quality* or ability to do useful work. The chemical potential energy concentrated in a lump of coal or liter of gasoline, and concentrated heat energy at a high temperature are forms of high-quality energy. Because they are concentrated, they have the ability to perform useful work in moving or changing matter. In contrast, dispersed heat energy at a low temperature is low-quality energy, with little if any ability to perform useful work. In investigating hundreds of thousands of different conversions of heat energy to useful work, scientists have found that <u>some of</u> the <u>energy</u> is <u>always degraded</u> to a more dispersed and <u>less useful form, usually heat energy</u> given off at a low temperature to the surroundings, or environment. This is a statement of the <u>*law of energy degradation*</u>, also known as the <u>*second law of thermodynamics*</u>.

Let's look at an example of the second energy law. In an <u>internal combustion automobile engine</u>, the high-quality potential energy available in gasoline is converted into a combination of high-quality <u>heat energy</u>, which is <u>converted to the mechanical work</u> used to propel the car, and low-quality heat energy. Only about <u>20 percent of</u> the <u>energy</u> available in the gasoline is <u>converted to useful mechanical energy</u>, with the remaining 80 percent released into the environment as degraded heat energy. In addition, about half of the mechanical energy produced is also degraded to low-quality heat energy through friction, so that 90 percent of the energy in gasoline is wasted and not used to move the car. Most of this loss is an energy quality tax automatically extracted as a result of the second law. Frequently the design of an engine or other heat-energy conversion device wastes more energy than that required by the second law. But the second

---

[2] Miller, *Living in the Environment*, p. 33. Used by permission.

law always ensures that there will be a certain waste or loss of energy quality.

Another example of the degradation of energy involves the <u>conversion of solar energy to chemical energy in food</u>. Photosynthesis in plants converts radiant energy (light) from the sun into high-quality chemical energy (stored in the plant in the form of sugar molecules) plus low-quality heat energy. If you eat plants, such as spinach, the high-quality <u>chemical energy</u> is <u>transformed</u> within your body <u>to</u> <u>high-quality mechanical energy</u>, used <u>to move</u> your <u>muscles</u> and <u>to perform other life processes</u>, plus <u>low-quality heat energy</u>. In each of these energy conversions, some of the initial high-quality energy is degraded into low-quality heat energy that flows into the environment.

The <u>first energy law governs</u> the *quantity* <u>of energy</u> available from an energy conversion process, whereas the <u>second energy law governs</u> the *quality* <u>of energy</u> available. In terms of the quantity of energy available from a heat-to-work conversion, we can get out no more energy than we put in. But according to the second law, the quality of the energy available from a heat-to-work conversion will always be lower than the initial energy quality. Not only can we not get something for nothing (the first law), we can't even break even in terms of energy quality (the second law). As Robert Morse put it, "The second law means that it is easier to get into trouble than to get out of it."

The <u>second energy law</u> also tells us that <u>high-grade energy can never be used over again</u>. *We can recycle matter but we can never recycle energy.* Fuels and foods can be used only once to perform useful work. Once a piece of <u>coal</u> or a tank of <u>gasoline</u> is <u>burned</u>, its <u>high-quality potential energy</u> is <u>lost forever</u>. Similarly, the high-quality heat energy from the steam in an underground geothermal well is gone forever once it is dispersed and degraded to low-quality heat energy in the environment. This means that the net useful, or high-quality, energy available from coal, oil, natural gas, nuclear fuel, geothermal, or any concentrated energy source is even less than that predicted by the first energy law.[3]

Although wording will likely vary, most of the information in your outline should be essentially the same.

I. Second law of thermodynamics—some energy always lost or degraded, usually in the form of heat energy given off

    A. Automobile engine—heat energy becomes mechanical energy; 20 percent of original energy actually used to move car

    B. Conversion of solar energy to chemical energy in food—in body, energy becomes mechanical (high-quality energy), to move muscles, and heat (low-quality energy)

---

[3] Miller, *Living in the Environment*, p. 34. Used by permission.

    C. First law of thermodynamics concerns quantity of energy; second law concerns quality of energy

    D. High-grade energy used only once—like coal or gasoline—when used, can never be used again

Exercise 8.5

Wording may vary, but paraphrases should be essentially the same as those in the key. Give yourself partial credit where you think it is appropriate.

1. Bilingual education is debated throughout the United States, especially where Spanish is spoken.
3. People in favor of bilingual education say that non-English-speaking students become fearful if all they hear at school is English.
4. People against bilingual education say that it only postpones the time that the child will learn English.
5. The argument continues each year when the government and states decide whether to give more money to bilingual education.
9. For many people, a workable bilingual program plainly tells students how long it will take them to learn English and use it well.

Chapter 10 Traditional Note-taking Techniques

Exercise 10.1

Wording may vary, but the condensed information should be essentially the same as that in the key. You may give yourself partial credit.

1. background to Darwin and theory of evolution
2. much research from travels to South America on *Beagle*
3. stopped many times; collected useful information
    Ex: finches
4. much research from Galapagos Islands
5. many plants/animals there
6. developed ideas for evolutionary theory
7. wanted to organize facts around principles
8. wanted to locate common ancestor with each species
9. natural selection
    Def: strength of certain animals to win out over others
10. pace of natural selection slow

Exercise 10.3

Phrasing may vary, but the information should be essentially the same. Be sure main ideas are separated from major details. Give yourself two points for each correct entry and partial credit where you think appropriate.

1. I. Characteristics of politics

    A. Power the basis
    B. Power makes change
    C. Most powerful groups cause change
    D. Inhumane interpretation of politics

2. I. History of the American city

    A. 200 years ago—95 percent lived on farms
    B. 200 years ago—only 24 cities, all under 100,000
    C. 1960—70 percent lived in cities
    D. 1960—6,000 cities

3. I. Black Death

    A. Struck Europe in 1300s
    B. England in 1348–1349—lost ⅓ of its population
    C. Carried by fleas on black rats
    D. Continued for 300 years

4. I. Characteristics of amphibians

    A. Have lived in water and on land
    B. Ex: frogs, toads, and salamanders
    C. Cold-blooded animals

5. I. Characteristics of monsoons

    A. Seasonal winds
    B. Found only in Asia
    C. Winter monsoons blow from land to ocean
    D. Summer monsoons blow from ocean to land

6. Nature of blood pressure

    Results from heart pumping blood in veins
    Systolic: action of heart when contracts
    Diastolic: measurement after heart relaxes

7. Parts of human heart

    4 chambers
    Pericardium: strong, protective covering
    Myocardium: heart's center driving blood through heart

8. Important latitudes on Earth

    Def: parallel lines north-south of the equator
    Tropic of Cancer—latitude north of the equator
    Tropic of Capricorn—latitude south of the equator
    Area between two latitudes has tropical climate

9. Conifers

> Trees bearing cones, with leaves like nails
> Leaves stay on for several years
> Ex: pine, spruce, fir

10. Capabilities of computers

> Can do only what humans can do
> Can perform large numbers of calculations quickly
> Infinitely patient
> Free humans from repetitive work so they can be creative

Exercise 10.5

1. =	**11.** without
2. >	**12.** compare
3. + or &	**13.** versus
4. ⊃	**14.** incomplete
5. re	**15.** important
6. nec	**16.** principal
7. pos	**17.** continued
8. incr	**18.** number
9. lg	**19.** therefore
10. max	**20.** is both cause and effect

Exercise 10.7

You may give yourself partial credit for 1–10. Do not give points for answers 11–20, where answers will vary.

A.
1. Picasso is an important figure with the majority of critics.
2. He helped develop the significant theory of Cubism.
3. Cubism makes objects look different.
4. Viewers see an object from several perspectives.
5. Cubism can be compared to Impressionism.
6. Picasso was influenced by primitive African art as well.
7. Viewers need to view Picasso with a different set of rules.
8. Picasso's art does not equal the real world.
9. Picasso's art work equals Picasso's interpretation of the world.
10. Therefore, it is necessary to understand some of Picasso's ideas regarding the world.

B.
11. George Braque began to wrk w P in 1st ½ of 20th C.
12. It is often diff to tell the wrk of these sig artists apart.
13. Both began to make old scraps of mats pts of their ptgs.
14. Their artstc creations ⊃ sig change in how vwr saw their wrks.
15. These old mats were both prt of their wrk of art and sep objs as well.

16. P and B were mkng sig statement.
17. Pieces of trash could become imp't subjts in art.
18. Their tech was usu called collage.
19. P's and B's C also → changs in style of sculptre and archtre.
20. ∴ we can conclude by saying that P → tremly aspts of mod. art.

Exercise 10.9

The following are sample responses.

Language Origins (L = language)

Need to look at L of human ancestors
    L devel't gradual process
    Ancestors moving from forest to grassland → wlking better on 2 ft →
        1. better vision
        2. better use of hands
        3. cmplx brain

Sound and nature of ancestors' L
    like chimp howls
    sounds chngd as they played
    tied to pres
    not prt of memory

When L tied to memory
    hunting → memory
    Hunters had to commcte to othrs
        Ex: "I killed anml!"

Settlng in lrgr comms → more cplx L.
    adv soc org → more adv speech

Chapter 11
Alternate
Note-taking
Techniques:
Mapping,
Laddering, and the
Cornell Note-taking
System

Exercise 11.1

Answers will vary. Give yourself credit if you think your study map clearly shows the relationship between main ideas and major details.

1.

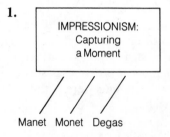

2.

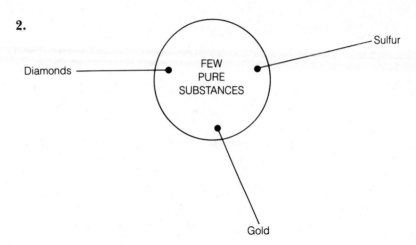

3. British Literature to 1800

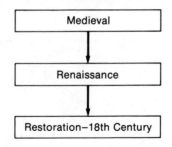

4.

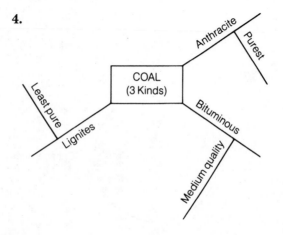

5. The Great Gatsby

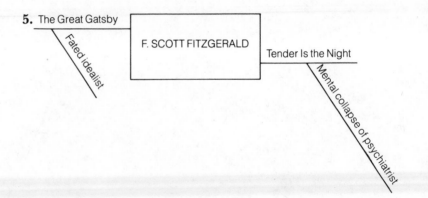

F. SCOTT FITZGERALD

Fated idealist

Tender Is the Night

Mental collapse of psychiatrist

6.   Great American Depression—1929

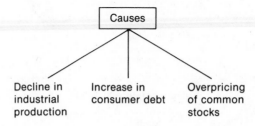

Causes

Decline in industrial production

Increase in consumer debt

Overpricing of common stocks

7.

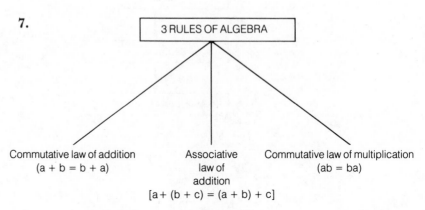

3 RULES OF ALGEBRA

Commutative law of addition
$(a + b = b + a)$

Associative law of addition
$[a + (b + c) = (a + b) + c]$

Commutative law of multiplication
$(ab = ba)$

8.   Both breast-feed young

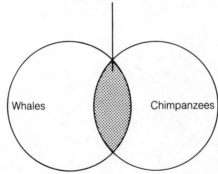

Whales

Chimpanzees

9.   Stages of language development

1) understanding ⟶ 2) speaking ⟶ 3) reading ⟶ 4) writing

10.

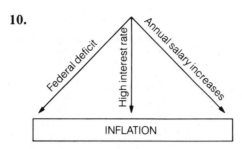

Exercise 11.3

Wording will vary, but answers should be essentially the same. Be sure that main ideas are clearly separated from major details. The study map that accompanies the outline is only an example. Score only the correct responses on the outline, not the study map. Count the number of correct responses, including the title. Each correct response equals five points; then add ten bonus points.

Nuclear Energy: Facts Pro and Con

Facts about
    produces 8% electricity in U.S.
    1990—may be slightly more expensive than coal

Safety
    less radiation emitted from coal plants of same size
    does not let out carbon monoxide

Nuclear accidents: meltdown steps
    1. fuel overheats
    2. turns water to steam
    3. steam makes plant explode
    4. radiation sent to environment

Nuclear wastes
    must be removed to central locations
    decay slowly
    put in steel cylinders in salt deposits
    salt areas not prone to earthquakes
    no guarantee

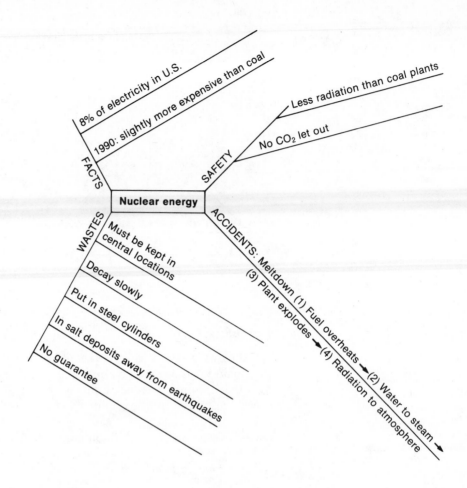

**Chapter 12
The SQ3R Study
System**

Exercise 12.1

The following are examples of correctly underlined and marked passages.

1. Catching More Fish and Fish Farming

Trends in the World Fish Catch   Fish are the major source of animal protein for more than one-half of the world's people, especially in Asia and Africa. Fish supply about 55 percent of the animal protein in Southeast Asia, 35 percent in Asia as a whole, 19 percent in Africa, about 25 percent worldwide—twice as much as eggs and three times as much as poultry—and 6 percent of all human protein consumption. Two-thirds of the annual fish catch is consumed by humans and one-third is processed into fish meal to be fed to livestock.

Between 1950 and 1970, the marine fish catch more than tripled—an increase greater than that occurring in any other human food source during the same period. To achieve large catches, modern fishing fleets use sonar, helicopters, aerial photography, and temperature measurement to locate schools of fish and lights and electrodes to attract them. Large, floating factory ships follow the fleets to process the catch.

Despite this technological sophistication, the steady rise in the marine fish catch halted abruptly in 1971. Between 1971 and 1976 the annual catch leveled off and rose only slightly between 1976 and 1983. A major factor in this leveling off was the sharp decline of the Peruvian anchovy catch, which once made up 20 percent of the global ocean harvest. A combination of overfishing and a shift in the cool, nutrient-rich currents off the coast of Peru were apparently the major factors causing this decline, which also threw tens of thousands of Peruvians out of work. Meanwhile, world population continued to grow, so between 1970 and 1983 the average fish catch per person declined and is projected to decline even further back to the 1960 level by the year 2000.[4]

2. Traditional Jazz

Two types of Afro-American folk music existed before and during the early years of jazz and later merged with it. One of these was **ragtime.** It featured the piano, occasionally in combination with other instruments. The music sounds like a polished, syncopated march with a decorated right-hand part. Early musicians associated with ragtime are Scott Joplin in Sedalia, Missouri, and Ben Harvey, who published his *Ragtime Instructor* in 1897. In 1974 the film *The Sting* caused a renewed interest in Joplin's rags.

The other type of music involved with early jazz was the folk **blues.** Its musical characteristics will be discussed shortly. Some of the most famous names associated with blues are Leadbelly, whose real name was Huddie Ledbetter; W. C. Handy, who was known for his "Memphis Blues" and "St. Louis Blues"; and Ferdinand "Jelly Roll" Morton, whose first published blues appeared in 1905—the "Jelly Roll Blues."

Like folk music, jazz was created by generally untutored musicians who could not have written down what they played or sang, even if they had wanted to. Jazz is different from most folk music in two respects. It has sprung from the cities rather than the fields and forests; it is an urban form of music. And for most people, it is a spectator experience. Usually only a few people perform, although listeners may contribute a little hand clapping and foot stomping.[5]

3. Matter: Types, States, Properties, and Changes

Types of Matter: Elements and Compounds   A lump of coal, an ice cube, a puddle of water, air—all are samples of matter. Matter is anything that occupies space and has mass. **Mass** is the quantity of matter in substance.

---

[4] G. Tyler Miller, Jr., *Living in the Environment,* 4th ed. (Belmont, Calif.: Wadsworth, 1985), p. 153. Used by permission.
[5] Charles R. Hoffer, *The Understanding of Music,* 5th ed. (Belmont, Calif.: Wadsworth, 1985), pp. 492–493. Used by permission.

A substance or pure substance is one of millions of different types of matter found in the world. Any substance can be classified as either an element or a compound. An element is one of the 108 basic building blocks of all matter. Examples include iron, sodium, carbon, oxygen, and chlorine. Scientists have discovered 90 naturally occurring elements on earth and have made small quantities of 18 others in the laboratory.

A compound is a form of matter in which two or more elements are held together in a fixed ratio by chemical bonds. Water, for example, is a combination of the elements hydrogen and oxygen, and sodium chloride (the major ingredient in table salt) is a combination of the elements sodium and chlorine. About 5 million compounds of the 108 known elements have been identified, and about 6000 new compounds are added to the list each week. With proper guidance, you could make a new compound yourself. At least 63,000 compounds are contained in the food we eat, the air we breathe, the water we drink, and the countless products we use.[6]

Exercise 12.3

A.

1. a
2. b
3. a
4. b
5. c

B. Answers will vary

1. What is the definition of less-developed countries?
2. How are strategic materials related to less-developed countries?
3. How are closer social and economic ties related to less-developed countries?
4. How does political stability relate to less-developed countries?
5. What is the normal issue surrounding less-developed countries?
6. How is the world running out of food?

C. Answers will vary.

Chpt 21   Less-developed Countries, pp. 229–231
Much of the world very poor
  ¼ of the world pop. very poor—1 bil ppl
  called less-developed countries

Need for natural resources—1st reason for U.S. getting involved w
                    less-developed countries (LDCs)
  many res come from LDCs
  will need more from LDCs as time goes on

Need to be economically and socially close to LDCs—2nd reason
  LDCs forming cartels
    control supply and price of materials
  U.S. needs to be on good terms w cartels

---

[6] G. Tyler Miller, Jr., *Chemistry: A Basic Introduction*, 4th ed. (Belmont, Calif.: Wadsworth, 1987), p. 2. Used by permission.

Chpt 21   LDC, pp. 229–231

I. Political stability in LDCs—3rd reason
    A. usu run by dictators
    B. U.S. help would eliminate dictator

II. Moral issue—4th reason
    A. world sees U.S. as indifferent to poor countries
    B. ranks low in terms of foreign aid

III. Food problem—5th reason
    A. pop. increasing—more poor are born
    B. world's grain reserves running low

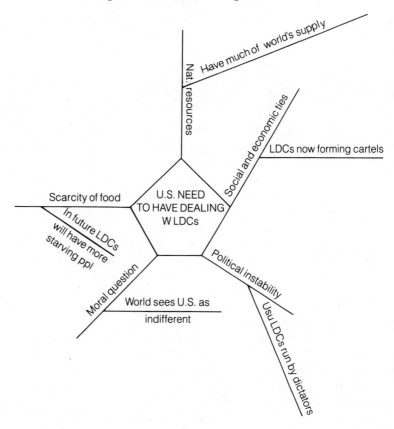

D.

1. d	6. b
2. c	7. c
3. a	8. b
4. b	9. b
5. d	10. a

Following the study map is the entire excerpt with the sample under-linings, markings, and comments. Compare this excerpt with yours.

Chapter 21
The Less-developed Countries
Challenge for the Future

Philip C. Starr

This last chapter is about poverty among nations. Poverty is, of course, a relative matter. Whenever there is any inequality in the distribution of income, some people will always be poor *relative* to others. But much of the world is so abjectly poor that some observers speak of absolute poverty—"a condition of life so degraded by disease, illiteracy, malnutrition, and squalor as to deny its victims basic human necessities."[1]

One billion people—one-quarter of the world's population—are in this category. One-quarter of a million people in Calcutta are homeless. They eat, live, and die in the streets. Three million people in Bolivia out of a total population of 5 million have a life expectancy of 30 years of age. The average Bolivian eats less than one-half of one ounce of meat per year, which in effect means that the peasant population is too poor to eat any meat at all.[2]

These problems are hard for Americans to appreciate. The problem is not like that of an American black male who cannot get a college education or like that of a female of any color who cannot get admitted to medical school. The problem is that two-thirds of the world's population have not made it in terms of income to first grade, while the other one-third has relatively easy access to wealth and income. The problem is not the typical American one of reducing the number of high school dropouts: The problem is how to give more than 2 billion people the means and the opportunity to make some investment in their own human capital. Our point is that only when *individuals* begin to have some perception of their own impact (positive or negative) on our planet can we begin to appreciate our *collective* responsibility to help one another.

Note that the chapter title refers to *less-developed countries* (abbreviated LDCs). Several terms are used to describe countries that are poorer than others: Underdeveloped countries, developing countries, Third World countries. We prefer the term "less developed."*

Economists have no specific dividing lines or explicit definitions of such terms. A nation's position on the ladder is usually determined by dividing its GNP by population (*per capita GNP*) so that there is a spectrum of nations from rich to poor—from $6,300 per person per year in Sweden to $70 per person per year in Burundi (both in 1973). (There are probably poorer countries than Burundi, but in those cases GNP and/or population is usually unknown.)

This chapter reviews the plight of the less-developed countries from the point of view of economic analysis. The chapter is divided into four parts: (1) Why should we bother? (2) Problems that must be solved. (3) What can be done to help. (4) Conclusions.

---

* All countries, rich or poor, are to some extent "developing." The difference is relative; so, by "less developed," we simply mean that such countries are less developed than others. The term "third world" is a conversational term implying poverty, but occasionally one will hear of "fourth" and "fifth" world countries, depending on how far down the economic ladder they are.

Starr, Economic Principles in Action, *pp. 350–352. Used by permission.*

CONCEPTS TO REMEMBER

Less-developed countries (LDCs)   Social overhead capital
Per capita GNP   Zero population growth (ZPG)
Organization of Petroleum Exporting Countries   Physical Quality of Life Index (PQLI)
  (OPEC)   Group of 77
Revolution of rising expectations   Official government aid (OGA)
Nonrenewable resource   Intermediate technology
Capital-output ratio   Green Revolution
Infrastructure   Triage

Why Should We Bother?

There are <u>five basic arguments</u>.

(1.) Our Need for Strategic Materials

An industrial society like the U.S. cannot function without certain raw materials. One estimate[3] is that there are 13 such materials essential to the U.S. Some examples are asbestos, bauxite (aluminum ore), chrome, cobalt, copper, lead, manganese, nickel, petroleum, platinum, silver, tin, and titanium—not to mention bananas, coffee, tea, and Scotch. <u>Many of these essentials come from the less-developed countries</u>, and our <u>dependence</u> on other countries is growing. In 1950 we relied on other countries to provide us with more than half of only 4 of the 13 materials. By 1985 we will want more than half of 9 of the 13 from other countries.

ex

(2.) Closer Social and Economic Ties

We are more closely bound than ever to all countries. Americans worry about the international traffic in drugs, some of which comes from the LDCs. We worry about inflation that comes from higher coffee, tea, and oil prices. <u>Many</u> of the <u>less-developed countries</u> are following the lead of *OPEC,* the *Organization of Petroleum Exporting Countries,* and <u>forming cartels</u>. Cartels have formed among the countries

that export bauxite, tin, coffee, bananas, tea, rubber, and pepper, to name a few. The <u>intent of</u> these <u>cartels</u> is to <u>control supply and raise the price</u>. The United States will have to learn to deal with and be on good relations with the countries that belong to these cartels.

(3.) The Need for Political Stability

It is sometimes said that "only the rich can afford democracy." Consider a nation of starving, bewildered, uneducated people. It is <u>easy for them to turn to a dictator</u> who persuades them that he or she can solve their problems. If the dictator becomes the source of international tension, or even war, as in some of the African or Latin American states, the <u>peace of the world may be threatened</u>. No one (rich) nation like the United States can afford to permit a people's suffering to threaten the orderly progress of economic development throughout the world. We mean to be cautious here. We do not suggest military intervention to remove the dictator but rather sufficient help for such a people to make the dictator unnecessary.

poor econ → dictatorship

(4.) The Moral Question

We are often viewed as the rich kid who pays no attention to the kids in the slums. Americans consume 40 percent of the world's resources with 6 percent of the world's population. Many people believe we are indifferent to the problems of the poor countries. The United States has a reputation for being miserly with its foreign aid. In terms of economic assistance as a percentage of GNP, we rank 14 among 16 developed nations.[4] For our own peace of mind, we cannot afford to be viewed as a "global parasite"[5] that consumes the world's resources while millions starve.

interesting DX

5. Time Is Running Out

By year 2000 almost 90% of new ppl in LDCs

In a world of growing populations and declining food reserves, the time left to solve the world's poverty problems is getting short. The world's population is increasing at the rate of 64 million* per year now, rising to 100 million per year by the year 2000.[6] Roughly 87 percent of these new mouths to feed will be in the LDCs.

Running Out of Food To feed this present yearly addition of 64 million people will require nearly 20 million tons of grain each year, which is more than the total Canadian wheat crop. (The population problem will be discussed in more detail in a later section.)

The Malthusian moment of truth has arrived. Although all countries are currently using only about 44 percent of an estimated 7.9 billion acres of arable land for food production, *all* of that land will be in use by the year 2080 if present population trends continue—*even if the yield per acre is quadrupled.*

The world's grain reserves are dropping as they are used up to meet increasing demand. Table 21-1 shows how the world's grain reserves have declined to a point where we had only a 35-day supply in 1975.

---

* We obtained this by multiplying 3.92 billion people by 1.64 percent, the growth rate in 1975.

Table 21-1
Declining Grain Reserves

Year	Reserves (days of consumption)
1961	105 ✳
1965	91
1970	89
1975	35 ✳

Source: Lester R. Brown, "The World Food Prospect," *Science,* 12 December 1975.

Notes

1. Robert S. McNamara, "The Moral Case for Helping the World's Poor," *Los Angeles Times,* 28 September 1973, pt. II, p. 7.

2. Harvey Morris, "Life of Bolivian Indians Remains Harsh," *Los Angeles Times,* 31 March 1977, pt. I-A, p. 1.

3. Charles W. Maynes, Jr., "Are the World's Poor Undeserving?" *Los Angeles Times,* 8 December 1974, pt. VI, p. 1.

4. McNamara, "The Moral Case for Helping the World's Poor."

5. Maynes, "Are the World's Poor Undeserving?"

6. See Nathan Keyfitz, "World Resources and the Middle Class," *Scientific American,* July 1976; "Running Out of Food," *Newsweek,* 11 November 1974; Lester R. Brown, "The World Food Prospect," *Science,* 12 December 1975; Thomas Y. Canby, "Can the World Feed Its People?" *National Geographic,* July 1975; and Douglas N. Ross, *Food and Population: The Next Crisis,* The University Library, 1975.

Chapter 13
Mnemonic Strategies

Exercise 13.1

Here are possible answers:

1. Station*ary* refers to cold and warm air front. *Air* rhymes with *ary*.
2. People who have *ill*usions may be psychologically *ill*.
3. *Between* means that no more than two items are compared, and "b" is the second letter of the alphabet.
4. Capit*ol* buildings are usually *old*.
5. Hunters carry spears and *rods*. I see a hunter with a *rod* in his hand chasing an *animal*.
6. Roy G. Biv (a name)
7. We are just mighty mice.
8. MTM
9. ERS
10. zeal, zealously, zealot, and zealousness

Chapter 14
Examination Strategies; Objective Tests

Exercise 14.1

1. c
2. b
3. c
4. b
5. d

Exercise 14.3

1. e
2. d
3. a
4. c
5. b

Chapter 15
Examination Strategies: Essay Tests and Math or Science Tests

Exercise 15.1

Wordings will vary, but the information should be essentially the same. You may want to use the following scoring formula: score = number of correct answers × 10.

1. Give yourself one point if you note that China after liberation was a better place to live.

2. Give yourself six points if you mention three of the following: (2 points each) famine, drug addiction, and prostitution, unreasonable taxes, large cities owned by companies, people treated like animals, workers worked long for little salary, or babies sold for pennies.

3. Give yourself three points if you mention three of the following: all people eat; all people have housing, clothing, medical care, and free education; no illiteracy, starvation, or prostitution; no sexually transmitted diseases or drug addiction; or cities clean without flies, mosquitoes, or other pests.

Here is a sample paragraph receiving all ten points:

> China before liberation was in a dreadful state. It was a country experiencing famine and having a high incidence of opium addiction and prostitution. Economically, the workers worked long hours for a meager salary. Today, all Chinese get something to eat. Illiteracy, starvation, and prostitution have also been eliminated. Finally, cities are clean, free of disease-ridden insects.

Index